MORE!
RAGS TO RICHES

All New Stories of How Ordinary People Achieved Extraordinary Wealth!

Gail Liberman and Alan Lavine

Dearborn™
Trade Publishing
A **Kaplan Professional** Company

Vice President and Publisher: Cynthia A. Zigmund
Editorial Director: Donald J. Hull
Senior Project Editor: Trey Thoelcke
Interior Design: Lucy Jenkins
Cover Design: Design Alliance, Inc.
Typesetting: the dotted i

Published by Dearborn Trade, a Kaplan Professional Company

Printed in the United States of America

02 03 04   10 9 8 7 6 5 4 3 2 1

Library of Congress Cataloging-in-Publication Data

Liberman, Gail, 1951-
    More rags to riches : all new stories of how ordinary people achieved
    extraordinary wealth / Gail Liberman, Alan Lavine.
        p.   cm.
    Includes index.
    ISBN 0-7931-4554-6
    1. Rich people—United States—Biography. 2. Wealth—United States.
    I. Lavine, Alan. II. Title.
    HC110.W4 L52 2002
    332'.092'273—dc21

                                                    2001005331

DEDICATION

This book is dedicated to our terrific nieces and nephew. We wish them much love, health, success, happiness, and riches:

Taryn Liberman

Brooke Liberman

Beth Greenberg

Lenny Greenberg

CONTENTS

ACKNOWLEDGMENTS

This book would not be possible were it not for the cooperation of the successful people we have interviewed. We thank them sincerely for taking their valuable time to very openly tell us their stories. We contacted them cold and probed them long and hard with some tough questions. We truly appreciate their honest and candid responses.

They include: Joseph A. Kruse, Angela Adair-Hoy, Seymour "Sy" Sperling, Kenneth A. Smaltz, Jr., Mary E. Foley, Anthony David Parks, Paul E. Kieffer, J. Peter Uys, Donna M. Auguste, and Harlyn and Karen Riekena.

These people deserve a great deal of credit for helping to open up communications about money, which, the more we write about it, seems to be a very emotionally charged subject. We hope their stories help to foster greater understanding about this inanimate object that seems to elude so many of us!

We'd also like to thank our publisher, Cynthia Zigmund, for her understanding and undying faith in us, and our new editor, Don Hull, for his hard work. Plus, we thank Jack Kiburz and Trey Thoelcke for helping to eliminate any errors.

We can't forget Courtney Goethals, Robin Bermel, and Mary Reed for their conscientious efforts to get the word out about our books.

INTRODUCTION

You evidently liked our first book, *Rags to Riches: Motivating Stories of How Ordinary People Achieved Extraordinary Wealth*. It hit two best-seller lists and was featured on Oprah's television show!

So we've combed the country to track down even more motivating stories to tell.

Besides love, work, and faith, financial security is one of the major cornerstones to a healthy and happy life.

To achieve it, you can go to school. There also are thousands of good books that will teach you about money—if you don't mind looking at tables, charts, and graphs.

However, both *Rags to Riches* and *More Rags to Riches* aren't like those. You won't find standard formulas or financial planning jargon about how to manage your finances. After all, even if you happen to ace a course or absorb the information in many of those other books, what you do with your knowledge afterward depends solely on you. Books or classes can't teach you how to respond to success or failure. That's something you must learn from experience.

Books, classes, college degrees, and professional designations, don't necessarily tell you how to get out of the rut of a miserable job. They won't teach you how to keep religious, ethnic, or racial discrimination from ruining your life. It's also tough to find instruction on how to get a creative idea.

With *More Rags to Riches,* we try to deal with these issues by serving you up firsthand experience. You'll hear directly from others who amassed wealth exactly what they had to go through to get it. You'll learn the mistakes they made along the way and what happened *after* they achieved it. By reading stories of what others experienced, hopefully you can get exactly where you want to be on your own with a little less stress.

Money, as you've no doubt already been warned, doesn't always buy happiness or solve all your problems. Health and love often weigh in a lot more heavily. Some of our subjects went so far as to confirm that.

Nonetheless, we figure that if we can provide you with specific wealth-building strategies that worked and show you the mistakes others made, you'll be that much ahead in your own life.

In both *Rags to Riches* and *More Rags to Riches,* we highlight the lives of regular people. We tried very hard to get our subjects to let it all hang out. As in our first book, you won't find lottery or sweepstakes winners, nor will you find people who inherited wealth.

No one gave anyone in *More Rags to Riches* their money. Each earned it in his or her own unique way. What you will find in both books, where possible, are one-on-one interviews. Where it was not possible, we conducted objective analyses as to what the significant forces were in the individual's effort to build wealth.

We try to tell you exactly how it's done, including the costs and figures involved.

There is one major change that has occurred since we wrote *Rags to Riches.* After being blessed with a healthy economy for more than a decade, the economy slowed. Some of our subjects admittedly had given back some wealth when the stock market declined more than 15 percent over the 15 months ending in June 2001.

Economic experts predict that the economy will pick up steam in 2002. So there could be more people on the road to riches. Hopefully, you will be among that elite group if you're not already.

Regardless, you'll hear how some millionaires weathered the 2000–2001 bear market.

As we wrote *More Rags to Riches,* statistics indicated that there were more opportunities than ever before for more Americans. The U.S. Census Bureau reported that minority-owned businesses grew four times as fast as U.S. companies overall between 1992 and 1997. African American–owned businesses totaled 823,500 while Hispanic businesses totaled 1.2 million.

"This portrait of the American economy shows rapidly expanding opportunities for minority entrepreneurs and a more diverse universe of small businesses," said U.S. Undersecretary for Economic Affairs Kathleen B. Cooper.

Women-owned businesses in the United States numbered 5.4 million. That represents a 16 percent increase between 1992 and 1997—almost triple the rate of all firms, excluding publicly held corporations.

We wanted to share some of these stories.

For both of our *Rags to Riches* books, we had to deal with the age-old question, "What is wealthy today?" It's clearly not as much as it used to be. Wealth also varies by geographic market. Many magazines lately have cited a net worth of $5 million as wealthy.

In fact, Spectrem Group, a Chicago research firm, had claimed that the affluent market is growing five times as fast as the general population. It predicted that by 2004, there would be 31 million households with annual incomes of at least $100,000 and/or net worths of $500,000 or more.

If you're not among this group, though, don't despair. We decided instead to aim for subjects with a $1 million net worth. We based that figure on a study by Merrill Lynch and Cap Gemini Ernst & Young. In 2000, they reported, there were nearly 7.2 million people worldwide who had at least $1 million in investable assets. Although that's up 180,000 from 1999, it's peanuts when you consider a worldwide population of a whopping 6.1 billion!

The Federal Reserve pegged the median U.S. household's net worth at a mere $71,600.

The first step, we still firmly believe, is to earn your first $1 million. Once you do that, it's easier to grow your assets even more. Moreover, even if you happen to be among those who already have $1 million in assets, we're willing to wager you'll pick up some information you didn't already know.

After all, not everybody has followed the same path as you.

What are you best off doing to build your wealth?

We've read books that gave some very interesting characteristics of millionaires. We've read, for example, that they're typically married, 57 years old, and more likely to shop at Kmart. While this may be true, you'll find, based on our interviews, myriad exceptions. We tried to bring you the widest variety of experiences we could find.

Repeated studies have indicated that most millionaires today are first-generation millionaires.

A survey by Financial Market Research for U.S. Trust Co., which looks at the top 1 percent of wage earners based on Internal Revenue Service (IRS) statistics, seems to confirm this.

The majority of those polled said they derived their wealth from business or professional practices. Nearly one-third worked for corporations. Only 10 percent had inherited their wealth.

Most of those surveyed rose from middle class or poor backgrounds. Plus, a happy marriage was an important factor.

Once again, if you don't fit in these categories, please do not give up hope. Many of our interviews of people with at least a $1 million net worth showed various other characteristics. In fact, we're willing to wager there are tons of variations!

Our goal is to help you understand these people's secrets.

More Rags to Riches is slightly different from our first book in a few ways.

We have been more diligent in asking certain questions. We wanted to know the exact role that religion and faith in God played, how our subjects were managing their money, and the absolute biggest lessons they learned. We also were more diligent in asking for their personal advice.

In our first *Rags to Riches* book, we wrote about some celebrities. We picked people in professions you wouldn't associate with financial success—like poet Maya Angelou, golfer Chi Chi Rodriguez, and magician David Copperfield.

In *More Rags to Riches*, we took a somewhat different tack. We focused on famous people who put their noses to the grindstone and overcame years of struggle to become successful. B.B. King (Chapter 9), the famous blues musician, has reported that he didn't become successful and wealthy until he was in his 60s. He spent 40 years on the road playing his music before he became a big hit.

Gloria Estefan's family (Chapter 6) left Cuba and came to Miami after Fidel Castro took over the country. As immigrants, the family not only had to struggle with a lower standard of living than they were used to in their native land, but they had a language barrier to overcome.

We also want to see how some famous Generation Xers made it to the top. We probed the success of Tony Hawk (Chapter 13), the skateboard champion and ESPN broadcaster. We even sought the truth in some younger success stories, including Venus and Serena Williams (Chapter 14), the tennis phenoms.

Unfortunately, some of the celebrities we highlighted in the book could not give us interviews. B.B. King was off on a European tour and had no time. The Williams sisters were writing a book, which their agent, IMG, Cleveland, told us would conflict with our chapter. Meanwhile, Tony Hawk's New York publicist, Sarah Hall, said he and his wife were busy getting ready to have another child. Zeida Gonzalez in the office of Jorge A. Plascensia, marketing chief of Estefan Enterprises, initially told us the Estefans were swamped because they had just released a record. Despite repeated additional phone calls to that office, neither Plascensia nor anyone else representing the Estefans returned our phone calls. Although a Sony spokeswoman said she would try to reach Emilio Estefan, nobody had contacted us prior to this writing.

We thought these people illustrated important enough success stories to make it worthwhile for us to analyze how they did it. So we scoured public information and records to find out everything we possibly could that would reveal what they did differently from the majority of people who haven't quite made it yet. We wanted to know everything we could about their relationships with money.

That's because we believe that one of the best ways to learn how to achieve financial security is to hear how others already have done it.

We did talk to Sy Sperling (Chapter 3). You might recognize Sperling from his Hair Club for Men commercials on television. He was so popular that during Bill Clinton's second presidential campaign, *The Tonight Show*'s Jay Leno did a comedy routine with Sperling. Sy acted as a reporter spotting politicians that needed more hair on their heads.

Did you know that he was once a shoeshine boy in Times Square? A couple of years ago, he sold his company for a whopping $40 million. Along the way he had some tremendous setbacks. We detail exactly how he got himself out of them.

There is one major lesson we have learned while writing the *Rags to Riches* books. There's no shortage of ways to amass wealth. Everybody who has done it has a different story to tell.

Who would think that after growing up on welfare and struggling for years, one millionaire would give much of his fortune away? Yet, Anthony Parks (Chapter 7) did exactly that.

Some, like Parks, had to struggle to put food on the table. Others came from middle-class families, but upon starting on their own, experienced hard times. Single mothers can learn from Angela Adair-Hoy (Chapter 2), a single mom who divorced an alcoholic husband. Now she owns a successful online publishing company. You'll also read the story of Harlyn and Karen Riekena (Chapter 12) who were small-town farmers in Wellsburg, Iowa. They built their fortune buying small parcels of farmland over the years.

Not everyone in this book is a college graduate. Kenneth A. Smaltz, Jr. (Chapter 4), for example, lacked a college degree. He also worked his way out of $40,000 in debt and maneuvered his way to become a partner in a rare coin dealership.

Of those who are college graduates, we probed exactly how much of a factor in their success college truly was. We hope their responses help in your effort to chart the course of your own life. By reading about the strategies these people have undertaken—told, in the majority of cases, firsthand—we're hoping you'll gain the information you need to mold a better life for yourself.

Gail Liberman & Alan Lavine
MWliblav@aol.com

CHAPTER 1

JOSEPH A. KRUSE

Tet Offensive Survivor
Strikes It Rich

The son of a steelworker, Joseph A. Kruse, 58, was a first lieutenant overseeing 100 soldiers during one of Vietnam's bloodiest battles, the Tet offensive, in 1968. Before leaving his wife and one-year-old son on what he believed could well be a death mission to Vietnam, he bought 200 shares of Mary Carter Paint. The company's stock, which he had read about in the newspaper's business pages, was about the cheapest he could afford at $5.50 a share. So he invested $1,000 of the money he had obtained from selling his 1956 Thunderbird. Upon his return, he noticed the company was mysteriously absent from the stock pages of the newspaper.

He subsequently learned from his broker that the company had been taken over by Resorts International, and his investment was worth more than $10,000! Today, his stock-picking prowess and creative salesmanship have combined to build him a net worth of some $10 million.

Kruse has two Jaguars and a 5,000-square-foot home on three acres in Naperville, Illinois, complete with a workout room, whirlpool, sauna, and steam room. He pays himself about $250,000 to $300,000 annually. It's more than enough, he says, to cover his taxes, daily expenses, his mortgage, his mother's mortgage, and frequent travel. The rest of his money is invested—split about 30 percent in bonds and 70 percent in stocks.

Kruse was able to retire in the mid-1990s after his 30-year career as a sales rep for Lees Commercial Carpets, a division of Burlington Industries, Inc. Now, he sets an alarm clock only when he has a tee-off time or he's traveling somewhere. His days are spent playing golf, traveling every few weeks, taking care of his property, and managing his investments.

Kruse is divorced with one grown son and a fiancée that he expects to marry someday. "Since we're not having children, there's no real reason to push the button," he says of marriage.

He comes from a conservative Polish family. "I was brought up [to believe] that you paid for it if you have cash," he says. This upbringing has paid off. Even today, he says, he charges nothing that he doesn't pay off within 30 days. "I don't think I ever had a credit bill except a house mortgage when I was growing up. Even when I bought cars, I bought [them] with cash."

His life has changed quite a bit from the time he grew up as a child in the factory town of Natrona, Pennsylvania. In those days, Kruse, who attended Catholic grammar school and served as an altar boy, was aggressively pushed into sports by his late father, Joseph Kruszewski. "Dad was a very good athlete in his time," he said. "Every day he would take me out when I was eight or nine years old and convince me to pitch a baseball to him." His father put him in Little League baseball. Then, he went on to play basketball.

"I used to set up bowling pins and make $10 a week when I was in sixth, seventh, and eighth grades," he said. "I would shoot basketball in the evening under the lights. We didn't have a car. I don't think my dad learned to drive until he was 60." Kruse and his older sister always had clean clothes. His parents often spent their last dollar so that he and his sister looked presentable for church. In fact, he says he still has a picture of himself as a child dressed up in a sportcoat, tie, and hat.

Kruse says his mother, Regina, was the go-getter in the family. She came from a large family. When her mother had died at an early age, she was the one who stayed home to handle the chores and help raise the family.

Much like his mother, Kruse definitely enjoyed the finer things in life. Often, he would save the money he earned setting up bowling pins to buy himself little luxuries. Once he purchased a cashmere sweater.

Kruse remembers being awed by the $25,000 annual salary earned by one of his idols, Pittsburgh Pirates Hall of Famer Bill Mazeroski. He always admired Mazeroski. After all, there was nobody else in the Natrona area with much money. "One guy had a new convertible," he said, noting that that was probably before 1961. "We're talking 1957, 1958, and 1959."

Kruse remembers eating mashed potatoes and buttermilk for dinner five days a week when he was in seventh grade while his father participated in a 180-day union strike. The whole town had shut down and union payroll was nonexistent in those days.

Always a good student, Kruse also became a basketball star in high school. In fact, he set a scoring record at Har-brack High School, now Highland High School, in Natrona Heights, scoring 456 points for the 1960-1961 season. He succeeded in obtaining a full basketball scholarship to Virginia Military Institute. The scholarship went so far as to include his uniforms, haircuts, and food. His father didn't have to spend any money, and Kruse was able to save additional money he obtained from his stint in Reserve Officer Training Corps or R.O.T.C. While in college, he boosted his income further by selling shirts. Upon seeing an ad in the paper, he contacted a shirt manufacturer and arranged to buy shirts for $4 apiece. He'd then sell them on campus for $5, making a $1-per-shirt profit.

Throughout college Kruse remained a good student and athlete. "I had good grades," he said. "I was better in math than in English, which is pretty common. I was very competitive. Sports taught me to be very competitive and very aggressive." He enjoyed sports. It was a diversion from the rigorous military life. In college, he played point guard and secured a position in his college hall of fame. In his junior year, his team became the first in Virginia ever to win the Southern Conference Basketball Championship. He remembers finally getting defeated in the regional finals by Princeton University.

It's no wonder. Princeton's team was led by Bill Bradley, who went on to play professional basketball for the New York Knicks before becoming a U.S. senator.

Kruse majored in chemistry and graduated from college in the top 10 percent of his class in 1965. He took a job as a metallurgical engineer for Bethlehem Steel, in Johnstown, Pennsylvania. His father had given him $1,000 for graduation. With that and his other earned money, Kruse bought a nine-year-old 1956 Thunderbird for $1,600. He married immediately after graduation and soon a young son was on the way. After the couple had the child, Kruse went into the service for one year. His wife was going to live with her parents in Lexington, Virginia, and she already had a car, so the couple realized they didn't need a second car. Because his car had no back seat, they decided it was the logical one to sell. He sold it for $1,700—slightly more than he had paid for it. He used the money to make his landmark first stock investment.

"I was just looking through the newspaper and saw a stock at $5 to $6 a share," he said of his first stock selection. "I think I read an article that indicated [the company was] building a bridge from Paradise Island to the main island of Nassau and looking into a hotel or gambling—something alluding to the fact that they were doing stuff other than paint manufacturing. It was pure speculation."

While in combat, Kruse didn't need his army pay, so he sent $400 monthly back to his wife to bank.

What he experienced in Vietnam may well have shaped his character for years to come. There is very little in life that is quite as intense as facing death and destruction every day in combat. Kruse already had developed self-confidence. His Vietnam experience provided added strength.

The Tet offensive, which began in early 1968, was a coordinated surprise attack by the Vietcong on a number of towns and hamlets around South Vietnam. The Vietcong ultimately withdrew, but the landmark battle raised questions about the United States' ability to win the controversial war in Vietnam and it poured fuel on the escalating antiwar movement. Some 32,000 people were reported killed in the battle.

"We were overrun," Kruse said of the experience. "It was nasty! I was an officer in charge of 100 guys in the artillery. I didn't have to go out chasing Vietcong. We were in the midst of the jungle. When you get orders to go, you get on a plane and eight hours later you're in a war. You expect to die. After a while, you get the hang of it because you don't know what to expect."

Kruse, who earned a bronze medal for his service in Vietnam, was in his early twenties at the time.

"What gets me is the amount of power they would give someone who is 21, 22, or 23 years old. I was in charge of all those guys!"

Kruse, a first lieutenant, was in the First Cavalry Division. He helped clear the jungles in the Que Son Valley area for a landing zone, where troops could bring food and ammunition. "There might have been 2,000 of us," he said. "You work like a dog digging holes and building tents and putting up barriers, setting up guns and cleaning up the area."

The pending landmark attack was no secret. U.S. intelligence had captured documents indicating that there would be a major activity. It was expected to be around the time of Tet, the Vietnamese lunar New Year. "We were pretty well prepared," Kruse said. "We just didn't know what day."

Kruse fired 175 mm guns—guns which he says are as long as telephone poles. The guns had a range of nearly 20 miles and could shoot a 200-pound explosive. Just before the attack, Kruse had received daily orders to make certain he held fire between 5:45 AM and 6:30 AM. No matter what happened, he was not permitted to fire. That's because U.S. B-52 planes were being dispatched to drop napalm some two miles away surrounding the landing zone. If his large guns fired too high, it was feared they could hit the U.S. planes. "You wouldn't think an ant could get through that fire!" he said of the area where the napalm was dropped. In fact, he has a video of it. "The Vietnamese must have been living in tunnels or whatever." Around the third day, the attack started.

Although nobody under Kruse's command was hurt, some of the infantry fielded shrapnel from the attack. He said, "We were just lucky." One of the shells hit an ammunition dump, which was a backup in case the gunpowder Kruse and his men had stored under the bunkers ran out. "That meant shells and powder started exploding." There were no fire trucks to come and extinguish it. They had to just wait for it to go out.

Kruse said that at about 2:00 or 3:00 AM, they could see the Vietcong coming and trying to get to the barbed wire. "We took our guns. We would lower our guns and were shooting at people. We could see their mortar fire. We would see them shooting the bad mortars. You would see a flash of a gun just like you do in the movies. I'd never done this before. This is nothing you learn at school. We lowered our guns and fired directly at them." The attack lasted until around 7:00 AM. He says the infantry, coupled with his men, ultimately killed about 300 Vietcong in the barbed wire.

The experience, while traumatic, later helped him see business from a very different perspective than other people. Often, people say something is critical or a matter of life or death. After fighting in Vietnam, his feeling is, "Eh. It's not that critical."

Upon his return, he tasted the rewards of investing, which would later help him build his wealth. His first stock investment had skyrocketed from $5.50 a share to $62, and Kruse's interest in investing definitely was stimulated. He continued to dabble in the stock market. But he also had to make the transition from a combat veteran to a civilian worker.

Initially, he returned to his job at Bethlehem Steel. But from the time he had set foot on the plane to go to Virginia Military Institute, he started realizing that small town life was not for him. Everybody at Bethlehem Steel was doing the same thing year after year. The company didn't seem to provide a way to move up the ladder quickly. "I said, 'this is too slow for me. I have to get into something more active.'"

Although he considered coaching basketball, he wound up taking a sales job with Lees Carpet in Lexington, Virginia. With a sales job, he figured he could be compensated according to how hard he worked. His first territory was Saginaw, Michigan, where he was able to use his stock profits to put a downpayment on a house and buy a car and furniture. Unlike so many who take out loans and use credit cards for their first homes, Kruse was ahead of the game. His only debt was a mortgage.

In his new sales job, Kruse was paid a salary plus a bonus. Initially, he made $8,000 to $10,000 annually for his first $400,000 in sales. Plus, there was a bonus if he exceeded the quota.

But as with many sales jobs you are not allowed to exceed the quota very often, he reports. Once you begin to exceed your quota, you get moved to a larger territory, which is exactly what happened to Kruse. After working in Michigan for nine months, he was transferred to Iowa, where he lived in Bettendorf. He was responsible for a territory equal to half the state. He had to sell his house and buy another, and earned just a slightly bigger salary—about $12,000. His sales quota had increased to $900,000.

"There was always a cap," Kruse said. "You could never make any big money. You might have made maybe $500 by exceeding the quota." Also, he had to travel for business three weeks out of the month.

Kruse did well and was promoted to the Chicago area, where the sales quota grew to $1.1 million. His salary increased to between $12,000 and $14,000 annually. He says he was able to pick up a brand new starter house in a development for $26,000.

He remembers that when he got his first paycheck—which he received every six months—in Chicago, he went downstairs into the lobby of the Merchandise Mart, the building where his office was located. "I looked to the left and saw a bank," he said. "I looked to the right and saw a travel agency." For a moment, he pondered what to do with the money. "I went to the travel agent and booked a trip to Jamaica," he said. "Even though I worked [really] hard, I would take a major vacation. I loved to travel."

After Kruse was in Chicago for nine months, the company offered to transfer him to an even larger territory—New York City. Tired of moving, he refused.

Investingwise, Kruse started getting involved in options and stocks in the early 1970s. "I lost money then and didn't get in the market for a long time." Then, he bought real estate and bonds. For the next 15 to 20 years, the market was pretty flat. "Bonds and bond funds did better than the stock market."

At work, however, he finally started meeting with some success. He had gotten into the commercial carpet business, before commercial carpet was routinely used in schools, office buildings, and hospitals. His job was to convince businesses to buy carpet instead of hard surfaces. Typically, his job would be to call on dealers, which at that time often were department stores like Marshall Field's, and try to get them to carry his products. Kruse didn't think that system made much sense.

"I just started looking at this and wondering why I would be calling on dealers. These are middlemen. Why wouldn't I just go directly to [the] people who are making the decision? Why would I tell my story to a dealer, who may have to tell the story to United [Airlines]. He might not tell my story. He may get a better story from Karistan."

Kruse decided instead to approach the architects, designers, and facility managers directly. These were the people who actually placed jobs up for bid, and decided on the specifications of the carpet they wanted. If he could get them to specify his carpet, dealers would be forced to order from him. He'd be in control.

It was a controversial move. "I started going right to Household Finance, United Airlines, or CNA Insurance," he said. "That was not supposed to be the way you did things because then the dealers would not sell the product."

Once his carpet was specified in a bid, distributors seeking to bid on the job started coming to him to make sure he would sell his carpet to them. Kruse, then in a position of power, would turn the process into a two-way street. He'd respond, "I'd be more than happy to sell it and I'd be more than happy to give you this price," he said. But in exchange, he'd ask the dealer to give him another client, like Zurich Insurance, for example.

The strategy caused his sales to snowball to $10 million within a few years.

At that point, Kruse sat down with his bosses and requested to work on straight commission rather than a salary. "I just saw this whole thing developing," he said. "Most people want to work on [a salary] because it's security. I felt I had a lot of confidence in my ability. I knew this was going to blossom and that things were going to do very well."

He was willing to pay his own expenses to work on his own commission. By working on commission, he saw the potential to earn $100,000 annually if he made $5 million in sales. His bosses agreed to the change.

Although Kruse had diverted far from his initial interest in chemistry, he says his education helped dramatically. His life in a military college taught him discipline. He had no problem waking at 5:30 AM, getting to his office at 6:00 AM, and leaving at 7:00 PM. By majoring in chemistry, Kruse knew everything about the chemical makeup of the carpet he was selling. He was able to make sure that the end users selected the correct carpet for their needs.

"Sometimes when you work with designers, they want to put a light blue carpet down," he said. "It's a product that's pretty, but not durable or functional. Sometimes I would lose an order because it wasn't what they wanted." His chemistry background, he added, also made him very conversant in industry terms, such as *noise coefficients*.

United Airlines once hired a major architect and designer to create a new terminal, he said. The carpet they selected was plush light gray carpet. "I said to United that I've been doing a lot of work. This is going to show coffee stains."

United Airlines went against his advice and picked the plush light gray carpet. Two years later the airline called him back to have it redone. "Everybody knew I was honest," he said. "They knew I specified the right carpet. They knew that walking through minefields, they wouldn't get blown up."

Kruse admitted that his decision to bypass dealers backfired at least once. One of the company's larger dealers, angry that he was being cut out, decided to pull his business. "I said 'Fine, I'll come and pick up the books.'"

Although Kruse said he received protests from his boss over the loss, he wasn't concerned. Once Kruse got his carpet specified in a bid, the pressure was on the dealer to be the lucky low bidder. "If the dealer didn't get it, Dealer Two would get it." Either way, Kruse still would have sold his carpet. That dealer, Kruse says, hadn't been generating that much business anyway.

"Probably back in 1974 and 1975, I was making $150,000 to $200,000 [annually]," Kruse says. He notes, that is the equivalent of $400,000 to $500,000 today.

But there was a fly in the ointment. Once you start making that much money, a company typically brings in partners which cut into your business.

This is exactly what happened to Kruse.

Although he wasn't happy about getting his first partner, he figured he had two options. One was to quit and work for another company. The other was to stay. He chose the latter.

He would work with his partners—he subsequently got another—and split the commission. "The partner didn't come in automatically and get 50 percent," he explained, so it was not an immediate loss of income. A partner might start at 10 percent and after six months, get another 10 percent.

Kruse's income remained the same. "I was offered many [corporate] presidents' jobs," he said. But he was doing well financially and probably earned more than the salaries of many executives. Plus, he said, "I was my own boss."

He admitted that in the 1970s, the trend among his friends was to move up the corporate ladder. However, he did not necessarily see that as his path. He wasn't ashamed to sell.

Kruse continued to put in long hours. He led a fast-paced life with a lot of late-night entertaining. Often, he would take clients to Chicago Bulls games. "You have to spend money to make money," he believes.

Kruse simultaneously had gotten more involved in investing. Initially, it was real estate. "I would team up with people I trusted," he said. "I never had time to do it myself." Around 1975, he bought into a building partnership that owned an apartment building. The partnership installed carpet, painted walls, and turned it over to a condo converter. "Within one weekend, they sold 300 condos in that building," he said. "We bought it for $1.4 million. We sold it for $2.5 million. Then, I got back maybe $300,000."

What he did following that investment, he says, was the "dumbest thing" of his life. He got into the oil business and lost those profits. "That was going to be my home run," he said. "It was 1974 and 1975, and gas prices were going crazy. I got sucked into the whole situation."

The major lesson he learned from the experience is not to get involved in anything he doesn't know about—even if it sounds wonderful. "In the carpet business, I knew the minefields. I knew what to do and what not to do. In the oil business, I didn't know anything." Instead, he put his trust in somebody. He also tried investing in pork bellies because his neighbor was on the Board of Trade. "I gave him a certain amount of money. I lost money."

In retrospect, Kruse says his investments would have fared much better in the 1970s if he had put his money in a mutual fund that invests in stocks that make up an index, like the S&P 500.

Nevertheless, the experiences prompted him to spend more time reading the financial sections. The information he picked up ultimately paid off. "Timing is everything in life," he said. Back in 1992 and 1993, when interest rates started falling, the market was down. He started buying Cisco, Intel, and Microsoft. Those did very, very well. He also started investing with his son and a friend in a golf course real estate investment trust—a publicly owned company that owns real estate.

Finally, having built a net worth of at least $3 million by the mid-1990s, he decided to quit his job after 30 years. He continued as quasi-consultant to clients he had obtained, but at the time of this writing, he was getting out of the consulting work.

The chief reason he left the carpet company, he says, is that they brought in "bean counters." "The whole company was going through a hard time. It was not fun any more." It's around the time he decided to quit that he first felt wealthy, he says. "If you have [$3 million to $4 million] and you're making 10 percent a year, that's $400,000 in income," he said. Even if you spend $200,000 or $250,000 annually, you're still ahead of the game. "I felt that was pretty comfortable. My son has a nice job. The girl I'm dating—my fiancée—has a nice job. That's when I sort of hung it up and figured I'm going to take it easy."

He said he actually wanted to retire at age 50, but stayed on largely to help get his son get started as a partner in the carpet business. But as much as he was trying to help his son, his customers still wanted to deal with him. He still had the same workload and was getting bored. Finally, he decided to leave. His son is now a stockbroker.

Sales work was not easy, Kruse admits, and may well have played an instrumental role in the demise of his first marriage. "You're always high or low. There's no even keel. You either lost an order or got an order. There's a lot of rejection in your life."

"You come home and figure why do I have to be nice to [my wife]," he said. "I've been nice to people for 14 hours."

However, he stops short of blaming either his hard work or his efforts to make more money on the demise of the 23-year marriage. Instead, he blames the fact that he was married at such a young age. He just wanted the experience of spending some money on himself for a change.

Now, Kruse says he is smelling the roses. He travels constantly on short trips—generally not lasting more than 7 to 11 days—and he remains an active investor.

Kruse admits that his net worth was a lot greater in 2000—prior to the dot-com crash. But he is unconcerned.

He has about five or six brokers including his son, Joseph Stuart, who is with Bear Stearns. In the mornings, Kruse says, he will call around to his brokers and decide what he should buy and what he should sell. Sometimes, he sets his computer to buy or sell a stock online. "If it hits, fine. If it doesn't, fine." Then, he'll leave and play golf.

He currently has a company, JK Ventures, Inc., which deals with private placements and research. "I have a real close friend, Jim Johnson, and we'll go investigate companies to see if we want to invest in them."

"Where I lost a lot last year [in the stock market decline of 2000] was in venture capitalist funds," he said. "I took a certain portion of money and decided to go into new businesses. One or two did fairly well." Many, though, were restricted. By the time he was able to sell them, they had dropped.

Kruse says he bought Sun Microsystems at $2 a share, which is at $50 at this writing. "I bought 400 shares five years ago. I have 12,800 shares. It split every year."

He admits he has sold about 20 percent of his technology stocks. "The Internet is not going to be the all-saving grace," he believes. "People are still going to want to go to Marshall Field's or Target and look at a shirt. People aren't going to sit in front of a computer for 10 hours shopping."

On the other hand, he believes children today are brought up with computers. "When I'm seeing my nieces and nephews, they're completely fixed to those computers."

"I just bought Microsoft," he said. "Software is where it's going to be. Phone systems will have a hard time for the next couple of years until they invent a new reason to buy a phone. But the Microsofts and Oracles—you're going to need that whether it's for video games or a PC." He also believes those are well-run companies with plenty of money in the bank. "I did get into more secure stocks, like Johnson and Johnson, for diversification. I have a certain amount of bonds that are going to be there forever. They pay me a dividend of 7 to 8 percent. I've got muni bonds. That is money to live on. The rest is just play money."

Once, he said, he watched one account he trades rise $2 million over a four-month period. "Then it all corrected and boom!"

Although you might consider Kruse a day-trader—a vocation that can be extremely risky—Kruse insists he limits his computer trading.

He might, for example, buy 500 shares of Lehman at $69 or $70 a share and put a sell at $75 a share. "If it sells, fine. Then I'll wait for it to go back down. If it bursts out and goes to $80, I'll find something else."

He stresses that he sets some rules on trading by computer.

First, he only does it with a limited amount of money. Then, he calls five or six brokers to get a diversified opinion on the stock. Plus, he only buys stock in a company he wants to own for the long-term anyway, so it doesn't bother him if it goes down.

"The management of a company is important," he believes. "You've got to make sure you research it."

Recently, he had a home built for his mother. While his father was still alive, he took his parents to Hawaii. He also bought them a car.

He wants to see his nieces and nephews have money for college and he wants his mother to have a comfortable life.

"If you loan money to relatives, it's not a loan," he notes. "It's just a gift." His sister has five children, and through them, he has nine great-nieces and one great-nephew. He has given each some stock so that when they reach college, they will have money.

Although he has donated money to his alma mater, VMI, he says he largely has shunned philanthropy due to the enormous responsibility he already has with his own family.

Looking back on his accomplishments, Kruse reflects on his working class roots and on what all his wealth means in the overall scheme of life.

The downside of wealth, he says, is you stop every once in a while and ask yourself what's enough? "It's hard to spend over

$250,000—unless you have villas in Rome [or] Florence, planes or boats. I'm not that type of person."

Kruse doesn't believe that more is necessarily better. "How many lobsters or steaks can you eat? How many pistachio-encrusted tunas with reduction of red wine sauce can you eat? Sometimes, basics are better."

He is happy with the security the money brings, "but then you get greedy."

Kruse says that if he had it to do again, he probably would have taken a certain amount of money in the 1970s and put it in a stock mutual fund or an index fund instead of the quick high-flying investments he made. "I probably should have bought a place in Palm Beach. It doubled in price. I just don't like to be committed to having a place. Then you're compelled to have to go there."

He appreciates variety when he's traveling. "Next week, I'm going to Charlottesville. I'm going to Lake Tahoe and New Orleans. I booked a trip to China. I love to see the mountains and oceans. I enjoy getting on a plane and just going somewhere."

His fiancée, he says, works in a straight commission business and lives on the top floor of a high-rise on Chicago's Lakeshore Drive. If she's free, she can travel with him. When they want the city life, they go to her place, and when they tire of concrete, they go to his place in the suburbs.

CHAPTER 2

ANGELA ADAIR-HOY

Single Mom to Online Publishing Diva

In March 1999, Angela Adair-Hoy, now 35, was out of work with three children, and newly divorced from an alcoholic husband. A year later, due to some unique moves she made to promote an online publishing business, she was a millionaire.

Her worst nightmare spanned a three-month period in 1999. Shortly after her divorce, she became unemployed when the Internet marketing company she worked for went belly-up. On top of that, her refrigerator had given out and she could not afford to get it fixed. It was a struggle to feed her family. She skipped meals for herself, and survived largely by eating the leftovers on the plates of her three young children.

In the two years since, her life has radically turned around. Remarried and expecting a fourth child in the fall of 2001, she now works comfortably with her new husband in her 3,500-square-foot home on the Penobscot River in Bangor, Maine. A millionaire on paper, she pegs the worth of her company, BookLocker.com, at "no less than $5 million or $6 million." She is reported to have rejected a minimum of three offers by venture capitalists to buy the company, but was considering obtaining investors at this writing. Plus, she earns close to $5,000 monthly from sales of her own electronic books. Her husband, Richard Hoy, left a $70,000-a-year job in Massachusetts to work with her on BookLocker.com full time at home.

Adair-Hoy's electronic publication, *WritersWeekly.com,* is circulated to 51,000 subscribers. It's a freebie she distributes largely to freelance writers to help advertise her five electronic self-help books. In it, she writes a popular column, "News from the Home Office."

She also claims more than 850 paying subscribers to *Write Markets Report,* a monthly electronic newsletter that charges $8.95 for the first year and $11.95 each year after that. The newsletter lists 30 new writers' markets monthly and each editor's current needs.

Adair-Hoy didn't exactly start out poor, but her life wasn't easy. Born in Columbus, Indiana, she spent much of her young life in Woodlands, Texas. Her father died of a brain tumor when she was five. With two brothers and one sister, she grew up with her mother and her mother's second husband, who owned a real estate company and later adopted her. "It was a beautiful big house and nice neighborhood," she admitted. She had her own room and a tree outside her window. "It was a nice tree that I could shimmy down." She often got to take her mother's credit cards to the mall. "I don't remember cherishing the fact that Mom would hand me a credit card," she reflected. "But I cherished having my own bank account, and having hundreds of dollars in it."

Adair-Hoy's mother was careful to teach her a few important lessons that carried her through the tough times in her life. "One thing that Mom taught me from day one is that I had to be able to make it on my own," she said. "You could never count on a man to take care of you forever. Her husband died when I was five. She had no college and no work experience. She was left with nothing but a small life insurance policy."

Her mother also taught Adair-Hoy another important lesson at an unusually young age. That is: The harder you work, the more money you can earn, and there is virtually no limit to the amount you can earn. Her mother worked at home as a bookkeeper for her husband's business and actually paid young Adair-Hoy to help out with the books. "She taught me accounting and bookkeeping," she said. "There was never too much to do. I could make as much money as I wanted." Adair-Hoy found that she didn't mind the hard work, and enjoyed making money. When she was 10, she actually wanted to work ten hours a day.

She also loved to read, pouring over *Readers Digest* from cover to cover when she was seven or eight years old.

School was a different story, though. In school, she was more interested in making friends than in obtaining good grades. "I was definitely an average student," she said. "My big brother always made straight As and graduated a year early from college. I was more creative."

You might say her calling came when she was in tenth grade and had to write a book report. "I can't remember what it was on because I didn't read the book." Nevertheless, the report still impressed her teacher, who gave her an A-plus and wrote on the report: Good B.S. The experience remained an inspiration to her. At that age, she knew she was able to write. Further inspiring her in that direction was a personality test in high school that indicated she would make a good journalist. She was thrilled to get a chance to live that dream while a senior in high school. She was selected at a school audition to work as a reporter for TV 10, a local cable television station. She covered the school beat. "I really wanted to be on camera," she said. "I thought that of all the jobs anybody had in high school, a TV reporter definitely would be the coolest one to have.

"I really liked being recognized wherever I went. It's like when a writer publishes a first magazine article and sees the writing before the public eye. It's a tremendous high."

Upon graduating high school, she went on to University of Houston. Her mother and step-father paid for the first year, but warned that she would have to pay for the rest of her schooling on her own. Not only did they wish her to be entirely independent, but they also had exhausted their college funds on her other siblings. That first year, she received $50 spending money weekly. As it turned out, she never finished college. She became pregnant at age 18. She dropped out of school after a year and a half and had her first son at age 19.

Adair-Hoy married in 1986. Her husband worked for a rental car company.

"I didn't believe in abortion," she said. She and her husband each wrote their own wedding vows, and Adair-Hoy says she must have had a premonition. She deliberately made sure that the wedding vows omitted the traditional words, "til death do us part." The two lived in a rented condominium in Woodlands, Texas, and she stayed home with her new baby for six months. Then she happened to note an ad in the newspaper for a bookkeeper job. It paid $1,000 monthly. To her, that was a fortune! She got the job.

Although she enjoyed her new job, her employment was cut short when her husband was transferred to an office in Clear Lake, Texas, one hour away. She had to quit, but was able to find another bookkeeper job near her new home that paid even more—$1,200 monthly. "That company got into financial trouble," she reported. The president bluntly told her she might want to get her resume out. She followed his advice and, within one month, had found yet another job. This time, she was making $2,000 a month as a bookkeeper for Space Industries in Clear Lake.

She was encouraged in her ability to continuously earn more. However, despite the increase in pay, she was having difficulty paying bills. She realized her husband was drinking away all their hard-earned money. He was spending virtually everything on 12-packs of beer. What made matters even worse was that he also was having difficulty holding a job. After she started working at Space Industries, her doctor put her on antidepressants. "I thought about killing myself," she said. "No matter how much I made, we were still broke."

There were fights, as well as yelling and humiliation at home. "He embarrassed me at company functions," she said. At Space Industries, there was an annual summer picnic, and she had always joked about how much her boss hated smokers. Her husband, who sat across from her boss, purposely blew smoke squarely in her boss's face. "He wouldn't have done that if he weren't drunk,"

Adair-Hoy said. It was not uncommon for him to sit in the backyard, play the guitar, and sing at the top of his lungs. He showed up at work drunk. Then he tried going to Alcoholics Anonymous for two years. He sobered up and everything seemed great.

In December 1996, he started drinking again. He didn't start drinking in small quantities either. "He started out right where he left off."

At first, Adair-Hoy says she thought it was best to stay married for her children. She later discovered that staying married was the worst thing you possibly can do for children in that type of environment. Do that, she says, and you risk having your children grow up to be just like their father. She fears now that one of her sons is taking on some of her ex-husband's characteristics.

"Get the hell out as fast as you can," she now advises women who are married to abusive husbands. It only gets worse. No matter what they promise; no matter how long they get sober. It gets worse every single day. If you take a look back at your life, you're not going to believe what you're humanly capable of withstanding."

Adair-Hoy says physical abuse was not the major issue. She only recounts one physically abusive incident.

"There's physical battering and emotional battering," she explains. "I was mentally abused—brainwashed, manipulated. I was told what a terrible person I was, what a loser I was, how fat I was, how ugly I was. Sometimes that's worse than getting smacked across the face or punched in the nose. That's an everyday thing—day and night. Women who are victims of emotional abuse don't understand how badly it's affecting them."

Although she is now happily married, she continues to feel the effects of the abuse from her earlier marriage. "Richard (her current husband) just got upset the other day with a customer. I cringed, like a dog who had been abused. I'm still squeamish about getting yelled at. I react to people who are upset just like an abused puppy does. I had no idea . . . for a dozen years, how it [would] affect me the rest of my life. And God only knows what it did to my kids. They're watching Mommy being abused. They're hearing every word."

She is working hard to change the behavior of her oldest son, who has picked up some of his father's bad habits. Sometimes, like his father, he is manipulative, she says. There also is downright lying. "He lies to my face, and then it's so easy to make up for it later. Well, I forgot. Or, that's not exactly what I said, Mom, what I meant is this."

She says she has been trying to stress how counterproductive such behavior is in the hope that he will change.

After years of abuse, Adair-Hoy says she threw her hands up and gave up on her first marriage. "I didn't move out. I went out and got myself a boyfriend. I knew [my husband] would find out and [I] didn't care."

Adair-Hoy says she, her alcoholic husband, and her family were living in a house in Shore Acres, Texas, along with her mother-in-law. Her husband was working as a waiter. She realized that his family was going to try to get custody of her children in the hope that they could live on her paycheck. One day, when she came home from work after her mother-in-law had been watching the children, her children grabbed her and sat her down. They told her that her mother-in-law had grabbed Adair-Hoy's young daughter by the hair, dragged her down the kitchen counter and gripped her throat. "I don't know if it was a menopausal type of rage," she said. After she complained to authorities, the mother-in-law was ordered to move out of the house.

At one point, she said, the police came to her house nightly for about a week. Police acknowledged that her husband was always drunk, but they thought it was a temporary situation. One time, her husband punctured her car tire with a screwdriver. He then chased her car to the police station, which she reached while driving on a bare rim. Police came out with their guns drawn. [The police] acted like I wasn't under any threat. . . . I went to court two days later and got a protective order."

In the meantime, her employer, Space Industries, had gone under. But her unemployment was short-lived. A former employee of Space Industries contacted her and asked her to work for his new

Internet company. "He offered me a lot of money and showed me how to open an Internet browser. I thought it was the coolest thing! I was making more money and really liked what I did a lot."

Again, her salary rose at the new Internet firm, and she liked the job.

The key to success can lie in spotting opportunity. Adair-Hoy had developed skills in writing early in life which lay dormant for years. But the chance to use them again arose.

"I was surfing the Net and thought about writing." She found a Florida-based magazine, *Gulf South Sailing,* online and sent in a query letter. She wound up writing a funny but true story about a sailing adventure the family had taken in Galveston Bay. "They ran a color picture of my son and me. I was hooked."

Adair-Hoy was thrilled to see her words in a magazine, and had managed to accomplish this feat while still working for her Internet company. Having her photo on the front page, she said, rekindled the joy of recognition she had experienced as a television reporter.

Seeking more writing opportunities, she obtained a book she heard about called *Writer's Market,* which tracks publications and their editors. She decided to use the book to query more publications about buying her articles. The e-mailed response she received from the first publication she contacted indicated that she needed to update her records. The editor she wrote to had left that publication a year ago.

That e-mail made her realize that there was a substantial void for freelance writers. *Writer's Market* is the writer's bible for sources of publisher information. Yet, it was substantially out of date.

She considered starting a magazine that listed current paying markets for writers. Within one month, she printed 1,000 copies of *The Write Markets Report.* She posted notices at various Internet sites frequented by freelance writers. "Anybody could get the first issue." She started a Web site on Tripod, a free Web site service. At $39.95 for an annual subscription, she picked up 600 subscribers after six months.

The paid subscriptions reflected added income over and above the $36,000 annually she was earning in her job, which subsequently increased to $50,000 annually.

At one point, she tried starting a syndicate, selling articles of other writers to newspapers. The business flopped, but taught her a lesson. Never start a business without carefully surveying your competition. The problem? She was competing with major syndicates that could supply a newspaper with several camera-ready columns daily and sell them for a mere $10 each.

All was not lost from the experience. She decided to write a book, *How to Be a Syndicated Newspaper Columnist.* She started marketing the print book to her newsletter subscribers, complete with a disk containing a database of 6,000 newspapers. "I hate paperwork and hated copying disks and stuffing them in envelopes," she said. "That is what led me to start selling this book as an e-mail attachment."

She sold a Microsoft Word attachment to people with her book, and lowered its price from $19.95 to $14.95. Because the book was available instantly, more people bought it." She already was accepting payments by credit cards and she paid a company $30 to set up a simple online order form. "That really took off and increased income."

At that point, she was making $1,500 to $2,000 a month working at night. "It was a huge source of arguments in the household," she said. "My husband really enjoyed drinking all the money. He felt guilty while I sat there and worked my ass off. One night, he poured beer on my keyboard. That was the only night he ever hit me."

She decided to send out an abbreviated issue of her *Write Markets Report* for free via e-mail. Even though it was free, she thought it would be a means to advertise her book. "Instantly, I had 3,000 or 4,000 subscribers." Her book sales increased. The newsletter, though, was monthly. She figured if she sent it weekly, it would make the marketing messages about her books that much more visible. Marketers often say people need to see a message about a dozen times before they actually act on it. "Book sales quadrupled!" By sending an electronic version, she had no printing costs and eliminated the need to lay out the newsletter, which was a chore she hated. "I sent a notice lowering the subscription fee and extending subscriptions. I only lost three subscribers." Now all her publications were electronic only. She had eliminated printing and postage costs. Altogether, she has published five books. She sold so many copies of one e-book, she says she sold it at auction to St. Martin's Press for a high five-figure advance.

By November 1998, she was divorced from her first husband. Her 12½ year marriage was over. "The month I got my divorce, the doctor took me off of antidepressants," she says. Her boyfriend, Richard, was vice president of marketing of the company she worked for, but immediately after her divorce, the company went out of business.

She was dating Richard despite her financial troubles. "Having faith in God really helped me get through the hard times," she said. "We used to go to church, but I hated going. Maybe because Texas is the Bible Belt. But every time we went they would talk about how much money the church needed. I started going to an Episcopalian church. There we learned tithing. They wanted 10 percent of my income. I thought that was ridiculous. I didn't go back there.

"I read the entire Book of Revelations. I teach [my kids] what they need [to know] to be good people. We're Christians, but I'm not shoving religion down their throat."

Her faith came in handy then, however.

Adair-Hoy and Richard were married in a surprise ceremony in March 1999. "Richard's mother was in town visiting. I had just met her. Richard was about to leave for Massachusetts and we were going to get married—but not then. He was leaving for a new job."

Adair-Hoy was going to ship the rest of his things, but he responded, "You can't." The two started arguing. She asked why not? "Because I'm marrying you on Saturday," he said.

It turned out everyone, including his mother, had known about the wedding that weekend, except her.

A month after they were married, they moved to Massachusetts because Richard had gotten a job for an Internet publication. "I was working at home running *WritersWeekly.com.*"

In September 1999, she was contacted by the owner of a company called BookLocker.com, who had been running the electronic book publishing company out of his home. "He was a stay-at-home Dad," she said. "He wanted to know if he could list and sell my book, *How to Write, Publish, and Sell E-books,* on his Web site. He would pay me 70 percent royalties and not take any rights. I said all right."

Within one week, her book was the best-selling book on his Web site. "Later that month, he called us and asked if we wanted to buy his Web site. It already was very well-known. Somehow he had managed to get press everywhere." It had gotten to be too much [for him] to handle by himself."

Adair-Hoy and her husband managed to buy it for $5,000 cash.

By March 2000, BookLocker.com and WritersWeekly.com were doing so well that Richard quit his $70,000-a-year job in Massachusetts. Adair-Hoy says she was netting about $60,000 annually, including book royalties.

The couple moved to Bangor, where, coincidentally, they live about five minutes from the famed fiction writer, Stephen King. Even though King happens to be the man who put e-books on the map when he became the first legendary author to offer his books to readers online, Adair-Hoy says she has never met him. She has gone by his house, but "he's never there," she says. "His gate says, 'Keep out,' but it's always open."

The couple lives and works out of a 100-year-old home, which has a stained glass window.

She began realizing her success, she says, in late 1999, when she was making enough money to be able to take her children to their favorite stores. Her son loved electronic stores, and her daughter loved antique jewelry. "If they say, 'Mommy, I need a new pair of shoes,' I don't have to worry that there's enough in the checking account."

Single Mom to Online Publishing Diva

It was almost as though the clouds opened when she divorced. "I could see I was going to make it. Right after I got divorced, everything accelerated. I learned it was because [my first husband] was holding me back."

Yet, in those three months after she lost her job at the marketing company, she never told anyone how bad things were at home. "I was getting no child support. He owes over $11,000 in child support now," she says. "The only income I had was from the Web site—which was considerably less than my salary." Although she had started dating Richard, she never thought to ask him for money. She also refused to ask her mother for anything. The independence her mother had taught her at a young age prevented that. Plus, she believes, "when you borrow money, after you pay them back, you still owe them something."

BookLocker.com has more than 700 authors and she pockets 30 to 50 percent of each sale, depending upon how the e-book is priced.

Unlike when she tried to broker newspaper columns, she carefully observes the competition. Most, she says, are e-publishers, which operate like vanity companies, charging authors to reproduce their work. "Our competitors concentrate on how much they can get from authors," she said. "We concentrate on how many [books] we can help our authors sell. We're a bookstore."

E-book publishing is a burgeoning business. Adair-Hoy is in on the ground floor with a brand name. She estimates that by 2002, more than 70,000 previously unpublished books and shorter works will be available online or through print-on-demand.

Adair-Hoy says the demand for her publishing services is strong. The average author published by a traditional publishing company gets an advance of less than $10,000 to write his or her book. Then the author typically gets between 10 and 15 percent in royalties based on the wholesale cost of the book. The wholesale cost of a book is about half the retail price. Only after it has made back its advance does a publishing company pay authors royalty checks from book sales.

By contrast, e-books pay no advance. However, royalties run between 40 and 70 percent of the point-of-sale cost of the online book. An online publisher makes about 30 percent.

A popular online book can pay off handsomely.

"The advent of the superstore bookstore, the decline of the independent bookstore, the mergers of so many publishing houses, and the megadeals authors get have all drastically lowered the number of new authors published each year," Adair-Hoy says. "Most big publishers want books that can sell at least 25,000 copies."

The key to her success, she firmly believes, is finding a niche. "I was just lucky enough to find something that was missing in the market," she says, "and I was able to serve that need. I'm continually looking for things that are missing."

She feels a great way for writers to make money is through *e-serials* in which readers pay per chapter or installment obtained electronically. "I was the first to write books on e-books. I look for a need and heavily market."

To anyone who wants to be wealthy, she advises, find a niche of your own. "Don't copy somebody else. If you must copy, do it in a different way. Really promote the fact that this is the only place you can find this product."

For her business, she says, she employs a freelance part-time formatter in Washington, D.C., and a freelance writer in Houston, who takes care of customer issues. She already plans for one of her book coauthors, M.J. Rose, and another author Doug Clegg, who she says is the first e-serial writer, to write eight columns in *WritersWeekly* *.com*. The arrangement is designed to give her a break after her new baby is born.

Her husband, Richard, she says, is their company's online marketing expert. Plus, he handles the technical back-end, recently negotiating with a Web site development company it hired. "He speaks far and wide. He comes up with brilliant marketing ideas for *WritersWeekly*."

Here is an example. Writers were up in arms when the Web site Themestream went out of business and failed to pay 40,000 writers money owed them. "Not all were *WritersWeekly* subscribers," she said. Her publication took an active role in trying to get the writers paid by creating a site to survey how much people were owed. Richard created the simple survey online which was accessed through a hyperlink from her WritersWeekly newsletter. At the top of the site was an e-mail address to subscribe to the free newsletter.

Although *WritersWeekly.com* typically averages 100 new subscribers daily, she says, the day the survey was posted, it registered 433 subscribers. It also landed media coverage. Meanwhile, a *WritersWeekly.com* subscriber, who happened to be an attorney, helped provide directions as to what unpaid writers should do.

Adair-Hoy believes that the greatest secret to promoting online is to have a free e-mail newsletter to distribute. "Offer free quality editorial content and your readers will keep growing and stay with you."

If you're a fiction author, she advises, distribute a free online serial. Even give away the first three chapters, she suggests. "Listing in a search engine does not work."

Adair-Hoy figures that every new subscriber to *WritersWeekly .com* is a potential buyer of books. "We're pretty sure that just about every subscriber buys books," she says.

The Hoys operate a specialty bookstore at WritersWeekly.com that sells books about writing. The BookLocker.com store sells online books on everything. "We don't just advertise BookLocker," she adds. "We advertise specific books. That's why sales are so high."

She estimates that each *WritersWeekly.com* issue promotes about three books from BookLocker.com and 20 from WritersWeekly.com. All the books are available through BookLocker.com.

If you're considering writing an online book, she suggests that a writer never sign an exclusive online publishing agreement. "These companies are too new to risk giving all your rights," she says. She suggests that you never accept less than 50 percent royalties for electronic books, and urges "don't ever sign a contract that you can't get out of within a day." Say you put your book online and sell 1,000 copies in one week. Suddenly, you get a call from Random House. "If you're in a contract you can't get out of for one year, they're going to drop you."

BookLocker.com recently "paid a company a fortune," she says, to upgrade. It wants its systems and databases converted to other Web sites so it can help other companies start their own e-book stores.

"Every time something gets too big or takes too much time, we automate it," she reports. "We just had to pay a developer $1,500 to automate orders that come in for print books, so we don't have to handle it. That's $1,500 well-spent."

Her at-home business gives her an opportunity to stay home for her children, much like her mother did for her. Often, she says, she would come home from school and smell cookies baking. The downside, though, is she is in high demand. "I get more than 700 e-mails a day now. It's hard to keep up and maintain a one-on-one relationship." Although her assistant in Houston helps, she says there are some e-mails that only she can answer. "It's a big drain on time."

She handles working at home with her husband by putting on two imaginary hats. Her writer's hat stays on all day long. "I have to get below 100 unread e-mails in my mailbox before I can turn off my computer," she said. "I try not to let any e-mail get more than 10 days old before I take care of it."

Typically, she shuts off the computer at 6:00 PM, goes downstairs, and becomes "mommy and wife." "Richard and I never argued until we were trying to name the new corporation," she said. "It took us three days. It's called Hoy Publishing. It doesn't appear anywhere. That was the first argument Richard and I ever had. We get along so well and respect each other so much and love each other so much.

"When we have a business disagreement, we know we are talking to a coworker—not to a husband or wife. We can have an argument whether we're going to carry this book or that book during the day. At night, that doesn't stop us from cuddling."

Things have gotten easier financially, but she is careful not to let her children get too spoiled. Each time they go to a bookstore, each is given $10 to buy a book. "It feels great to be able to spoil the kids that way." They also each get a $5 weekly allowance. In return, they have chores to do around the house.

Adair-Hoy admitted the couple was seeking a financial advisor. "Seriously," she says. "We need help. We're making too much money. We have absolutely no idea what we're doing with the money except spending it."

Yet, the two are not entirely debt-free. She said the company, which had been debt-free, recently took out a small loan. The couple still has leftover credit card debt. In fact, she says, they had just paid off one credit card, and were taking that $500 monthly payment and applying it to their other debt. "I think all the personal credit cards will be paid off within three years. She anticipated having the house paid off in five years.

In the aftermath of the dot-com bomb, the period in 2000-2001 in which many investors lost more than 50 percent on tech stocks, Adair-Hoy says her company has not suffered.

The dot-com bomb, she claims, is the result of entrepreneurs getting themselves in hock up to their ears. "They've got a tremendous amount of debt and investors to keep happy. They got caught up in the big whirlwind of IPOs."

Many dot-coms, she complains, had a business plan to go to an initial public offering (IPO). "That's the way to fail," she believes. "We never intended to go IPO. We always kept the business model as a self-sustainable business model. Our expenses will never exceed our income. We may be growing slowly, but we've got steady growth. At the end of the month, we always have plenty of money in the bank to pay authors royalties. Sure, we could have cashed out and gotten tons of investors."

She also has shunned venture capitalists. Venture capitalists invest money in growing companies. Later on when the company's earnings are growing, they hope to profit by helping take the company public. Then they cash out their shares of stock in the firm for a fat profit.

But venture capitalists are not always the silent partners they say they are, she believes. She says she would not be able to grow the company the way she wants with involvement from a venture capitalist. Plus, she would lose editorial control.

There's no guarantee that you can get investors, she says. Also, a lot of entrepreneurs cash in for investors so they can have big salaries temporarily. "We live within our means," she says.

CHAPTER 3

SEYMOUR "SY" SPERLING

Balding and Divorced to Hair Club Czar

Seymour "Sy" Sperling, 60, grew up fighting once or twice a week to protect his lunch money from the gangs in South Bronx and had his college career cut short by a shotgun wedding. Today, the founder of Hair Club for Men lives in a 3,000-square-foot oceanfront home, with a gym and 70-foot balcony overlooking the ocean in Hillsboro Beach, near Boca Raton, Florida. He is best known for his popular television ads that showed his bald head "before" and his hair-laden head "after." He repeatedly made honest claims on television that he's "not only the Hair Club president, but also a client."

Having sold his company in 2000, he claims a net worth of $18 million. In addition, he is under a five-year contract, earning $800,000 annually as a consultant to his old company and another $600,000 annually not to compete. He and his third wife each drive a Lexus.

"I'm still a consultant for Hair Club," he says. "They use me for public relations, marketing, and motivational sessions. They felt that was a very important part of what I did. I was on Deco Drive [Miami Beach, Florida] last week talking about the hair styles of Hollywood people. What [comedienne] Joan Rivers does for clothing, I do for hair."

He also is a partner in another company, Sperling Marketing, which specializes in buying television time at bargain prices.

Born Jewish, Sperling, a father of two grown children, goes to temple on Mondays and Thursdays. "I'm the official Torah carrier," he says. "It brings me back to my early roots. My mother and father were very, very traditional. I rejected it for many years." Sperling found it hard to absorb his parents' teachings of orthodox Judaism while everybody in his neighborhood was involved in gang wars. However, his sister, Rosalie, started going to synagogue twice daily, and renewed his interest. He also has hired a full-time financial advisor.

Sperling is one of three children born to his father, David, a plumber, and his mother, Carrie, a homemaker and full-charge bookkeeper. He very much loved and admired his father. Yet he felt sorry for him and decided he never wanted to be poor like his dad, who had his own plumbing business and often saw months lapse between jobs. "We always had enough food on the table. We never went hungry," Sperling said. "But he always struggled to pay the rent. Clothing was sparce."

"He was a silly man," Sperling says of his father. "He would walk around with filthy hands. He didn't have a tool box. He carried his old tools in a burlap bag. My friends used to laugh at him."

In fact, while growing up, Sperling actually was jealous of his cousins, whose very wealthy father owned many apartment buildings in Manhattan and had left them millions. But as Sperling shoveled dirt on his father's grave in 1970, he realized that the gifts he had been left by his father were far more important. He pondered how his father respected his commitment to family and to charity. His father bartered plumbing services for tuition so that Sperling could go to Yeshiva Elementary School. His mother worked in the school's kitchen.

He also appreciated his father's sense of humor.

Sperling recalled the time when his father was 56, and was taken to the hospital with chest pains. A nurse, asked him, "Where's the pain? Where's the pain?" Quipped his ailing father, "In the pocket. In the pocket."

As life turned out, one of Sperling's once-admired wealthy cousins became obese and died in his 50s. "He never got a chance to spend his money," Sperling noted.

Sperling, on the other hand, is enjoying his newly realized wealth.

It wasn't always that way. As a child, Sperling had admired the entrepreneurship of his older brother, Jay. Now in the home improvement business, Jay Sperling, at the age of 13, had started delivering newspapers, and actually had friends working for him.

Sy Sperling had his first job at age 11. He would take the subway from South Bronx to Manhattan on weekends to shine shoes in New York's Times Square for tips. He'd earn $5 to $10 a day.

Sperling was far from the best student in high school. He averaged grades of about 75 percent. He recalls once scoring 90 percent on the Regents exam. He spent his time playing basketball and going out with friends. He loved westerns and often watched Roy Rogers and Gene Autry. He'd make believe he was on a horse and hop home from school. More than anything else, he wanted his parents to buy him a pony. He often begged his father—only to be told that there was no room for a pony in the two-bedroom flat shared by the family of five.

Sperling, though, reports that he managed to succeed at becoming "the first urban Jewish cowboy." He tracked down a horseback riding stable in South Bronx and offered to shovel horse manure in exchange for a free ride on a horse. Eventually, he was permitted to take the horse out, and he became a guide on trail rides. "I used to go there every day after school." In fact, he said, he sometimes skipped his bar mitzvah lessons to go to the stables.

It was Jay Sperling who subsequently encouraged his family to move to a much nicer area—North Bronx. He went so far as to offer to help pay the family's rent, if necessary, to make the move. By the time Jay was 18, he had taken over a major newspaper delivery franchise servicing the *Daily News, Daily Mirror, Journal American,* and *Herald Tribune.* Sy Sperling began working for his brother part time. By age 16, he was also helping out with his father's plumbing business part time.

Sperling says the turning point in his life came when he was 18 years old and enlisted in the air force. "If I didn't go into the air force, I got the feeling I might have gone down the wrong road on the highway," he says. "I was hanging out with gangs, smoking a lot of pot. I saw my future fading in front of me. I enlisted. I wanted to get away from the neighborhood. I needed a change in scenery."

He went through basic training in Texas. "My first week in the air force, the drill instructor asked for a volunteer to fight the champ of the base. I was the only one out of several hundred guys who volunteered to fight him," he said. The champ not only was good at boxing, but he also had been an all-state football star. Sperling definitely felt qualified for the job. He had grown up in a war zone. "We had about 100 fights a year. My experience strictly was street fighting. I used to watch boxing on TV." Sperling came very close to defeating the champ. He fought to a three-round draw. After that, he joined the air force boxing team.

"[Boxing] got me out of a lot of basic training mundane chores," he said. "I didn't have to do kitchen work or scrub bathrooms." He worked out in the gym and boxed weekly on Saturday night. "I guess you can take the person out of the community, but the community stays with you through your whole life," he said. "I was fighting until age 27. I had a short fuse. When you grow up in that kind of environment, it becomes a mentality. Rather than negotiate my way out of a dispute, I would take a short cut. I'd duke it out."

Through the air force, Sperling got to travel—further expanding his horizons. He also got to attend college. There was an extension of C.W. Post University on base, so he was able to earn most of his college credits through the Long Island–based university. While in France, he obtained additional credits through the University of Maryland. "I liked the idea of making money. That was important to me," he said. "I didn't know what I wanted to do with my life until I reached my mid-20s." He thought he might wish to teach political science, and he majored in political science and history. His grades, mediocre in high school, greatly improved in college. He obtained grades upwards of 3.5 on a 4-point scale. "I was very, very committed," he explained, "Once I got away from the neighborhood—I was 18 years old—I started to think like an adult. I was more focused on getting good marks and having a good career."

Sperling accumulated 96 credits and was 15 credits shy of finishing college when his education was derailed. His girlfriend told him she was pregnant. Sperling, feeling a sense of duty, agreed to marry her. He asked her father if they could stay in his extra bedroom in Queens for just a couple of months so that he could finish college. "No," her father had responded. "You made her pregnant. Go out and get a job." Although Sperling was very discouraged to hear those words, in retrospect, he considers his father-in-law's hardline stance a blessing in disguise.

Sperling initially moved with his new wife into a one bedroom apartment that cost $125 a month. He earned $65 a week in his first job, repairing Xerox machines. "I had acquired technical skills in the air force," he explained.

"After subway fare, dry cleaning, and buying food for the family, I didn't have enough [money] for rent. I used to try to eat at my in-laws' place as often as I could. I had no money."

Although he was poor as a child, his life as a married man was worse. At least when I was a kid, there was always food on the table," he said.

Sperling married in November 1964. The couple's first child was born the following May. He moved on to a higher paying job—selling carpeting. Now he was earning $100 a week. He wasn't getting rich, but he finally had money to afford food. Then, he went on to sell home improvements. As he obtained more experience selling, he grew more confident. His salary increased from $100 to $200 to $300 to $500 weekly. "I was doing a lot better."

During his two-year first marriage, which produced his two children, his wife didn't cook. The couple went out for fast food every night. He gained 25 to 30 pounds. "My hairline was going all the way back. I was sweeping it over and spraying it." Sperling's first marriage ended when he was in his mid-20s. He was at an emotional low and moved in with his brother, Jay, in Long Island, who had married and had several children and extra bedrooms. He also spent time at his sister's home.

Although Sy Sperling was single again, he was interested in re-marrying. "When you look like a schlepper [Yiddish for clumsy or stupid person], you're not the most marketable person out there," he said. "I decided at that time to get something done. My brother and I [got] together on [a] Sunday and saw an editorial [in the newspaper] about a new concept of hair weaving. He went to Florida and had it done. He was going to surprise me." Sperling, simultaneously, also decided to have his hair woven. "We both wanted to surprise each other and had our hair woven at the same time."

The hair weave changed his life.

"It made such a difference in my self-esteem. Now that my hair looked good, I took a more critical look at the rest of my body. It motivated me to go on a diet and lose weight. I bought new clothing and went to Grossinger's [a resort in New York's Catskill Mountains] on a singles week.

"I was so confident about the way I looked with the new svelte body. For the first time in my life, I actually liked myself. I felt self-confident. I was talking to young women and getting phone numbers. It was like a rebirth."

At the time his social life was improving, Sperling was working for his brother selling swimming pools. Because he was more self-confident, his sales improved. His brother, Jay, suggested that they go into the hair weaving business together, and that Sperling be the sales manager. "I had to help him," Sperling said. He borrowed a couple of thousand dollars on his credit cards, but the business lasted just a few months.

"Once we decided we were going to go into the hair business, my brother made a connection with a guy in Manhattan manufacturing hair pieces on a small scale out of a loft at 923 Broadway." The manufacturer employed a woman to do the hair weaving. They had provided hair weaves for some Hollywood celebrities. The group made a deal on a handshake. Jay and Sy Sperling would do the advertising and the manufacturer would do the hair weaving application. The Sperlings would charge $750 for the hair weave and pay the manufacturer $200.

After the first month, they were stunned at the results. They had 30 new customers—much more than they had anticipated. "We would have been happy with half that!" When the hair manufacturer saw how high sales were, he decided that he could make more money if he cut the two brothers out of the picture. Yet, the two already had "put a couple grand into his place," Sperling said. They had put up panels, repainted, and carpeted the front reception room.

"After the first month, he kicked us out. We argued with him. We said, 'Look, we have to spend a lot on advertising. We're doing the selling.' He didn't even want to complete the 30 clients. These people had given us deposits, but we couldn't finish the work. We were without a place."

Sperling says that in hindsight, he realizes that the three should have put their agreement in writing. Nevertheless, the two brothers had a plan. The manufacturer had been training Sperling's sister-in-law to do the hair weaves. They decided to pick their new clients up at their homes, drive them to Jay Sperling's house in Long Island, and have his wife complete the weaves in their basement. They pocketed the money and used it to help build their first store in Long Island. They called their business Hair Weave Creations. Sperling says he put out about $7,000 to $10,000 for the space—which largely came from cash flow and credit cards. They bought barber chairs, put up panels, and painted. "We started making sales before we finished construction," he said. Sperling started placing ads in the sports pages of *Newsday*. "I didn't have an ad agency," Sperling said. The ad showed before and after shots featuring Sy Sperling's own once-bald head and his head after having a hair weave. "The results were so impressive."

The two sold three franchises immediately—in Queens, New Jersey, and the Bronx. But after all their effort, Sperling and his brother were not getting along. Finally, they split up. Hair Weave Creations was bought out by a public company, Doric Distributors, after three months. It gave Jay Sperling $750,000 worth of stock. Sy Sperling was to receive $75,000 worth of stock. However, Sy was so angry at his brother, that he returned the stock. The stock later proved worthless because the company went bankrupt during the recession that began in the late 1960s. Though the stock initially sold for $7 a share, Jay bought the company back for one penny on a dollar and renamed it Hair Replacement Centers.

In the meantime, the franchise that opened in the Bronx had been bought by a high school buddy of Sy Sperling's. The friend invited Sperling to become a partner. "We made a whole bunch of sales," he said.

Sperling notes that when somebody offers you a partnership, generally, there is an economic motive behind it. In this case, his friend was not a good salesman, and Sy Sperling was. After Sy Sperling was with his friend six months, splitting profits, Sperling wanted half the corporate stock. His friend refused because his father had helped put in money for the business. He demanded that if Sperling wanted stock, he would have to put an equal amount of money into the business. "I said, 'That's not fair. We had a gentleman's agreement and you're reneging.'"

Sperling left the business and, ultimately, it folded.

Next, Sy Sperling joined the Queens franchise after that owner had split up with his partners. "We were making a go of it. Then, in 1970, my father died."

Although Sy and Jay Sperling had parted in their initial hair weave business, the two sat shiva together—or mourned according to Jewish custom—for their father. The two reconciled. "My brother and I both loved our father," he explained. Although Sy Sperling still was mad at his brother, Jay reported that his business was on the brink of failure and invited his brother back. Sy Sperling was reluctant to return to Long Island, but Jay Sperling, by that time, had opened another hair center in Manhattan. He offered to split it 50-50 if Sy Sperling could go there and turn it around.

There was one stylist at the Manhattan center that he suggested Sperling meet. "I took a ride up there and met my second wife, Amy. She was a one-person operation."

Sperling told her that his brother wanted him to take 50 percent of the business, and the only way he intended to do it is if she stuck around. "She liked me. I met her on other occasions. We got along very well."

He immediately got several other hair weaving centers to form a co op advertising program. All the franchises his brother had sold were having problems and everybody was mad at each other. "They broke up because they didn't like my brother. I had very good rapport. I said, 'Look, you can't make it individually. You don't have advertising clout. If you want to make it, you've got to go into the *Daily News* and *New York Post*. Let's do it cooperatively."

The co-op campaign began generating leads for potential clients. "We started doing sales in Manhattan and I turned it around. My brother started seeing more revenue." Ultimately, the center moved from a 2,000-square-foot office to a 5,000-square-foot location. Prior to the move in 1973, however, Sperling decided to break up with his brother for a final time. In 1974, Sperling married Amy, his second wife, and in 1976, Sperling formed Hair Club for Men.

Sperling already had begun to recognize that he had a flare for publicity and was among the early users of celebrity endorsers in advertising. "In the early 1970s, my first celebrity client was Ron Bloomberg, a balding Yankees slugger. I had recruited him to be a client of ours and do print commercials." After doing Bloomberg's hair, Sperling went out and hired a public relations firm. The company was growing and obtaining new clients.

At the time, hair pieces had a bad reputation. People were buying them only to find that three to four years later, an embarrassing line between the toupee and the client's remaining hair would form.

The reason, Sperling explains, is that the toupees were made of human hair, but unlike human hair, a hair piece does not continue to grow. So if someone swims in a chlorinated pool, the hair gets bleached. After a period, the hair starts to oxidize. As hair oxidized, it had to be dyed again. When a hair piece was dyed, the line of demarcation between the natural hair and the hair that was added became more pronounced. It looked unnatural, and the industry needed to overcome this negative image of the average toupee wearer.

When a sale was being made, "the idea was to try to convince the client that the investment won't be as great as he thinks it is." The image of the industry and the sensitivity of each man to the problems with hair pieces were Sperling's chief concerns. "It's like buying Viagra," he says. In fact, hair weaves were such a touchy subject for men that Hair Club promotions promised to mail information to prospects in an unmarked envelope.

After talking extensively to clients, Sperling came up with a plan that revolutionized the male hair piece business. He would charge a monthly fee and allow the client to come in at any time for new hair. This way each hair piece would always look authentic and clients would be more satisfied. At this writing, Hair Club typically charged $1,500 initially for the hair and $200 monthly after that. There is no contract to sign, just a commitment on the part of the client to maintain the hair piece.

The concept changed the public's perception of toupees. Because customers were paying to maintain the piece monthly, they were more careful to maintain it so that a distinct line didn't show. The new payment plan simultaneously created an annuity for Sperling's company, bringing in monthly income. The attrition rate from people who were dissatisfied with the toupee because of the visible lines dropped to virtually zero. Once Sperling was able to recruit a client, he was fairly certain to receive $200 monthly for life. "[With] the majority of men now [wearing a hair piece], you can't tell that they've had anything done. Even [actor] Burt Reynolds. If you remember, he had a bad rug. Look at him today. Not only is it more reasonable for the client, but he looks better, he's happier, and because he's happier, he stays with it."

Business started to thrive. By 1976, Sperling had moved into his larger location on 57th street. Sales doubled. Sperling says that it was important to keep his stores nicely decorated and elegant. "I put $100,000 into that," he said of the first move in Manhattan. "I didn't borrow money. It came from normal funds going through the business. I signed a lease. [The landlord] gave me six months free rent." Sperling admits he had been fortunate to decide to move his location during a very depressed real estate market. "I knew that was the kind of deal that might not be available if I hesitated. Bargains are not out there all the time. When you see a bargain, take advantage of it."

The company grew, opening three or four new centers annually. In the mid-1980s, his business started to expand more rapidly. He started running print ads in magazines—including the *New York Times* magazine section on Sunday. "I used to take full-page ads," he said. "I was aggressive in advertising. In 1982, I went on TV and did a commercial. I hired a small ad agency. They came up with the idea of me doing my own spot. They thought I'd be a good pitch man for the product. I looked good with the product and believed in it. I believed in what I was saying."

The TV campaign started with 60-second prime-time commercials that provided toll-free numbers for viewers to call for a free brochure. Direct response is considered among the most precise types of advertising because the responses actually can be counted. Sperling used professional production houses for the spots. In 1985, he reported that 25 percent of the company's $10 million in revenues went toward the television spots.

"In the beginning, it was strictly before and afters," he said. "I tried to become more Madison Avenue and go slick. It never worked. We always wound up going back to the basics—before and after." There is nothing as effective, he says, as showing a visual of a before and after. He also has used testimonials.

Later, Sperling thought he needed more airtime to get the point across, and became one of the pioneers of 30-minute infomercials. "This is not an everyday product," Sperling explained. Most people were unaware of what the product was—whether it's a toupee or a transplant. A half-hour provided more time to explain the process.

While he successfully handled the promotion, his now ex-wife, Amy, handled the technical end of the business. He says there were about a dozen major technical advancements with the product. "Amy was a technical genius," he said. Today, the company has set up a whole product development department.

As the business grew, Sperling reached a point where he couldn't handle it himself. "I didn't have an MBA background. I wasn't very good at making the transition from an entrepreneurial smaller company to a mid-size, regional company to a national company. That transition is a quantum leap."

Sperling needed help, so he hired an MBA from Harvard and made him chief executive officer. His new CEO had led the aggressive growth of Nathan's and Dunkin Donuts. Initially, there was an employment agreement for two years. In 1989, it was reported that he planned to add at least 25 new company-owned facilities with a $2.5 million investment. "He was going to help me grow the company on the national level."

Sperling made the decision to go with a major expansion. "I was like an old Wild West cowboy," he said. "I never worried about failure. I was a very big risk-taker. I had a very healthy attitude toward business and growth. I didn't mind rolling the dice. I was a true entrepreneur.

"A lot of it had to do with the way I grew up—with gang wars and fights at an early age. If I went into the subway at 3 AM going through South Bronx, that didn't bother me. Why would opening up more locations or taking risks in business bother me? I wasn't a selfish kid in suburbia afraid to fall on [my] face a couple of times."

Sperling says he also had toughened up due to his early business experiences. For example, while he and Amy were in Manhattan in 1972, the two had been alone in the store. They had been working on a single client from 1:00 PM to 1:00 AM. Nobody else was around when the client decided that he didn't want the hair piece—after the two had been working 12 straight hours on it. The client ordered the two to take the piece off his head, and demanded all his money back. "If I gave him all the money back, I probably wouldn't be able to pay the rent that month," Sperling said. "He was about 6-foot-8—a bad dude. He said, 'Look. If you don't give me all my money back, I'm going to bust the place up.'"

Sperling told the client that his girl had been working on the man for 12 hours. "Don't you think it's worth it to split the difference?" "No," the client firmly had responded.

At that point, Sperling, summoning up his streetfighting experience from South Bronx, was prepared to hurl something at the client, if necessary. "I said you're going to have to take the money from me," Sperling said. "'Let's go.' I was ready to duke it out with this guy. I felt we deserved it. I wasn't going to let this guy walk out without paying a fee. He finally gave in."

After experiences like that, Sperling had become fearless in business.

"When you have that mentality, you don't have fear," he said.

Later on, when the CEO started helping Sperling hire regional managers, he displayed no fear. "Go west or bust. Now I'm ready. I figured let's open up a few hundred locations. We opened store after store. In my mind, the cash flow is there." Sperling figured it would cost him $25,000 to open each new center. "My mentality was where we were in 1969." In those days, new centers cost between $15,000 and $25,000. "By the time we started opening new centers, we no longer were on a minimal budget. We would open up a whole center." Some centers were 13,500 square feet, costing more than $85,000! "Before [we] start[ed] turning a profit, it [cost] another $150,000 at least. [We had] to wait a year or two."

By the mid-1990s a problem arose. "I was always in the dark [as to] where we were financially. [The CEO] never gave me an accurate financial picture. After [expanding for] two or three years, he tells me we're $6 million in the red. For a small, growing company, this is an enormous amount of money. I was in shock, I said, 'Wow. That was a lot to be in the red! If you gave me the financial reporting, I wouldn't have expanded at the same pace.' It wasn't that our business was not profitable. We were not getting the right financial reporting."

How could Sperling be kept in the dark about his own company?

"If I wanted to find out about how we're doing financially, I would ask him, 'How are we doing financially?' I would ask him, 'How are we doing with the bills? Are we late with anything?' I never was able to get a good accurate accounting from him. If I did get a good accounting, there's no way in the world I would [have] expand[ed] at the rate I [did]. He didn't say, 'If you look at the projections, we're not turning a profit right way. We're going to out-of-pocket spend $250,000 before we're profitable.' I didn't know that."

The experience taught Sperling a major lesson. "My advice would be before you become a national company, don't do it the way I did it," Sperling declares. "If you're only a good marketing and sales person and promotional person, make sure your partner—your wife, or whoever you're getting involved with—[has] a very, very good understanding of finance and infrastructure. You have to build an infrastructure. I was totally dependent on an outsider. The best alternative is to earn an MBA before you get started."

Sperling notes that in his new venture, Sperling Marketing, he is partners with a Wharton MBA, Peter Koepell. Because Koepell is part owner, hopefully, such an experience shouldn't happen again.

Nevertheless, despite a near bankruptcy, Sperling succeeded in bailing out his company. He hired a new CEO—"somebody who specializes in doing turnarounds. He was a 'Chainsaw Al' type," Sperling said, referring to Albert "Chainsaw Al" Dunlap, the former CEO of Sunbeam Corp., renown for his ruthless cost-cutting. "He came in with the intention of developing a relationship with creditors."

The new CEO started closing stores that were not yet profitable. If they were going to take another two or three years to make a profit, he didn't want to carry them. "Once you have a big nut to crack, you've got to start getting rid of nonprofitable stores. The advantage to being in a position where you're almost in Chapter 11 [bankruptcy] is [that] the landlord will be a lot more lenient with you."

Sperling said the Hair Club for Men got itself out of bad leases and trimmed its labor force from 600 to 400 people.

The problem was that the new CEO was strictly a budget-cutting specialist. "He didn't seem to have a good feel for the marketing of the business. We did all the budget-cutting we could."

To succeed, the business had to generate cash flow. Sperling's marketing skills were needed.

Before Sperling took over, he had to meet with creditors for eight hours. He convinced them that instead of selling the company—forcing him into a Chapter 11 bankruptcy—they should give him another shot.

"I convinced them that they'd be better off with me. I'd give them 50 cents on a dollar. I said, 'Look, I need some time to work it out. If you hang in with me, I'll take it back over. I'll do the marketing, traveling from city to city, and go on TV. I'll work 24 hours a day.' They bought me. I said, 'I'm not a crook.' Usually, when you accrue a debt like that, the reaction is this guy pulled a sham. They assume you're dishonest. When things aren't going well, everybody accuses you of wrongdoing. I had to sell them on the fact that I'm for real and the debt I accrued was legitimate. I told them 'I put 25 years into it. Give me another shot.'"

In the meantime, Sperling's second wife started Hair Club for Kids, offering the company's services to kids who were undergoing chemotherapy. "She loves kids. We were always very charitable."

Sperling talked to them about the social involvement the couple had. "They opened up their hearts. It goes to show you that charity doesn't have any immediate benefits, but it creates a good karma. It gives you a little mazel [Yiddish for luck].

"I don't do it for something in return. You're brought up that way and want to make a difference. I was chairman for a homeless program. I was the biggest contributor to the temple."

After Sperling convinced the creditors to give him another chance, he hired a public relations person. Generally, public relations firms charge steep fees—regardless of how much publicity they generate. Sperling said he was fortunate to find a public relations man who was very inexpensive and worked on a per-hit basis. In other words, Sperling paid nothing unless the agent actually placed him in the media. You find these things, he says, "when you're at the desperation level and you're looking for survival. I was very fortunate to find the guy."

He targeted radio programs nationwide and paid the public relations person "a couple hundred dollars" per hit. Once he got on the shows, he offered free hair to the first 300 people who called up. Then, once potential clients got in the stores and received the hair, Sperling sold them an ongoing maintenance program. "I did it as a last-ditch effort to put a few thousand people through the door right away. I got the airtime for free, gave away free hair, and generated thousands of new clients. The cash registers started to ring up big time."

While traveling to do the radio spots, he would visit the stores to motivate employees. "I would do rap sessions with them. Everybody's fearful they might lose their jobs. I said, 'I'm personally getting involved myself. You're going to see hundreds of new clients in three days [from] some of my radio promotions.'" For one year, he said, he put on the "Sy Sperling Road Show."

The effort started generating cash flow. "I couldn't afford television spots and an infomercial is expensive. I didn't have much money to play with. We were three days away from bankruptcy."

Sperling had bought a six-month reprieve. Although he didn't quite meet his promise, morale started to improve at the company. Sy Sperling became a recognizable figure in people's living rooms through his television commercials. "One of the guys on the board of directors of the creditors was my printer. He convinced the creditors' committee once he saw I was making a difference, to go five years rather than six months. They signed off on the long-term deal with me and I wound up paying them off completely by 1998."

During that period, he also moved the company headquarters from New York to Boca Raton, Florida. "That saved us $1 million a year in overhead. Plus, I was already living in Florida." It eliminated his need to commute.

As his company grew, however, he and his wife Amy had been growing apart. The once mom-and-pop operation had changed dramatically. Other companies copied his monthly fee "hair club" strategy. "Now you're hiring CFOs, CEOs, and a whole new environment of people. If you don't agree on a philosophy, you're going to have a hard time with marriage."

The two already had been having a hard time. Sperling had two children from his prior marriage and she had one from her prior marriage. It wasn't easy merging families. The kids had gotten older. "Even though the marriage had its ups and downs, we had a common bond of building the business together," he said. "The business was our child. In the early years, we worked 12 hours a day, 6 days a week together." As the business had grown exponentially, that bond had weakened.

"I walked a straight line. I was monogamous," he stressed. "Things started getting shaky in the last year."

He cites the breakup of his eighteen-year marriage as a chief reason he decided to sell Hair Club for Men for $40 million in 2000 to Kaetech, a company formed by a group of investors. He split the proceeds with his ex-wife. "After Amy and I got divorced, [we] could not stay partners . . . and expect it to work. You have to keep in mind that in the early years, [it was] very, very easy for [her] and I to get along. We only had one center to worry about. I would do sales, marketing, and promoting. As we became a national firm, the differences in our philosophy started to surface. She was on the technical level. We both decided it was time. We got a great offer." The company was sold to a group of Canadian investors. They were rounded up by an international manufacturer. "We were his number one account," Sperling said. Sperling since has married for the third time. Upon selling the business, Hair Club for Men had 80 offices. At this writing, he says, there are 85.

In addition to his new company, he also has written a book, *How to Make Money at the Flea Market and at Online Auctions,* which he plans to sell on the Internet. He also plans to do infomercials for products or new books. His company, he says, is developing relationships with Internet companies that will allow them to promote on their site and only charge on a per-sale basis.

Sperling Marketing will do things like buy a full-page *Playboy* ad for $30,000, which normally costs $100,000. "We buy a remnant page," he explains. "Once you know that end of it, it's a matter of coming up with main products to promote through the media."

Sperling said that even though he had managed to save a couple million dollars on his own while he owned the company, he never felt wealthy. It wasn't until he looked at his bank statement for the first time after he sold the business that he finally realized he was. "Once they wired the money into the account and when you see all those numbers on your statement . . ."

Prior to the sale of the business, Sperling had money in stocks and bonds and other investments. "Even though the company was almost bankrupt, I was in business for many, many years, and personally saved some money. It's not like Hair Club was almost bankrupt over many, many years, so the creditors could never say I tried to milk the business. The money I had was savings."

Sperling says he also owns commercial property in Long Island and collects rent.

"I don't want to be recognized by friends and relatives as a millionaire," he said. "I never talk about money with other people. Maybe I have more than the next person, but it's very private to me."

The nice thing about having money, he says, is that "you develop a feeling of financial security. No matter what, you know you're going to be comfortable for the rest of your life. You're going to pay your bills, feed your family, take care of your kids, take care of any charities. Philanthropy is a very important part of me."

On the downside, he said, "you're more visible, and although there are so many positives, by being visible, you lose your privacy to a certain extent."

Sperling hired a Certified Financial Planner, Andrew Welt, who works out of his house in Deerfield Beach, Florida. Welt, he says, is married to an attorney and is both legally astute and astute from an accounting standpoint.

It was an essential move. One thing Sperling realizes is that if you want to achieve success, it is very important to understand your own shortcomings. "I've seen too many people lose their life savings on the market. They wind up buying tech stocks at $100 and they're down to $2 and they lose their fortunes."

Sperling said he hired Welt after he was considering investing in a private equity investment opportunity—a company that acquires companies and takes them public. "It was very different from buying conventional stocks or bonds," he said. "I had to tie up at least $1 million."

Before hiring him, Sperling gave him that investment to evaluate. He offered him $1,000 to prepare an analysis and report. "He prepared a 25-page booklet," he said. "I could see this guy really did his homework. I said, 'You know what, I'm going to give you a shot with other things.'"

Sperling says that anytime he buys a bond, Welt researches the company and will shop the market. "I got a call yesterday about a municipal bond paying 12.8 percent that was triple-b rated," he said. His investment guru checked it out on the Internet and said, "I don't think I can beat the price." Other days, Sperling says, Welt thinks he can get 10 basis points better. There was one issue in Nevada where instead of 5.7 percent tax-free, he was able to get 5.8 percent.

Often, Sperling explains, investment houses will buy out estates and get odd-lots of bonds paying a much higher yield than is currently offered. "He wound up getting a 17 percent yield on a J.C. Penney bond. If you went to buy it right now, you wouldn't get more than 10 percent to 11 percent. [Welt] earns his fee in the amount he saves me from day to day."

Sperling says he pays a flat rate, which allows Welt to be objective.

Although he invests in a few exotic things, like hedge funds, Sperling says he is conservative, keeping 70 percent of his money in bonds and 30 percent in stocks.

"I became a very, very cautious and conservative investor who gets a very healthy return." When he plays the market, he often buys absolute bargains. He admits he even counsels his ex-wife, Amy, on her investments.

Sperling acknowledges that money is extremely important in today's society. "Even though we call ourselves a democracy, the influence of money is enormous." It can buy you better doctors, a better lifestyle, and a better education, he says. It can solve a lot of problems. "How many marriages break up because of economic difficulty?"

If you're single, he adds, money also has an influence. "There is power in fame and fortune. Make no doubt about it. I try not to allow that to enter into my behavior toward other people. If I were single, I wouldn't want a woman to know what my assets are until we were serious about each other."

When he met his current wife, Susan, at a singles club, she came up to him and said, "Aren't you the hair club guy?" Sperling admits "I know what influence money does have. I would rather have a woman fall in love with me for who I am rather than what my financial status is in life."

Sperling said that because of money, he was able to buy a condo for his mother 30 years ago. Now that she is 92, he pays to have a woman take care of her 24 hours a day.

He is firmly committed to philanthropy. "My gameplan is I wished I could be wealthy so I could make that much more of a difference. I believe when you're altruistic with your thoughts, it creates what you call good karma or spiritual energy. . . . Wealth is something you have to be deserving of. Why would somebody have to earn $40 million just for themselves?"

At this writing, he is a large contributor to both a reformed and a conservative temple. He was working to help the conservative temple attract more interest and raise money. "I'm going to buy radio time for the rabbi, who will promote himself to attract new members," Sperling explains. "Instead of being ritualistic, it will have more of a human touch to it."

Sperling said that the rabbi, on the radio, would be a little like Dr. Laura Schlessinger, the popular syndicated radio talk-show hostess, and invite people to a Saturday service.

Sperling says he also was working on trying to get the rabbi to cut the service from four hours to two hours.

"Judaism is the oldest religion, but has the smallest constituency," Sperling explains. "Christians are great marketing people. They came up with Santa Claus and Easter eggs. Unless you market religion, the religion is going to die. My biggest commitment is to make a contribution to the perpetuation of religion. Most of my resources are going toward preserving the culture. It's very important to me. I'm taking my marketing expertise I was able to get through my experience with Hair Club and applying it to philanthropy."

You needn't be a genius to be successful, Sperling believes. "Listen to your people. Have an open ear. Learn from others. I never went to Harvard. I never achieved an MBA. I was always a down-to-earth guy. I'd roll up my sleeves. I would sit in the waiting room and talk to clients about what they thought could make us better for them."

They would ask for up-to-date magazines, a television set, bagels and cookies, or fresh coffee. "You'd be surprised how little things, when you add them all up, can make you successful."

Also, if you're going to succeed in any industry, he says, "your message and your product should be head over heels—far superior to anybody else's. You never want to be one of the pack. You want to come off as a shining star." From his early days, Sperling insisted on improving the product and finding the best manufacturer in the world.

Sperling says his rough South Bronx upbringing also helped him in the long run. "When you're trying to grow a small business from ground zero to a highly successful company, there are going to be many times when your back is against the wall," he said. "There's going to be nobody to help you out. What you learn on the streets, that stayed with me. I question whether somebody who didn't have that would be able to deal with adversity."

Sperling says he always believed that the curtain is never fully closed—as long as there is a ray of light shining through. His near-bankruptcy might have been one of his lowest points, but he perservered.

"Anybody who's your friend when you're at the top, you don't hear from when you're at the bottom," he warns. "There are very few who hung out there with me. There are very few friends you make in the corporate world—a few here and there—but they are few and far between.

"When things are going well, you make a lot of friends while you're on top. But the ones who stick with you throughout—cherish those friends."

Despite his near-bankruptcy experience, Sperling says he always has managed to avoid stress and frequently counsels his sister to do the same.

"Even when I was going through my near-bankruptcy, I just turned it off at 5:00 PM or 6:00 PM, went jogging, watched a ball game, or went out with friends or family," Sperling said. "I didn't even allow myself to go there. You condition yourself. If you want to be successful with your life, stress management is extremely important. I'm very good at that."

Sperling firmly believes that when stress gets to you, your immune system breaks down and you become susceptible to illness.

"Health is too important," he says. "If you walk away from an accident with nothing broken and you're still alive, don't worry about your car. Material things can always be replaced."

CHAPTER 4

KENNETH A. SMALTZ, JR.

Salesman Grows $1 Million Out of $40,000 Debt

Kenneth A. Smaltz, Jr., 38, though $40,000 in debt in the early 1990s, refused to declare bankruptcy. When we talked with Smaltz, a college drop-out, he had totally paid off his debt and was receiving new offers of credit—for good reason. He had built his net worth to slightly over $1 million and had bought a partnership in New World Rarities, a Hauppage, New York, rare coin dealership. The deal was believed to make him the first African American to have an ownership stake in a rare coin dealership.

Smaltz, who never married but would love to find the right woman, was back in the saddle, living in a Hempstead, New York, co-op, working out mornings in a gym, and driving a leased Jaguar. He owned another co-op as an investment. Leasing a car is attractive businesswise, he says, and he enjoys driving a different car every two years. But he says that he learned some major lessons about both money and humility on the way to reaching this point.

For one thing, close to 90 percent of Smaltz's earnings now go toward a savings plan, including a SIMPLE IRA (a type of retirement plan for employers with 100 or fewer employees). He uses credit cards only when there's a very good reason—such as a special deal that offers 10 percent off. Otherwise, he only uses a debit card, which allows him to have a purchase deducted directly from his checking account.

"I am so financially savvy now—to the point where it's ridiculous," he said, "to the point where I don't have any fun any more with money because I am so fearful of going back to that situation. I have to make sure [I am] going to be taken care of now, tomorrow, and when [I] retire."

Some people start treating people poorly when they become very well off financially, he says. Smaltz's experience proved that no matter where you are in life, you very easily can lose everything you've accumulated. It has served to drive home in a special way the teachings of his parents. "The people I work with, the people who work for me, the people on the street—every one of those people [is] just the same as I am," he declares. "I just have a whole different outlook on life."

Smaltz got off to a rough start growing up. His family put a lot of psychological pressure on him to achieve and go to college—so much pressure that he began to have self-doubts about his abilities. It took years for him to overcome his insecure feelings. But once he did, he excelled.

Smaltz's parents were very hard working. His father worked two jobs, one as a firefighter and subsequently a fire marshall. He also worked as a postal carrier for 20 years. His mother, who passed away in 1988 from a rare form of Mad Cow disease she contracted during a blood transfusion, was a bilingual teacher. She was fluent in Spanish as a result of her mother's roots in the Dominican Republic.

Born in Queens, New York, Smaltz and his family, which includes an older sister, initially shared a large house with his cousins, their parents, and his grandparents. By the time he was seven, his parents took him and his sister to live in their own apartment in Queens. His mother stopped working when the children were young, but subsequently returned to school to earn a masters degree in education.

Smaltz and his sister received a small allowance—$5 or $10 weekly, he says—in exchange for performing daily chores. His job was to take out the garbage and complete his homework. While his sister managed to save her allowance, Smaltz says he clearly was the spender in the family. His money went out the door all too quickly—to comic books and candy. He found himself often asking his sister for cash.

Smaltz says his father, though very intelligent, was unable to go to college, and always had wanted to be an engineer. He did not want his son to make the same mistakes. At first, both Smaltz and his sister met their parents' expectations and did well in school. Smaltz got As and Bs, and upon encouragement from a teacher, took a test to get accepted to one of the area's top technical high schools—Brooklyn Tech. He passed without even studying. He was on track to become a commercial artist.

"My first year was fine," he said. Then the high school experience suddenly turned miserable. He stopped going to class. "I wasn't getting As and Bs because there were no tests I was taking. I majored in lunchroom."

Smaltz started discovering freedom. "It had nothing to do with my learning capabilities." He failed to do well at Brooklyn Tech and was later transferred to Westbury High School in Long Island, after his parents moved to a nicer home. His failure to stay with the elite technical high school upset his parents to no end.

His lack of interest in school, unlike many others who follow his path, had nothing to do with getting involved with drugs or getting into trouble, he stresses. His parents had done a good job teaching their children right from wrong, although, he acknowledges, "a lot of parents teach children right from wrong and they still went the wrong way. We just stayed away from anything illegal on our own. I never had peer pressure. If my friends did drugs and I didn't want any, they said OK. They never shunned us for not participating in things."

Smaltz did graduate from Westbury High School, however, more trouble followed his graduation. "My father was very upset with the fact that I didn't excel in high school the way he wanted me to," Smaltz said. "[My parents] were constantly on my back with, 'You've got to get good grades. You have to go to college.' Every single day I heard this."

Smaltz was particularly close to his mother, who was a bit easier on him and tried to get her husband to work more gently with their son. His father, though, was forever critical. "I don't blame any of this on my father," Smaltz now says, "but it did give me an insecurity complex. I realized I wasn't doing what I was supposed to, but didn't know how to stop it. I always wanted to be more than what I was."

Often Smaltz's father talked about his own failed dreams to be an engineer. "I always said I never want to be in a situation where I said, 'God, I wish I had done that.'" In the meantime, Smaltz began believing his father's criticism of his abilities.

Seeking to please his parents, Smaltz attended various colleges off and on for about a year. He began by attending New York University, but quickly dropped out and got a job at a shoe store near the NYU campus. "I would still hear the constant complaining of my parents about having to go back to school."

So, he gave college another shot—enrolling in Queens College. "I couldn't do it," he said. Once again, he quit. He went to work in the shipping department of a Long Island electronics store, but rents in the area simply were too high for Smaltz to venture out and live on his own.

By this time, Smaltz was 19 and still was hearing from his parents how important it was that he further his education. He gave college one more shot, this time, at Nassau Community College. In fact, he says, there was one point where he worked at the electronics store, attended school, and, afterward, cleaned offices at Chase Manhattan Bank. Finally, Smaltz dropped out of Nassau Community College. His college career had permanently ended. Nevertheless, he promised his parents he would not disappoint them. He would make something of himself. "I didn't want school. My parents did."

Smaltz was unhappy working in the shipping department of the electronics store and living at home. He also learned all too quickly that an African American with no college education would have a tough time moving up the corporate ladder.

His primary goal was to get into the corporate building of his company, where the higher-echelon employees worked. Whenever he visited the corporate area, he'd see job postings and wonder why they weren't also posted in the shipping department.

When Smaltz inquired why job openings weren't posted in shipping, he was shunned. "I would make a stink about it quite often. One day I took the people in shipping and organized a petition." The thrust of the demand was to give shipping personnel the same chances they were giving people in the corporate building.

Following the petition, job postings began to appear in the shipping area. Finally, Smaltz was recognized. He was asked to go on a trip to a Boston suburb to help set up another store. Smaltz was to be one of the people in charge of the project. "I was so happy!" he said. "It was my first time on a plane. They put me up in a hotel. I [was] 20 years old. They got me a rental car."

Unfortunately, he says, his plane ticket and some cash had been stolen on the plane. Because he was the only employee with an expense account, meals of other workers on the trip were charged to his account. Given that his cash had been stolen, he asked a supervisor if he could charge the purchase of a $40 teddy bear for his girlfriend to the expense account. He said he would reimburse the account when they returned. The supervisor agreed, but the move turned out to be fatal to his career at that organization.

The day after his return, Smaltz was summoned by company higher-ups and asked about all the charges on the account. "They made it sound like I was partying and having people eat with me," he said. "They told me I tried to take funds from the company."

Although the issue of racial prejudice had not been on his mind, he later realized that there were no African Americans in the corporate office. The experience strengthened his resolve. He knew that to get ahead, he would have to work extra hard—harder than anyone else.

Meanwhile, Smaltz says he had been aware of some improprieties committed by the supervisor who had authorized him to put the teddy bear purchase on the expense account. "I told him if you don't write me a letter of recommendation, I'm going to let them know what you did." The supervisor, he says, evidently succeeded in getting the company to write him a glowing recommendation.

Through a friend who graduated from Harvard and landed a good job, Smaltz was put in touch with a job recruiter. Armed with his letter of recommendation, Smaltz met with the recruiter who found a job open in the shipping department of MTB Banking Corp., a company which sold coins.

Smaltz did not want to work in shipping, feeling as though he was capable of much more. But the recruiter convinced him that he was extremely limited without a college education and little work experience. The recruiter felt that because his prior experience had been in shipping, there was little more he was qualified to do.

Smaltz met with one of the owners of the banking company, and took a math test. After the interview, the coowner gave him $20, and told him to go downstairs and have lunch in Rockefeller Center. Although she reported there were three more people she wanted to interview for the job, she let Smaltz know she wanted to hire him.

Smaltz had few other options. "It was terrible because I had such a bad life in the house," he said. "I wanted to be somebody. I wasn't yet. I wasn't making enough where I could actually get a place."

At age 21, Smaltz still was living at home. His parents never asked him to contribute toward the mortgage or food, but he covered virtually all of his other expenses. The first day he showed up for the shipping job at MTB Banking, he wore a suit and tie. "My father told me that whenever you apply for a job, always go in and look like you're going to run the company," he said.

In addition, the one thing that he had learned at Brooklyn Tech was excellent penmanship. Because of his handwriting skills, he immediately was taken off heavy physical duties. He largely handled registered mail.

On the job, Smaltz had opportunities to work overtime. "No matter what time it came, I never rejected overtime. Whenever it was offered, this other guy [and I] were fighting for it."

Overtime pay was time-and-a-half. By the end of the week, he said, it made for a substantially larger paycheck. Plus, it put him in good graces with the company.

Nevertheless, Smaltz was not saving money. "I was doing overtime because I just wanted money. I pictured myself being wealthy beyond compare."

Smaltz said he was greatly influenced by two movies. In *American Gigolo,* actor Richard Gere's character was his idol. Smaltz wanted all the suits that were in his closet, his Mercedes convertible, and his women. "I was him," Smaltz said. "He was so cool!"

He also idolized Charlie Sheen's role as an aggressive young stockbroker in the movie *Wall Street.*

Fortunately, he also found a more realistic role model and mentor at MTB Banking, who would help him find his way in life and business.

Smaltz often chatted with MTB Banking's vice president, Louis Vigdor. "He had been a hands-on vice president," Smaltz said. "He dressed well, but always came down to shipping." He would help with packages and confided to Smaltz that he had started his career in the shipping department.

Vigdor greatly encouraged Smaltz, and helped him in his career throughout his life. Vigdor stressed that there definitely were opportunities for him at the company if he worked really hard. In the meantime, Smaltz had observed that the sales department was one area of the company where he might make lots of money. Even better, Smaltz noted that being a salesman required no college degree.

Smaltz already knew the large amount of money that could be made in sales. He would see the orders written by the salespeople upstairs as he packaged coins. He decided to make his desires known. "I said, Louis, whatever you need me to do. Whatever it will take to get upstairs, I'll do it."

After spending two years in the shipping department, Smaltz finally got his wish. "Louis came to me one day and said we're going to bring you upstairs. What that was like, I can't tell you!"

Once Smaltz got there, however, nobody went out of their way to help him. "Salespeople are very arrogant. They don't trust you. They don't want anyone else to come and do better than them." Smaltz said the sales manager was not even notified of his arrival.

"I think [Vigdor] thought he was going to face opposition because I was the only black guy there," he said. "They didn't even have black guys in shipping. When he got me upstairs, he sat me at a desk. It was sink or swim. He told [the salespeople] to show me things. They didn't show me anything. They let me know they didn't want me there."

Although Smaltz finally was in a classier banking atmosphere, he didn't exactly feel welcome. "I thrive on challenges like that," he said of the chilly reception. "Whenever someone makes me feel as if I'm not capable of doing something because of my race, it's like the worst thing to do to me. I wasn't in any way intimidated."

Instead, he focused on trying to determine who the best salesperson was in the department by how much money was made. When he found the best salesperson, he sat behind him watching every single thing he did.

His new job did not involve making cold calls. Rather, sales efforts were directed at previous customers, people who had responded to advertising or catalogs, or persons who had written in.

Before Smaltz's new role model, the star salesperson, called anyone, Smaltz noticed that he put an order on the desk. "He assumed the sale. He wrote in the date and put the contact's name on the order and then called. Automatically, he would talk the customer into buying coins."

In imitating him, Smaltz adapted his own style. "He was very smooth," Smaltz said. "His voice was very deep. He was direct. He didn't really make many jokes. Sometimes people like to discuss things about a person's background. He didn't do that very much."

Smaltz began comparing this star salesman's approach to the telephone solicitations he personally received. You have to be direct and give the benefits of the product and reasons people should buy it, he figured. "But there's nothing wrong with finding out how a person's day was."

Smaltz also liked to write down key points about a client—the person's birthday, his or her children's birthdays, anniversaries, and likes and dislikes. "Any type of [information a] conversation can be built upon."

The information he'd collect would be kept on file. "The next time you call a person, you remember that last conversation. If they were doing the lawn, you can say, 'Hey, did you ever finish your lawn?'" That way, he says, the person doesn't feel like you're just a salesman.

Also, Smaltz said, he didn't merely call clients to make a sale. Sometimes he called to wish someone a happy birthday, or just to find out how everything was going. "So when they hear from you, they don't think you're wanting to sell them something."

While it's true that your employer owns the list of your clients' names, Smaltz says, the customer typically goes with the salesperson. "If you handle your customer the right way, no matter where you go, the customer will follow you."

In his sales job, Smaltz started realizing his dream. He worked at MTB Banking from 1984 to 1991, and made as much as $82,000 annually. During that period, he finally was able to move out of his parents' home. "I remember, I had the first month's rent, first month's security, and had literally nothing else."

Smaltz settled into a one-bedroom, two-bathroom apartment in the Clinton Hills section of downtown Brooklyn. Once he moved out of his parents' house, he rarely called. He never brought home laundry. "It wasn't because anyone did anything to me. It was just, I'm out of there! It [was] partially [because] everything [belonged to my parents]. The house was theirs, the car, food. I had to live by my parents' rules. I was getting to an age where I was independent, but I couldn't be that independent because I was still living at home. The day I started furnishing my apartment, I couldn't have been any happier. I would go in the [apartment] and sit there and smile from ear to ear. But I really didn't keep a family bond. I started going out on my own."

If you are successful, but don't take steps to manage your finances properly, that success can go by the wayside. When the economic recession hit in 1990, he learned some hard lessons. Smaltz had been living the Wall Street life. "I bought the suits and ties. My entire persona was that of a Wall Street broker." In 1988, he even paid cash for a two-year-old BMW.

However, his dream come true was short-lived. MTB Banking started having trouble in 1989 as the rare coin market faltered. Fortunately, salespeople were the last to go. Salespeople are critical to the foundation of a company, Smaltz observes. However, by 1991, he was laid off. "All my credit cards were at the top—MasterCard, VISA, and American Express."

Although he had been making good money, Smaltz never saved. He was going on vacations and associating with more affluent people.

Today, Smaltz says, whenever he lectures salespeople, he explains that there are three things you need to know about "off the books": (1) Pay your (estimated income) taxes. (2) Pay your taxes. (3) Pay your taxes. "Most people don't. When you're getting your money and no one takes [any taxes] out, you get a little happy. Some of it [belongs to] the IRS. You've got to pay [taxes] because sooner or later, you're going to have to. New salespeople always fall because of that. I was one of them. I was traveling all over the place, driving a nice car, going to the Hamptons, trying to live a [life] I [pictured] myself living. This is where I was supposed to be. I finally got there."

When he was out of work, he was forced to stop paying his bills. "I didn't declare bankruptcy," he said. "I had $14,000 in a 401(k). That money I basically used to sustain myself until I tried to find work. I found work—in odd jobs for two years."

Smaltz said he initially had some hope when his well-known aunt, Audrey Smaltz, a former model and owner of The Ground Crew, a business that supplies dressers for models, contacted him.

"To be honest, I didn't think I would have any problems," he said. "I'd worked seven years off of Wall Street."

Commenting on when his aunt summoned him, he said, "I kind of thought she wanted me to run the company." Upon visiting her in her midtown Manhattan penthouse, Smaltz had visions of meeting fashion models and hobnobbing with the nation's fashion elite.

He was in for a major disappointment.

Instead, his aunt invited him up to her terrace. "I'm thinking about painting," she told him. "I want you to go out tomorrow and get me some paint and I want you to paint my terrace."

Later on, she explained that she thought Smaltz had been a little too cocky and he needed to realize that what had happened to him was much more serious than he thought.

"She said I needed to have a sense of self-discovery. [She told me] 'What you did on Wall Street was great. You are now out of work. You'll get work again, but you have to get a little humility.' She broke me down."

Smaltz wound up handling shipping and deliveries for his aunt. But toward the end of his time with her, she had him take on more responsibility. She introduced him to the movers and shakers in the fashion industry.

Among those he met fashion photographer Francesco Scavullo, comedian Bill Cosby, and fashion designers Oscar de la Renta and Donna Karan.

"She wanted me to take the bull by the horns. I was very green. I'd never seen that kind of opulence. She wanted me to walk over to Francesco Scavullo and network myself into a career. I wasn't able to do it. I was nervous and kind of shy."

Often, his aunt put in a good word for him, introducing her nephew to some of the chief executives of companies she dealt with. "They didn't do the least bit to help me," he said. "There were a couple of people who were tops—the buck stopped at their desks. They had the capability of hiring me in positions. And the positions I went to them for were very lowly." Often, he sought trainee positions or office cleaning jobs. "I did everything I possibly could as far as getting to the interviews on time.

The rejections hurt. "The only person that saw I had potential and that gave me a shot each time was Louis [Vigdor]."

Smaltz definitely was at a low point in his life. Just before he was laid off, his mother had passed away. His father sold their house and moved to a one-bedroom apartment. Smaltz was forced to put his furniture in storage and move in with his father. Unable to pay his bills, the storage company sold all his furniture after two months, leaving him only with a futon and a stereo system.

Then another aunt of his died followed by the death of her husband. "There was funeral after funeral after funeral." Then, in 1991, his beloved grandmother passed away. "After those deaths, I got laid off. After getting laid off, I was dating a young lady who left me and called me later to tell me she's marrying her best male friend."

On top of that, when he moved back in with his father, his father resumed his criticism about Smaltz's lack of a higher education. "I'm feeling like this failure again because I'm hearing it from my father, living in his home, and living on unemployment."

Unable to live with his father, he begged a friend's parents to let him stay with them offering to contribute what he was capable of paying. He moved into their basement and continued unsuccessfully to look for work in New York.

A friend in Atlanta suggested that he move there. Smaltz moved and began working on music videos at $100 per job.

Then, he called his old boss, Louis Vigdor. "I was very, very proud. I never asked family or friends for money and never wanted to call back the company I worked for any help. I remembered Louis was a pretty good guy." Smaltz asked Vigdor if he knew of a coin dealer in Atlanta.

At Vigdor's suggestion, Smaltz applied for a job at Hancock and Harwell and became the company's vice president of marketing. The job, though, required Smaltz to take a draw against income. He was in charge of generating his own income. "It was a great title, but I wasn't making any money." He was living in HUD

Section 8 low-income housing and paying $385 a month in rent. He would walk to work. Meanwhile, the company was not that well known, and everybody he hired to work in sales would leave shortly afterward. "[It was] a small company. I was [hired] to come and build the sales force."

Although Smaltz said he succeeded in publicizing the company in the *Atlanta Journal-Constitution,* he received few calls. After one news article appeared, one of the secretaries mentioned that quite a bit of mail had arrived that nobody had told him about. "I never saw [the customer responses] and I'm in charge of sales!"

Smaltz was angry. Any one of those responses could have been important. "You never know which customer turns into a big customer," he said. "One customer can pay back a year's worth of salary."

Again, he figured he had to do something else, and he called Vigdor for advice. Vigdor gave him the names of two other rare coin dealerships—one in California and one in Minnesota.

Smaltz accepted a job in Minnesota but hated the area. "I didn't like the coldness." He stayed there three years before moving back to New York.

By that time, Smaltz had lots of sales experience under his belt. But something was missing in his life. He turned to God for help. Once he did, he says his life made a turn for the better. He began getting more involved in religion. Although he had gone to Catholic school for eight years, he'd joined a Baptist church while still in Minnesota. "It gave me centering. It gave me balance," he said.

His move toward becoming more religious began in Atlanta. He believed that once you put God first, everything will come together. "I would go to church every Sunday. I realized if I needed some money, all of a sudden I'd go to the mailbox and get a check from AT&T for $100 to transfer service. Out of the blue, things would just come up. I was eating every day. I was able to sustain myself with the little amount of money I was making."

In Minnesota, things started getting better. His salary, which started at $70,000 annually, grew to about $82,000. In Minnesota, however, the money went quite a bit further than in New York where expenses were higher. He was able to get back on his feet.

In 1995, he called the IRS, to whom he owed at least $15,000, and arranged to pay them. They worked out a deal, based on what he was capable of paying back. Smaltz succeeded in convincing them to take the minimum amount—$100 monthly. Unfortunately, Smaltz got some important news too late. Had he filed his 1991 income taxes, he would have received a $5,000 refund! But by 1995, the three-year statute of limitations had lapsed, and he was unable to claim it.

"I finagled, wheeled, and dealed with different [creditors]," he said. "When I didn't reach someone reasonable, I called back and spoke with another person. The only problem was the IRS." Smaltz realized that by paying $100 a month, it would take years to pay the IRS back. Although he began making the minimum payments in 1995, by 1999, he decided to pay everything. "I must have given [the IRS] $4,000 in just interest!"

Smaltz said he had been encouraged to pay back his debt by Vigdor, his aunt, and Brian Abrams, his partner at New World Rarities Ltd., where he started working in 1997.

"It's a very exhausting, tedious process," he said. "You're calling each [creditor] you owe and talking with different people." They want to know how much you are earning and how much you owe. "You have to explain you're destitute. You work out payment plans with them. You have to stick to those plans. You can't go back to them.

"You have to then call those people you were paying to make sure they call the credit bureaus. Once they call the credit bureaus, you have to make sure they have the information posted. You have to constantly check back and forth to make sure one person is talking to the other. You know people are going to be mean, nasty, and cruel. You're going to be on the line for ten minutes. A person will pick up and disconnect you. They're not going to be sympathetic. You just have to have patience."

By 1999, Smaltz had paid off all his debts and started saving.

As soon as Smaltz took a job at New World Rarities in 1997, the picture brightened substantially. Business soared. His annual income quadrupled. One reason, he says, is advertising. "We used to primarily go into papers like the *Wall Street Journal* and *Investor's Business Daily.*"

Smaltz says that when he was working in Minnesota, he learned of an advertising company that does space ads. For less money, the company can get you into almost every publication in the country. Initial use of this tactic generated so much business that it forced New World Rarities to hire more people.

Smaltz said he also overhauled the look of the ads. Color, background, and borders are important. "First, it has to be a story about what you're offering them. People like a story," he says. "Every coin we offer has a story. We give them the history." He added that within the history there has to be certain important points bold-faced. "Your telephone number has to be large. It can't be small," he says. "You can't have [the customers looking] all over for the telephone number."

Products, Smaltz says, don't just sell themselves. Too often, companies have their own way of advertising and explain what they're doing to salespeople. "When I started at my first company in New York, the salespeople had ideas as to how the ad should look. Every so often, we would give our input. When that input was given, we would always get more calls. We knew better than anyone what it took to make those phones ring." By observing the response to ads for several years, he had picked up many ideas about advertising.

Even more important, he managed to grow a nice customer base, retaining customers from each prior job. Any time you leave a company, he says, the company gives your customers to other employees. "I've always managed to have a customer follow me wherever I went." Many salespeople take their customers for granted. Yet, your customers are your bread and butter. "You have to take care of them."

When you're in sales, he explains, the object is to get hitters, people who are capable of helping you achieve your annual salary.

"I cultivated them. I take care of them. I make sure at Christmas time they get presents."

Smaltz says he gives a certain percentage of the money he makes off his customers back in the form of gift baskets and cards. "Every year it's something different." The size of the gift, he adds, is based on the percentage of business the customer brings in.

"Secretaries are vital," he stresses, noting that they generally get gift baskets too. After all, it is the secretary that has the power to hold your call until his or her boss gets off the phone. "They're the gatekeepers. Sometimes, when your customer is busy, they'll say, 'Ken. Hold on one second. Let me see if I can get him off the phone.'" On Valentine's Day, his client's secretaries always get cards.

"Sometimes you don't realize which customers are going to be your big customers," he said. "Sometimes, they'll stop for a while. Then they'll come back."

Upon generating so much business in his new job in New York, one of his first steps was to hire an accountant and financial advisor. He learned early in his career the perils of not considering the IRS. The financial advisor also helped him set up a stock portfolio.

Initially, he set up his own company, Kenneth A. Smaltz, Inc., which acted as a broker for New World Rarities. But Abrams suggested that he become a partner in the company instead. While Smaltz wanted to go off on his own with the client list he had built, he decided that New World Rarities was more established.

Now that he is a partner in the company, which he says has $25 million in annual sales, he expects the business to grow tenfold. "There is no debt in the company. The company is very solvent and has a lot of capital. Any future debt that comes, I'll be personally responsible for. We're very solvent. We have a lot of credit. There are a lot of people that can vouch for finances and backing."

Smaltz says he had to lay out money to buy into the company, but he says he is paying it over three years. "[Of the] monies that come into the company now . . . 35 to 40 percent are generated by me. So that's going to be put into the actual company itself." In the meantime, he says, he will be earning a salary.

Smaltz now collects the art of well-known black artists. He also paid a year's scholarship for one high school student whose scholarship application was mishandled by the school. Periodically, he volunteers to build houses for Habitat for Humanity.

Smaltz reads self-help books, such as *The Art of War* and *Nine Steps to Financial Freedom*. He also reads *Money Magazine, Fortune,* and newspapers. He watches CNBC.

He stops short of saying that he regrets the fact that he didn't finish college.

"Sometimes people look back and say I wish I had done that," Smaltz said. "Never regret your past. What you did then made you the person you are now. If I had it to do all over again, I probably [would] go to school, or I'd figure out why I had such a phobia or fear about school. It might have been my father. That might have been part of it. Or school might not have been for me. Obviously, it wasn't.

"There are some people I've met in the past who thought I might have graduated from college. I'm able to hold conversations intelligently.

"One of the things school doesn't teach you is how to handle the ups and downs of life. [Often] you leave school and can't find a job. Or you find a job [that's] not in your field. [Or] maybe you get laid off. You go through financial difficulties. So many things happen in your life that they don't discuss in school. Those things should be discussed. They should show you how to handle your finances and how not to get into debt. They don't discuss those things and those are the things life is all about."

Smaltz says the advice he would impart to people looking to achieve wealth is to pay back all your debt, and don't get into debt. "Realize that you're never going to accumulate wealth when you owe somebody. It won't be yours. It will be someone else's."

Too many people put money away while they remain in debt. "That's silly," he says. "They think the debt is going to leave you."

The other important advice he offers is "put money away—no matter how little. Forget about it. Put away $1 a day. At the end of the year, when you said you didn't have enough money, you'd have $365."

Many have the misconception that with wealth there is no sadness, he says. Everything is not smooth sailing. "The more money you make, the more problems you have," he says. "I'm not saying I'm at the level I hope to be. You have to work that much harder to stay at that level. There constantly are innovations to the market, and if you don't stay in step with it, you'll get left behind. With the Internet, we had to get our Web page redesigned. It was not in step with the rest of the market."

Smaltz says he hopes to avoid some of the troubles his other employers experienced. New World Rarities is more diversified. "The company is not just sales," he said. "It's retail and wholesale sales. The company is Internet sales and advertising. It's even, as we speak, venturing out into doing bank loans—loaning our customers money and using coins as collateral."

Smaltz always keeps a tattered Bible near him, and quotes from it. He frequently turns to one passage in Matthew: Chapter 6, verse 25. "What I am having to deal with is not worrying that I'll go back to that situation [when I was in debt]," he says. "If I do, God will get me through it again."

Smaltz admits he would like to find the right woman for a permanent relationship. "For whatever reason, I haven't been capable. I date. I go out. There were a few I thought were the right ones. It didn't work out.

"Men always have an excuse not to get married," he says. "One of the excuses is I don't have enough money to take care of her the way I should. When I was young and working off Wall Street, I didn't want to get married. When I got laid off, I didn't even go out anywhere. I didn't want anyone to know the situation I was in. I was so insecure, so uncomfortable."

He admits now that it probably is not right to feel that way. "That's just how I took it. I took it pretty bad. I never gave up. I didn't enjoy life as well as I probably could have or should have.

"I can't even say it was the women who did that. I made myself miserable. I would spend days and days in my room after work, go home, watch TV, and read. I didn't want to have to hear from people [whom] I knew or people I was going out with 'What do you do? Where do you live?' I didn't want to discuss it."

Now he has a different perspective.

He also loves to sing. His hope is to go to the Lennox Lounge in Harlem, where greats like Louis Armstrong and Ella Fitzgerald have sung. "My dream is on my fortieth birthday, I'd like to get a jazz band and have all my friends come out and do a set."

CHAPTER 5

MARY E. FOLEY

Customer Service Rep Retires at 33

Mary E. Foley, 36, launched her career in a red brick building as an $8-an-hour customer service representative for Quantum Computer Services, Inc. Fortunately for her, the company mushroomed into America Online (AOL). Now she is retired with a net worth of $10 million. Her father, Charles, a dentist, delighted in announcing at her AOL-sponsored retirement party that he had to take off work to attend.

As fate would have it, the company Foley joined in McLean, Virginia, grew. She credits her $10 million net worth entirely to stock option agreements. When she officially retired in 1999, she exercised all options and cashed out the stock, depositing most of the money in a money market fund.

Although the ability to sign out of the work force early with millions of dollars might seem like a dream come true, Foley does not feel like she hit the lottery. She definitely worked hard for that money. Ultimately, she rose to the position of corporate training manager, and survived a half-dozen rounds of layoffs at a company that, upon her exit, employed close to 15,000 people. When she left, she adds, her annual salary was $65,000—a figure she considered below market in relation to the amount of responsibility she shouldered.

Foley describes her stint at America Online as like "being on adrenalin for 10½ years." Upon finally leaving, she made a pledge to herself. She never wishes to lead such a fast-paced life again for such a long period. It took her as many as four months after her retirement to recuperate. She needed to decompress emotionally and physically. "I almost had to go to the doctor," she said. "I thought I might have Epstein-Barre [syndrome] or something."

Since her retirement, she has obtained a masters degree in organization development from Pepperdine University in Malibu, California—a degree she paid for herself. She finished her thesis in a rented furnished San Diego condo overlooking the water, where she stayed for two months. She made the cross-country trip to Palm Springs with her mother in her black Porsche Boxster. "We dubbed ourselves Thelma and Louise," she said. "We had a ball."

Today, her work week, which she organizes with a computer calendar, is carefully designed to include workouts in the gym three to four times a week. It also is filled with lunch or dinner appointments with friends or business associates. There have been trips to Italy with her mother and other travel with friends.

When we interviewed Foley, she was about to move into a luxury 1,700-square-foot high-rise two-bedroom, two-bathroom condo she purchased in Reston, Virginia. She also just spent four months writing a book, *Bodacious! An AOL Insider Cracks the Code to Outrageous Success for Women* (Amacom). Plus, she has started her own company, Bodacious! Ventures, LLC, aimed at giving talks and workshops on subjects discussed in her book.

The road to riches for Foley was not exactly the smoothest.

She grew up the shy daughter of a dentist and elementary school teacher in the quaint, historic town of Williamsburg, Virginia. She was the second oldest of four children, with an older sister and a younger set of brother-sister twins.

For first through fifth grades, she attended Catholic school. "My parents put a lot of emphasis in doing well in school," she said. They also were careful to help her figure out what other activities she might be interested in. There were plenty. Foley loved basketball. Although only five-foot-two, she frequently beat some of the boys in the neighborhood, and her father installed a basketball hoop for her at their home. She enjoyed tennis, which both of her parents also played. She also practiced piano. "I always had some little project going on—particularly crafts," Foley said. She enjoyed working with plaster of paris. When she was 12, her mother suggested that she run a crafts workshop for the neighborhood children. Foley convinced the other children's mothers to let them attend two-to-three-hour classes over the course of a few weeks, for which she charged no more than $10. Cooking and playing the saxophone were some other pastimes.

Foley was a quiet child with short hair. In fact, she remembers distinctly going out to dinner with her family when she was young and sitting very quietly. The server asked what the "little fellow" would like to have. "I looked a lot like my father," she said. "I had short hair and was a tomboy." The server didn't hear her response and inquired again. "It occurred to me to speak up," she chuckled.

Foley says she earned an allowance at home for which she was expected to keep her room clean and help with the dishes. As she became older and her desire for material possessions increased, her parents very cautiously helped her out.

Take the stereo set she wanted so desperately when she was 16. "It was a big purchase," she said. "By the time I had gotten a couple of speakers, tuner, and turntable, it was going to be about $400. It was around my birthday. My Dad said if I really wanted something, I could do something around the house or around the office. I remember one time painting the walls inside his office or the exterior to earn more money." He promised that if she earned half, he'd finance the other half for her birthday. Her father was generous and would always pay her far more than what the labor was worth. "But he knew I had a goal and was willing to do something additional. So he'd make an offer."

The experience taught her that if she wanted something, she was able to get it, but she'd have to earn it. "I'd just have to be clear about what I want and have a plan."

Her father worked very hard establishing a dental practice. As she looks back, she says, she realizes that her family never lived exorbitantly.

"The focus was never on money as a measure of who we were as people," she said. "[The focus] was how you care about people and treat them."

After the younger twins were born, her family moved from their three-bedroom, two-bathroom home into a two-story brick home on land they owned adjacent to their existing home. Her mother, Donna, gave up her teaching career to become a full-time mother. Often, her parents, whose own families were in the medical field, socialized with other doctors and dentists. Foley says she noticed how their children often had more possessions and went on more extravagant vacations than she did. "It wasn't jealousy," she said, "but I would think those kids are so spoiled."

She realized that even though her father eked out a good living, four children can put a crimp into your financial lifestyle. "As I've gotten older—even into college, I've really respected the fact that my parents connected with a lot of these people and they were making choices in terms of lifestyles. They scaled back more than some of their friends."

When her parents did opt to spend money, it usually was on something that brought the family closer together. A favorite excursion, she says, was when they simply loaded the Foley clan into a trailer and drove to Disney World in Florida for a week. "We stayed on the Disney property on the campground—which we thought was a big deal." After all, she noted, it would have cost a small fortune to put a family of six up in a hotel room. Often there were trips to Virginia Beach or nearby mountains that they could get to in just a few hours—minus costly airfare.

Foley never read much as a child, although she says she is starting to enjoy books now. She was more of a doer. However, she always was a good student and, in fact, graduated fifth in her high school class. Her mother helped her pick a college. When they realized that Foley did slightly better on math than the verbal portion of the PSATs, her mother suggested engineering. "My mom generally was a forward-thinking female," Foley says. "She wanted her daughters to be self-sufficient financially. She was a full-time mom. That was a choice. But she made it clear that even if you get married and your husband becomes a provider financially, you need to know that you can take care of yourself financially."

It was assumed from childhood that all the children would go to college. "My parents viewed having a college education as a prerequisite to earning a living and financially being able to support ourselves in the world," she said. "They made it clear they'd pay for it. So growing up I thought everyone went to college and that their parents financially supported them. It didn't dawn on me until high school that some people chose other options with or without direct financial support."

Foley liked the idea of engineering school. "I wanted an education, but I didn't want it to go on forever," she explained. Had she followed in much of her family's path and gone on to medical school, it would have been way too long before she had finished.

"I quickly came to appreciate my parents' offer [to pay for college] and didn't want to be a big financial burden." She chose a lower-cost option—Virginia Tech, a state school.

Her parents bought her a used Ford Escort so she could be involved in a cooperative education program. She was able to drive to work where she worked part-time as a junior engineer, gaining on-the-job experience. She rented a room in a house, and would save all the money she could from her paycheck. With her earnings, she was able to reimburse her parents for some of their expenses. The experience drove home one particularly important point. She didn't want to be an engineer for the rest of her life!

The cooperative program added another year to her four-year education. She would attend school for a semester and then work for a semester. After three semesters of working as an engineer, she made up her mind that the field was not for her. Yet, she was caught between a rock and a hard place. If she transferred to another program, she would have lost her credits. They were not transferrable. So, she decided to follow through and obtain her college degree in engineering.

"My gut [feeling is that] it was the lack of real people interaction," she said of her distaste for engineering. "You're solving problems that are mechanical or systemic in nature." She graduated with a 3.0 out of a maximum 4.0.

Although she had recognized that engineering was not for her, Foley credits her college career with both drawing her out of her shell and teaching her how to think methodically and analytically. Engineering training centers on focusing on a question, determining the facts, and getting a hypothesis, she says. Too often in business, mistakes are made because the initial question is unclear.

While in school, she joined a sorority, Phi Mu, in her freshman year. Initially, she was running rush parties, which required her to initiate conversations with other women. This helped her overcome her youthful shyness. "I learned the art of small talk and how to start conversations," she said. "I got tons of practice." She became historian at the sorority one year and, subsequently, vice president. That job, she says, provided her with some valuable training managing and motivating people, she believes. Against the prodding of her friends, she refused, however, to take a critical Engineers-in-training accreditation exam. Although passing the exam is a prerequisite to being at many companies, she made up her mind that she did not wish to go that route. "It was one of the first times I started to trust myself even though my classmates thought I should take it," she said. That experience and the positive outcome that ultimately resulted helped boost her self-confidence.

Foley got her engineering degree in 1988. Not exactly knowing what else to do, she went back to her family's home to live. "I had my head a little bit down," she admitted. "I was very clear on what I didn't want to do—engineering—but I was not clear on what I wanted to do."

Williamsburg did not provide many options for a young college graduate. There was little exposure to corporate life—which she desperately needed to help solidify her future direction. The town was known for William and Mary College, Colonial Williamsburg, and Busch Gardens. It was filled with college students and intellectuals.

Foley was beginning to feel like a loser and her mother, in particular, was getting very antsy. "She was concerned that I didn't have a direction. I also didn't know how to go about finding a job. So [I was] trying to figure it out."

She began looking at job ads in the *Washington Post* and *Richmond Times-Dispatch*. She had no idea what type of job she wanted. "I really wanted [to work in] northern Virginia or metro [Washington] D.C.," she said. Her path became clearer when a friend from high school had a room available in a townhouse she shared with several other women in McLean. Foley felt that if she could move there, she then could look around and at least figure out what she wanted. She found two job possibilities. One was the customer service rep job with Quantum Computer Services. The other was a position with a temporary agency. She was significantly overeducated for both jobs. But she was confident that her path would become clearer if she could get out of her small hometown and learn more about corporate America. She obtained interviews with both companies on the same day.

The visit to the temp agency was a bomb. She felt that she had flunked every assessment. "No, I can't type fast," she said. With all her training as an engineer, she was unprepared for many of the tests she had to take to become a secretary. The experience hit hard on her self-esteem.

Foley had grown up largely Episcopalian. "I had faith in God, but it wasn't very developed," she said. In college, she had become more involved, joining a student Christian organization and a nondenominational church. She believes God might have been the factor that steered her to Quantum Computer Services. "I had called Quantum Computer Services several times to speak to the recruiter and was about to give up when I decided to call one more time," she said. "This time the recruiter was available and took my call. I had a preliminary phone interview and was asked to come for an in-person one." Foley was impressed with the liveliness of the people. "The recruiter was very energetic," she said. Interested in getting the job, she strained her memory to try to recall any experience whatsoever that might help give her a shot. She had held a part-time job at a toy store. She worked as a waitress one summer before her senior year of high school. She worked part-time a couple of semesters of college in the cafeteria. Fortunately, Quantum Computer Services was not a stickler for direct on-the-job experience. She got the job and within 11 days, was living and working in northern Virginia.

Initially, Quantum Computer Services provided online services for consumers and entered strategic partnerships with computer hardware companies, such as Commodore Business Machines and Tandy, to expand. Foley hadn't been online yet, but had used a computer in engineering school. "I was trained on how to answer questions," she said. The company was just launching a new online service. "I really liked the people." Although she also was impressed by the entrepreneurial spirit, she felt very soon that she needed to move on. She was on the phone for 8 hours a day, 40 hours a week, one phone call after another. It was grueling.

The good news was she had no debt. Although she only made $18,000 annually, she lived in a group house, so rent and utility costs were low. Quantum had a very casual dress code, so she didn't need to buy expensive clothes. She had a checking account and credit card, which she paid off monthly. She even donated to charities such as her church. She sponsored a child through Compassion International, Colorado Springs, and was able to help needy friends.

Foley had joined Quantum Computer Services in an entry level position. At that time, there were no stock options. "There was a good amount of turnover," she added.

Eventually, she was promoted to training specialist, and four years after she started at Quantum she was granted stock options. The options—in the form of a 20-page legal document—came along with her evaluation. On the day America Online went public in 1992, the share price rose $2.50. Her profit if she were to sell them that day would have been an attractive $10,000. "I remember looking at that number and thinking, wow. That's a lot of money." She had a meeting with a senior manager, who is now Jean Case, the wife of AOL Chairman Steve Case, and was told to put the agreement away and consider it a nest egg. Obediently, she filed the document away at home.

Foley knew very little about stock options. Although her father educated her a great deal about money, the subject of stock options didn't happen to come up. There was some talk about them in the cafeteria at work. But most conversations focused on whether there would be layoffs as the company struggled with a thin staff through several major mergers. "I remember Steve Case saying to all employees, don't focus on the stock price. It's not always a good measure of how we're doing. Try to focus on what we're trying to achieve. Just focus on your job. It made sense to me. That's basically what we did."

Although she didn't receive stock options when she first started, she says that policy subsequently changed at AOL and newly hired personnel began getting them. "I thought I got gypped," she admitted. "I had put in hard work and heart and soul for the first four years." She let her feelings be known, but to no avail.

Even though she had an attractive option agreement sitting tucked away at home, Foley was not yet vested. In other words, she could not cash the options in for stock. The options were on a four-year vesting cycle from the point at which she received them in 1992. After the first year, she was allowed to exercise 25 percent of the options. The next year, 50 percent; the following year, 75 percent; and the fourth year, she could exercise all of them. The options had a ten-year expiration date from the time of the agreement. Because she couldn't exercise them anyway, she decided to take Jean Case's advice after the company went public, and she largely ignored them. Instead, she focused on her job. "Initiative and performance counted a lot," she said. "I thrived in this environment." It provided an opportunity for her to contribute, be respected, and feel what she and her coworkers were doing—bringing online services to the masses—was meaningful.

"I thought about leaving AOL a couple of times when the stress was really high and I wondered if I needed to scale back my life a bit," she acknowledged. "But it continued to be fun and interesting."

While she was a trainer, she used to ask Steve Case to speak to new customer service reps about how the company got started, his vision, and the current status. Listening to him again and again over several years made his vision almost second nature to her. "In training new employees, I also had to know a lot about where the company was headed, how all the pieces fit together, and who was who." In her early days on the job, this information was not available in any kind of training manual, so she had to seek out answers herself. "I quickly got in the habit of introducing myself to new people, finding out their roles, sharing mine, and offering assistance."

She built a network of people all over the company and created warm friendships. "Up until I left, I had people call and ask who might know something or who to talk to get something done."

The financial catalyst in her life, though, came in 1994, when she figured the value of her options was $400,000. "At that point, I went, 'Wow!'" she said. "I was a bit scared of it. I remember being with a girlfriend. She had no reaction. I felt immediately like I made her uncomfortable." That, she says, was her first inkling that not everybody reacts the same way when it comes to money.

In the spring of 1994, she took the role of call center manager and dramatically expanded the group. Originally there were three supervisors and 70 reps on the phone. She grew it to 15 supervisors and 230 reps. "Fourteen months later, I'm running a 250-person organization," she said. "Call that my crash course in leadership. I was 29 years old."

It was a tight management team, she said. There were no issues regarding age and gender. By June 1995, she switched from call center manager to human resources and began the corporate training function. She often worked nine hours a day. Some days were 12 to 14 hours long.

At age 25, she married a computer science major she had met at engineering school. The marriage, while childless, lasted eight years. With marriage, though, came some debt. There was a bit of credit card debt, car payments, and, finally, a $150,000 mortgage. She admits she tapped about half of her stock options to pay down the debt and help cut the mortgage loan on the couple's $405,000 house. Had she not touched the options, she estimates that her net worth might now be $20 to $25 million instead of $10 million.

When she divorced in December 1998, her husband got her house, and she moved into a two-bedroom apartment. She went back to using her maiden name, Foley.

"Work was not a factor," she said of the divorce. "Not to say that the high pace of working at AOL didn't put some strain on our relationship. It did. He would get frustrated with me working late. It wasn't easy, but I got to the point where I wouldn't do e-mails at night. I wouldn't do them on weeknights or on the weekend—only on an exception basis. That was really hard for me. I loved work and loved the environment. But I intellectually knew when I got myself away and did something different, I re-energized myself."

Despite the divorce, Foley is not turned off toward marriage. "I might marry again," she said. "I'm not down on the whole concept just because one wasn't right. In fact, I'm dating somebody right now [whom] I really enjoy." If she married again, Foley says she would not change her name. While she's not sure whether she would have a prenuptial agreement, she definitely would not want assets commingled. If she and a future mate do something together, like buy a home, that might be a joint asset.

"The biggest catalyst is realizing how much I had to be more proactive in my life. I can't relinquish finances to [a spouse] either."

Foley retired from America Online in 1999. "I had mixed feelings," she said. "I really wanted to continue to pursue a career path in organization development. I was not getting the ongoing opportunity to do that in the way I wanted. I decided that even though I loved the company, I needed to follow work that was fulfilling." She knew she wanted to go to graduate school, and could not envision working full time at her demanding AOL job while going to school. In fact, new hires at AOL just getting their feet wet at the fast-paced company could not believe she had survived there as long as she did. "I was just tired," she said.

As Foley pondered leaving, not all her option agreements had been completely vested. She was about two years into her last agreement. "I left some options on the table," she admitted. "I never calculated the exact cost. It might have been a couple hundred thousand dollars or so. I consciously had to say the cost of staying was a higher personal price in not being able to pursue my dream." Nevertheless, AOL's stock already had split six times while she was there.

Foley says that in retrospect, she might have made two mistakes in her career. One was she married the wrong person. "Out of that I learned a lot about myself and what it takes for a relationship to work," she said. She also believes that while she was at America Online, she could have paid more attention to office politics. "I thought of it as a negative thing," she said. "The reality was politics is a lot about relationships. I had a lot of very positive relationships. I had a good reputation and credibility within the organization. But I didn't fully leverage it."

In a very short period of two or three years, America Online had been flooded with new people who joined the organization and volleyed for leadership positions, she said. Many were around her age and up to 10 years older. They simply were more astute at handling corporate politics than she was.

Perhaps she could have reached out more and introduced herself to even more key players throughout more departments, she muses. "I could have tried to be more strategic. I could have spent more time sitting back and thinking about the political landscape and about the ways I'd like to advance and then proactively trying to make some move."

When she finally retired from America Online and took her money with her, she remembers thinking how she didn't want it to change her life. "What I really meant is I don't want it to change the character of who I am," she says. "It does change your life. I'd be in denial if I said it didn't.

"I almost froze," she says. "I remember that feeling of, yeah, I could do everything I want to do, but I can also screw this up and now I have [further] to fall. In all likelihood, I'm not going to get this opportunity again."

Foley says she was flooded with choices of how to manage her newfound wealth. "I felt like I could go to school to learn just about this whole arena."

Then she remembered Stephen Y. Park, vice president of investments with A.G. Edwards in Washington, D.C. He had been calling on her at America Online, trying to get her to agree to let him hold one-hour financial seminars for AOL employees.

Although Foley felt strongly that such seminars were needed, and America Online later launched a seminar program, the proposal initially was killed, she said. Nevertheless, while the two were talking, Foley realized that some day she was going to need someone like him. She liked A.G. Edwards because the company has no proprietary products. For example, they don't distribute their own mutual funds. When a financial services company distributes its own mutual funds or other services, employees may have incentives to push those more aggressively, she reasoned. They may or may not be in a client's best interest. "I'm no idiot," Foley says. "If you have proprietary products, you're going to want your agents to sell those. He didn't have that pressure." She said she had to wrestle with the idea of having the money take over her life as a full-time job, or giving up some control. She found a happy medium. She lets Park manage her money but he keeps her informed. "What I really like about Stephen is that he looks out for my best interest while respecting my right to choose," she said. "We've developed a partnership that I believe is the best strategy to handle the ongoing financial changes."

When we interviewed Foley, she was invested most heavily in growth stocks. She also had value stocks, small cap stocks, and international companies. "I favor the high-tech sector because I've lived it and believe it's the backbone of the new economy," she says. "The trick is picking well as there will be fewer winners and lots of losers financially as new industries are birthed, grow, and consolidate."

She also has invested in HumanR, a human resources technology and consulting firm, as an angel investor. She sits on the board of directors of the online startup. In fact, she spent 2½ months acting as the company's vice president of sales and marketing. We talked to her during a bear market in 2001. Even though the bulk of her money was in stock, Foley was not overly worried. "I am in the market for the long term," she said. She also had some money in lower-risk money market funds that paid 4.5 percent interest. Park told us that because Foley is young and expects ultimately to be drawing income from HumanR and her book, he put her heavily into stocks. When we talked to him, she had 30 percent of her money in value stocks, 30 percent in growth stocks, 15 percent in international stocks, and 10 percent in cash. However, Park admitted that the two were to meet shortly to discuss allocating some money into bonds for interest income and safety. She already had cashed out some bonds earlier to make her venture capital investment. Foley's money is invested through A. G. Edwards' private advisory service, a service that uses institutional money managers, yet requires smaller minimum investments. The investments, Park says, are more tailor-made than traditional mutual funds.

Think life would be easier if you had as much money as Foley? Think again, she suggests. "My experience is that it's different," she says, "but not necessarily easier. It changes what you have to focus on."

Once you have all that money, there are a number of issues to deal with. One is the way that people look at you and perceive you changes. "You don't get a choice in that." It also can result in changing friendships and family relationships. "You may find your friends aren't as good friends as you expected. In a way, you say, 'I didn't ask for this. I didn't know it came in a package with all these other things.' There's no way you can fully anticipate that unless it happens to you."

Everyone has a relationship with money—whether they're conscious of it or not—she believes. People react to success based on their own relationships with money. "I have to be able to accept the fact that some people are going to accept me positively or negatively, not because they know me as a person, but because they see wealth. I also now have to keep my antenna alert to people who want my money."

As an angel investor, she says, people constantly court her to invest in their organizations. "I've not dealt with this so much before."

Foley says that she needed to be very positive and strong with family members and is proud of the way they have reacted to her new wealth. She confided her net worth to her parents. She even experienced the thrill of giving them each a gift of a trip with her anyplace in the world all-expenses-paid. For two years, she says, she didn't talk about her net worth with her siblings. "They saw me doing things like going to grad school and not working," she said. "They weren't idiots." But when you have a lot of money, it can be touchy. It is important that everyone develop values and the ability to take care of themselves. You don't want to take away someone's respect and pride. On the other hand, she says, if any member of her family were in desperate financial need, "you'd better believe I'd help them out. We all would rally and do what we could."

Once you have a lot of money, and the initial partying wears off, "at some point, you have to look at yourself in the mirror and say, 'Who am I? What's my life about? Do I have a purpose and what does it mean?'" she says. "These are huge questions!"

With another 30-some years until she reaches the typical retirement age, she had to determine how she wants to spend the money and how not to lose it. That was a huge burden for a college engineering major.

Although she considers herself still new at this quest, she is taking it step by step.

For one thing, she is trying to pass some of her good fortune to others. Her new book is designed to help other women achieve. In it, she tells women to be bold and self-reliant. When you take charge of your life and begin making your own decisions, positive things start happening to you. You are no longer afraid. You have more confidence in yourself.

"Bodacious," she says, "means to be outstanding, bold, and audacious." The concept of work helped change her own life.

"When I look in the mirror, I see someone like no one I have ever seen before," she says in the first chapter. "I see someone who benefited from the New Economy in ways most people don't even bother to dream about."

She teaches women to take stands against issues and shows others how to use relationship skills more strategically. She hopes to do motivational speaking in conjunction with the book.

Much inspiration, she says, came from two books by Sark she read, *Succulent Wild Woman* and the *Bodacious Book of Succulent,* both published by Fireside.

She also has been sponsoring more children in other countries for Compassion International. "Every Christmas I'm going to add another child [to the list of] those I sponsor," she says. "Now I have four. It's a way not only to give back and help kids in other countries. It's a way for me to help a generation." She is particularly interested in sponsoring young girls.

In addition, she provides support to an organization, Women Helping Women, in Houston. It is an organization for women who have come to the point where they're serious about changing their circumstances—whether they're divorced or abandoned by husbands or lovers. "I very much liked the fact that it is directed specifically toward women."

Was Foley's good fortune at America Online a flash in the pan that few people will experience again? She admits that she was part of a bubble that started in the late 1990s that has gone back down. It might happen again, she says.

She advises that anyone considering working for a company in the new economy ask a lot of questions and "not just the standard ones." Your role in a company, responsibilities, and your experience and desires are a small part of it. Conduct a competitive analysis, she suggests.

"Ask questions [as] if you were an investor—the profitability of the company, revenue growth, projections, how well it has done in the last two or three quarters, new products or services."

She advises you ask about research and development—what the company is coming out with to continue to stay competitive.

"I would do that with or without stock options," she said. "In particular, I would do even more scrutiny if they were a start-up or youthful company and using stock options as one way to offset the immediate cash needed for salary."

Stock options contributed to Foley's success and she does not think they will disappear as an employee benefit. Nevertheless, she does not consider them the most important factor in selecting a company either.

"I didn't make my career decisions based on financial issues," she reflects. "I based it on fulfillment." Once you are fulfilled, she believes, there may even be other ways to benefit—your salary might increase, or a job could lead to a more financially fulfilling position.

CHAPTER 6

GLORIA M. AND EMILIO ESTEFAN, JR.

Cuban Immigrants Create Music Empire

Sometimes a husband and wife can combine to create just the right business team—not that we know anything about that, mind you. Gloria and Emilio Estefan, Jr. have paired to create a net worth that has been estimated at $40 million by *Hispanic Business* magazine.

The parents of two children, the Estefans own a six-bedroom home on a 80,000 square foot lot on Star Island, Florida, as well as a state-of-the-art production studio, and a host of real estate properties, much of it in the hot South Beach deco district.

Prior to their marriage in 1978, the lives of both had been shaken up when Fidel Castro took over Cuba in 1959. Although Gloria and Emilio did not know each other then, both of their families independently chose to flee the island.

Both families came to America with no money and had to learn a new language. Although well off in Cuba, they were poor in America. But they got an education, followed their passions, and took one step at a time to get ahead.

Emilio, 48, grew up in Santiago, Cuba, the son of the owner of an underwear factory. Estefan was seven when Castro took over Cuba and began to slowly nationalize all privately owned businesses. Estefan's family stayed on the island six more years in the hope of saving their factory. Emilio, in the meantime, had started playing the accordion after he received the instrument as a gift at age six. When he was 13, he and his father gave up on their effort to save the factory and left for Madrid. Although Emilio was young enough to escape military service, his brother, Jose, was prohibited from leaving Cuba due to his eligibility for the country's draft. So Emilio and his father went to Madrid without him and applied for visas to come to the United States. It was nearly two more years, during which Emilio played the accordion for meals, before he made it to Miami on a student visa. He shared a home with his aunt and at least 13 relatives.

Emilio had come from a business family. So he knew how to make things happen for himself. Once in Miami, Estefan was reported to have become an instant entrepreneur. First he ran errands in an old Volkswagen for the elderly women in his neighborhood in exchange for tips. He also sold T-shirts, and got involved in running beauty pageants. By the time he was 16, he became a mail boy for Bacardi Imports, most known for its famous Bacardi rum. He earned $60 a week, and finished high school at night. Estefan studied marketing at Miami-Dade Community College, and continued to be promoted at Bacardi.

In the meantime, his involvment with music was revisited. He offered to play for free at an Italian restaurant on Biscayne Boulevard, making his income solely off tips. Once, he reported that he convinced an uncle to cosign a loan for a $700 accordion, which to him seemed like borrowing $70,000. Income from his music continued to grow, and when his boss at Bacardi heard of Emilio's musical talent, he invited him to play at a party. Estefan realized that this party was a major opportunity. To make a good impression, he believed he needed to appear with more than just an accordion, so he recruited a drummer and conga player from among his high school buddies. Estefan soon found himself as a percussionist playing other rhythm instruments in the band that debuted in 1974 as the Miami Latin Boys. Initially, the band played Latin favorites.

Gloria Maria Fajardo, 44, was born in Havana, the daughter of Jose Manuel Fajardo, a driver and bodyguard for the family of

Cuban dictator President Fulgencio Batista. Her mother, also named Gloria, had been a school teacher.

It was Batista that Fidel Castro overthrew in 1959 to seize control of Cuba. Although the Fajardo family had lived a middle class lifestyle in Cuba, it no longer was safe for them to stay on the island once Castro arrived. They fled on a Pan Am jet to the United States. Because they expected the revolution to be short-lived, they actually purchased round-trip tickets. Gloria has retained her $21 ticket as a keepsake. She was one year old when the family left Cuba. The Fajardos lived briefly in Texas and then in South Carolina before settling in a ghetto near the Orange Bowl in Miami by the time Gloria was two.

Gloria and her family were poor. But she was smart. She took solace in music when, as a teenager, she had to care for her ailing father. She also got an education.

As a child, Gloria says she went to the Torre de la Libertad (the Freedom Tower) in Miami where the family would get Spam and welfare cheese. "My mother would cover the Spam in Coke to make it brown and sweet," she told *People* magazine. Her mother also reported putting newspapers under Gloria's bedsheets to keep away the cockroaches.

Her father, accustomed to being a military man, quietly left to fight as a tank commander in the Bay of Pigs invasion, which was orchestrated by the U.S. Central Intelligence Agency, in 1961. Within three days, the war was over, and Fajardo was among 1,173 reported to be taken prisoner. He had been captured by a cousin, a Castro supporter. Finally, after 1½ years, Castro released Fajardo and other prisoners of the embarrassing battle in exchange for $53 million worth of food and medicine.

Gloria was a shy, pudgy child, fondly encouraged to eat by her grandmother. She has said that some of her earliest memories were during the time her father was imprisoned. All the women and their kids were in one apartment, she said. "No husbands. One car that cost $50. They'd pile us all in the car and go do the shopping," she reported in the *Miami Herald*. Meanwhile, none of the women spoke English and the grocer spoke no Spanish.

Gloria says she never went hungry. But those were tough times for Hispanics in this country. There was a great deal of prejudice. Her mother was forced to start her teaching career all over. That meant learning a new language.

Although her mother found learning English difficult, Glorita, as her family called Gloria to distinguish her from her mother, viewed it as a challenge. The only Hispanic in her class, Gloria once won an award for her reading skills. She helped teach her mother English and even went on to learn how to speak fluent French.

Fortunately, music had been plentiful in Gloria's family. Her mother frequently played records from Cuba and would sing to her as she changed Gloria's diapers. In fact, her mother once had obtained a contract in Hollywood to dub Shirley Temple movies into Spanish. Two of Gloria's uncles wrote songs and sang. One, a classical violinist and salsa flute player, had a successful band in Cuba.

Gloria's mother and her grandmother always told her she could do anything she wanted. Her parents encouraged her to take lessons in classical guitar. Her grandmother, she says, always made her sing in front of house guests and vowed that Gloria's destiny was to sing.

All this musical background came in handy. It became a welcome diversion when tragedy struck the Fajardo household. After her father had returned from his imprisonment in Cuba, he became a captain in the U.S Army and volunteered to go to Vietnam. Upon his return from Vietnam in 1968, the family noticed something was drastically wrong with him. He would fall for no reason and stop at a traffic light when it was green. Ultimately he couldn't walk without a cane.

Although he was diagnosed with multiple sclerosis, the family believed that in Vietnam, he had been exposed to deadly Agent Orange. The chemical, used to strip leaves from trees and expose enemy soldiers, was reported to have sickened many Vietnam veterans. The condition of Fajardo, a one-time volleyball champion and recipient of a Pan American Game medal, steadily worsened. He was unable to work.

Gloria's mother was working feverishly and going to school at night. She was desperate to get her Cuban teaching credentials re-certified so she could teach and support her family. When she finally started teaching in a Miami school, Gloria, at age 11, was forced to take care of her bedridden father.

"We had a lady who came till three in the afternoon, but there was no one after that," Gloria said in the book *Gloria Estefan,* by Michael Benson (Lerner Publications Company). "My mom was working her butt off, too." From the ages of 11 to 16, Gloria had her hands full. She also took care of her younger sister, Rebecca, and cleaned the house.

Gloria went through high school with virtually no social life due to her enormous responsibilities at home. It was the guitar, she has said, that served to take her mind off of all her troubles and helped her express her deep emotions. She continuously practiced and would teach herself Beatles songs as well as Cuban melodies. She was a great fan of pop singers, including Elton John and Stevie Wonder.

Finally, her father was too sick to stay in the house and was admitted to a Veterans Administration hospital. He subsequently died in 1980. Gloria, despite all her hardship, had succeeded in becoming an honor student at the Catholic high school she attended. She obtained a partial scholarship to the University of Miami.

While at University of Miami, she worked part-time from 1:00 to 9:00 PM as an interpreter. She also gave guitar lessons at a community center. Gloria was only five-foot-one and still over-weight. Although she sang, she was not exactly in the limelight.

It wasn't until she met Emilio that her life started changing. She says she first saw him in 1975, when he was invited to her school to speak to music students. By then she had started social-izing and, with some friends, had put together a singing group. The father of one of the girls in the group worked at Bacardi and arranged for Emilio to come over and give them some pointers. Three months later, Gloria's mother coaxed her to attend a wed-ding. Emilio's group, the Miami Latin Boys, happened to be playing there. Gloria has said she was impressed at Emilio's musical creativity—particularly the unique way he played "Do the Hustle" on an accordion. Emilio, against the initial wishes of his band members, invited Gloria on stage to sing.

Emilio was so impressed with her performance that a few weeks later, he invited both Gloria and her cousin to join the band. Generally, though, only men played salsa and the move to add women to the band was controversial. Emilio liked the idea of breaking the taboo. Of course, with women in the band, the name of the band had to change. It became the Miami Sound Machine.

Gloria agreed to join the band on the condition that she could continue her studies at University of Miami. Education was an extremely important issue in Gloria's family. That meant she could only play on weekends and holidays. Initially, Gloria sang backup vocals. She still was shy, and did not like getting in front of the crowd. She preferred writing music and recording.

By forcing herself to get out in the front and sing, she reports that she grew professionally, and finally became more comfortable with her leading role. Emilio supplied her with encouragement, suggesting that she act in front of an audience the same way that she acted when she was with him. He also gently encouraged her to lose weight, noting that she could "improve 95 percent."

Emilio and Gloria's relationship grew slowly. They didn't date at first. Gloria had viewed Emilio as a bit of a playboy, who often dated older women. Emilio had said he was attracted to Gloria's skin and honey eyes, but had resolved not to make a move on her unless he was serious. "She's been through too much," he said.

They married on September 2, 1978, after Gloria graduated from college where she studied psychology and communications. The two had no wedding reception. Instead, they preferred to spend their money on a trip to Japan. Shortly afterward, they went to Cuba to help Emilio's brother, Jose, come to the United States. A year earlier, the Miami Sound Machine had recorded its first album, *Renacer*, on a ridiculously low $2,000 budget.

But even at this point, the music business was a hobby for Estefan. He continued to rise up the ladder at Bacardi Imports.

Like other successful people, Emilio was not afraid to take risks. Plus, he looked at failures as a learning experience and fought strongly for what he believed in. He didn't make the same mistake twice.

Estefan told *Forbes* he lost everything from his first two records. The band was under a record contract that paid the band a mere 4 percent songwriting royalty. "Fortunately," he said, "we learned from our mistakes."

The Estefans had to abandon rights to their old songs to get out of the old contract when Discos CBS Records, now Sony Discos, offered them a new deal in 1981, according to *Forbes*.

In the meantime, Estefan had risen to the director of Hispanic marketing for Bacardi Imports, and was earning $100,000 annually. The couple's first child, Nayib, was born in 1980. Deciding he wanted to devote more time to the job of managing the Miami Sound Machine, which had become the top party band in Miami, Emilio took the brazen step of quitting his full-time job at Bacardi. He also wanted to spend more time with his new son and wife.

The Miami Sound Machine, which recorded four Spanish-language records between 1980 and 1984 became a huge hit in Latin America. The arrival of American pop culture to Spanish-speaking countries was welcomed by sold-out crowds. In fact, the crowds were much larger than those the group had entertained in the Miami area. But as the Miami Sound Machine grew more popular, dissension took over the group. Gloria's cousin, Merci, and the band's keyboard and saxophone player, Raul Murciano, had married and quit the band. Emilio also stopped playing with the band to devote more time to its management and to his son.

The group signed another larger contract with Epic Records Group, now a division of Sony Music Entertainment, and Gloria was billed as the group's lead singer.

It is considered a phenomenon in the record business when musicians, who play a certain style of music, can woo radio stations that play other types of music. The industry calls it *crossover*. Generally, record companies tend to play it safe, and prefer the less costly tactic of targeting music to specific audiences. So, initially, the music of the Miami Sound Machine was largely limited to radio stations that played Latin music.

Sony, though, finally agreed to let the group record the flip side of one record in English. It was a song that Enrique "Kiki" Garcia, a band member at the time, had written, called "Dr. Beat."

"When an artist crosses over into the largest-selling market, it presents the artist with a higher level of recognition and exposure," Oscar Llord, president of Sony Discos, told *Billboard* magazine in 1999. "But much care must always be taken so as not to alienate the artist's core audience."

It is with "Dr. Beat" that the Miami Sound Machine achieved its monumental goal of crossover. The group suddenly heard the song being played on a Miami radio station, and a 12-inch dance single of the record reached number ten on the dance music charts in the United States.

Emilio firmly believed that he could sell the group's music to much more than Latin audiences, and convinced Sony to release an English album, called *Primitive Love*. In fact, *Forbes* noted, the Estefans added $32,000 of their own money to the $20,000 Sony would spend to produce it. The group hired its own production trio, known in Miami as "The Jerks." They were Joe Galdo, Rafael Vigil, and Lawrence Dermer. Emilio had heard an aerobics tape the three had produced and thought it was the exact sound he sought for the Miami Sound Machine. One of the songs released off that English album as a single, "Conga," hit the top 10 of *Billboard's* "Hot 100" list.

Gloria, at the time, wore heavy make-up, eyeliner, and straight hair, creating an image of Latin women she thought people wanted. Later on, as she felt more comfortable with the band's blend of Cuban-American music, she toned down her style and promoted a more natural appearance.

Getting the landmark hit, "Conga," out to worldwide audiences, though, was a battle for the Estefans. The record company executives thought it was too Latin for American audiences and too American for Latin audiences. The group had manufactured a new sound that was a controversial blend. It came at a time where the Hispanic population was growing significantly. Today that group represents about 13 percent of the U.S. population of 281.4 million, according to the U.S. Census Bureau. Many of the Hispanic population also were younger and thus a prime target for the Estefans' pop music. On top of that, sales of Hispanic records started growing faster than the sale of American records, attracting more attention from record executives.

The song gained momentum when Gloria sang "Conga" at the 1988 Calle Ocho Festival, and 120,000 people gathered to claim the Guiness record for the longest conga line.

The Estefans' successful crossover caused the group's popularity to ricochet. Once the Estefans conquered the U.S. market, they succeeded in doing what some have termed a reverse crossover. They became even more popular in the Latin markets.

In 1986, the Estefans formed their own corporation, Estefan Enterprises, Inc. They bought their home, built in 1959, for $600,000 which they later expanded. The market value of the three-story home, which the Estefans dramatically improved, now is listed on Miami property records as close to $2.8 million. More hit records followed in 1987 with the group's *Let It Loose* album.

But fame can cause a lot of changes among people. Additional band members left, including Kiki Garcia, the writer of their first crossover hits, "Dr. Beat" and "Conga." In 1989, Gloria Estefan released her first solo album, *Cuts Both Ways,* and from then on received sole billing. The Miami Sound Machine was dead, and Gloria and Emilio were on their own.

All was going quite well for the Estefans. They had become household names. Gloria had a personal trainer and had slashed her weight to 102 pounds. But the tragedies she endured as a child had not yet ended.

She put an elevator in her home to transport musical instruments, however, she later acknowledged that the elevator partially was built due to her innate fear that she one day would wind up an invalid like her late father. It almost seemed like a premonition.

Shortly afterward, in 1990, she was nearly paralyzed when a semi-truck rammed her tour bus in the snow-covered Pocono Mountains, as she was on her way to a concert in Syracuse, New York. The accident left her in excruciating pain with a broken back. Emilio suffered head injuries and their son, Nayib, who was nine at the time, broke his collarbone. The injury forced Gloria to cancel an international tour, and spend a year recovering.

Emilio, Gloria had reported, didn't leave the house for the first three months during her recuperation. "I've really learned that you have to enjoy every moment," she told *USA Weekend* in 1990. "Before, sometimes I'd get so stressed out that I wouldn't allow myself to relax and enjoy things. Now I do."

In 48 hours, she had received 1,100 floral arrangements, and in two weeks, 11,000 telegrams and 30,000 letters, *USA Weekend* reported. "A 12-by-24-foot card was signed by 20,000 people." The Estefans wound up getting an $8.5 million settlement as a result of the accident.

The accident left Gloria with two eight-inch metal rods permanently attached to her spine. But it didn't stop her from performing. After her accident, Gloria also ignored doctors' warnings against getting pregnant due to her back injury, and she gave birth to her daughter, Emily, in 1994, via a caesarian section.

Yet, Gloria's tragedies were not over. In 1995, a 29-year-old law student from Howard University was killed off South Beach when his Yamaha Wave Runner ran into the wake of the Estefans' powerboat.

A statement issued by the Estefans said that Emilio Estefan had been steering the vessel, while Gloria was relaxing. "Immediately following the collision, Estefan jumped into the water to try to assist the victim who was still alive at the time."

Emilio voluntarily gave blood to dispel any doubt that he might have been operating the vessel while impaired. The accident deeply moved the Estefans. Gloria personally was reported to have called the man's parents, offering to do anything she could to help.

Gloria also aggressively campaigned before the state legislature to get state boating laws changed. Today, anyone under 21 operating a vessel powered by a motor of at least 10 horsepower must have a boater safety identification card, signifying completion of an eight-hour course or the equivalent.

Meanwhile, Emilio Estefan was emerging as an impressive businessman. He learned early on how important it was to own everything he wrote. In 1996 alone, *Forbes* reported that the Estefans' wholly owned music publishing unit collected $10 million from a catalog of 1,000 songs. Those included soundtracks for *Evita* and Walt Disney's *Pocahontas*.

"We like to have the publishing rights," Estefan told *Miami New Times* in 1994. "I would not make a deal with someone who is going to sell 500,000 units worldwide if I do not own the publishing rights, because then we don't make a penny. We have an organization with almost 300 people working for us, and we don't make money on the live performance, we only make a small profit on the record deal. The only way we make a little bit of money is on the publishing company."

Even though the Estefans made millions from their music, they didn't rest on their laurels. They began to diversify their business. They put their money to work for them in other businesses and investments. They didn't keep all their eggs in one basket.

Besides learning the ropes of the music business, Estefan started building a real estate empire in the heart of the South Beach deco district. He bought the Cardozo Hotel for close to $5 million and opened a successful Cuban restaurant, Larios, for which the *Miami Herald* reported they paid $2.2 million. The trendy restaurant has been frequented by many celebrities, including Oprah Winfrey, Sharon Stone, and Quincy Jones. Much of the land they bought, which included lots, office buildings, and condos, was purchased through their company, Mau Mau Corp. Plus, they opened Bongos Cafe at Walt Disney World in Orlando. *Forbes* once reported that the Estefans get 80 percent of the profits from the Disney restaurant.

The Estefans' South Beach restaurant and hotel often are touted as major sites to see in Miami. They are successful, despite the fact that many restaurants with celebrities backing them have flopped.

"People will go the first time because of the famous name," Emilio Estefan explained to *Variety* in 1999. "The second time, they come back for the food and service."

Estefan, in fact, has claimed that his restaurant fails to suffer the off-season drop-off in business that plagues other South Florida restaurants. The Estefans, published reports indicated, were careful to go into the business with a family they knew already had operated a successful Cuban restaurant. The same family is reported to be involved with Bongos Cafe at Disney World.

Emilio Estefan made out big time, many say, due to a multi-million-dollar deal he signed with Sony in 1994. Under the contract, Estefan was to have received a seven-figure salary. He was provided with a budget for signing names, and receives a percentage of the sales of albums under the label.

Crescent Moon Records, a Sony spokeswoman told us, is a multicultural, multilingual, and multiracial record label. The company signs what it feels passionate about, and considers itself an artist development company. However, whatever is produced through the label must be distributed exclusively through Sony. Crescent Moon Records falls under the umbrella of the Estefans' own company, Crescent Moon, Inc., which includes Crescent Moon recording studio. The recording studio does not produce exclusively for Sony.

Estefan Enterprises also helps manage artists.

Estefan's businesses have been reported to, in some fashion, have had a hand in the development of such stars as Marc Anthony, Jennifer Lopez, John Secada, Ricky Martin, and Shakira. More recently, Sony Music Entertainment announced that Estefan's record label, Crescent Moon, would be part of a new Madrid-based joint venture label to discover, develop, and establish Latin music artists around the world. Sony Music Entertainment and Grupo Prisa were the two other parties to the venture. Unlike the Crescent Moon label, a Sony spokeswoman explained, the new label's primary intentions would be to sign Spanish-language artists.

The union came as a study by PricewaterhouseCoopers, which predicted that music sales in Brazil would increase 14.2 percent annually between 2001 and 2005. Over the same period, it said Latin American music sales would increase 11.8 percent annually to $3.52 billion. Factors cited are economic growth, improved literacy, greater personal computer and Internet penetration, and recent legislation cracking down on piracy, notes *Billboard*. More competitive pricing also was anticipated.

The Estefans, with their state-of-the-art Crescent Moon Studio, have been getting the reputation of being Miami's Hispanic Motown. Emilio Estefan also was reported to be entering the magazine business by cofounding a Spanish-language magazine, *Ocean Drive en Español*.

The Estefans very carefully manage their personal finances, published reports indicate. Aside from cutting real estate deals, which have been credited with helping to revive the South Beach area, Emilio Estefan has been vigilant with both his charitable causes and taxes.

In 1994, *Miami New Times* reported, Gloria and Emilio Estefan saved $6,649.97 by using a tax consultant to appeal their residential property taxes. In addition, *Forbes* has cited Gloria Estefan's foundation as being among the more efficient celebrity foundations. In 2000, the magazine reported, Gloria Estefan's foundation had an overhead of just 2 percent or less.

Part of a celebrity's success also depends on coordination of publicity. Although you often see stars on television looking as cool as a cucumber, there is much preparation involved.

Epic Records in 1996, for example, was reported to have made a one-year commitment to *Destiny*, Gloria Estefan's eleventh album for the label.

That March, *Billboard* reported, it made a single off the album, *Reach*, available for radio and club airplay. It hit retail outlets in June. The record was the theme to the 1996 Summer Olympic Games, which was televised on NBC in July. Estefan was slated to perform at the games' closing ceremonies. The release of the complete album followed.

Then, the new music was supposed to dominate Estefan's first major concert tour in five years. The tour was booked by the

William Morris Agency in New York. Simultaneously, the "Reach" video was getting played on VH1. That network also began selling advance tickets to her tour. Estefan was featured as the network's artist for July, *Billboard* said. Plus, an HBO concert was scheduled.

That was just the promotion slated for the United States! An international marketing blitz also was scheduled.

Evidently, it all paid off. Gloria Estefan hit number 31 on *Forbes'* 1997 top 40 list of entertainers, showing she earned $17 million in 1996 and $30 million in 1997.

Needless to say, the Estefans with all their promotion, are busy. More recently, Gloria has been getting involved in films. Emilio is reported to be a workaholic, who actually designs her clothes and picks out Gloria's jewelry. He also is a neatnik, according to Gloria.

The Estefans, with all their financial success, have not forgotten their roots, as well as their humble beginnings in the United States.

The Estefans are extremely popular for their devotion to charitable causes. It's been reported that they founded the Gloria Estefan Foundation, Inc., which provides financial support for good health, education, and cultural development for young people. They also have been generous donors to University of Miami and the Miami Project to Cure Paralysis. They especially endeared their fans when Hurricane Andrew hit the Miami area in 1992. Besides loading their trucks with emergency supplies, which they personally delivered to victims, the Estefans also organized a hurricane relief benefit concert. It was said to have earned more than $1.5 million. They conducted a similar effort when Hurricane Georges hit Puerto Rico and other islands in 1998.

Published reports indicate they also are good-natured in their personal lives. Emilio Estefan, while jogging on the beach one day in 1999, was reported to have come upon some Cuban refugees who had landed on shore after being at sea nine days. They asked Emilio if this was the United States, *USA Today* reported. "I said yes, and everybody started crying," Estefan said. He immediately ran into one of the hotels he owns and brought them some Cuban coffee and muffins before the border patrol arrived.

A downside of being a celebrity, however, is that you're at risk for crimes. Both Emilio and Gloria have been reported to have bodyguards. At least one threat on Gloria's life had been reported to the FBI and there was a report that antique watches had been stolen from her home.

The two cannot help also being a subject of controversy.

When Estefan and the Jerks, producers of the Estefans' *Primitive Love* album, split up, one of the Jerks, Joe Galdo, had criticized Emilio Estefan for taking too much credit for the work. "We put the Miami Sound Machine on the map," he told *Miami New Times.* "All you have to do is go and buy the albums they did before *Primitive Love* and compare them. It's the difference between night and day."

"But what about all of our number-one hits that came after [Galdo] left?" Emilio responded. Artists also have criticized the contracts he has with them as unfair.

Emilio Estefan in the *Miami Herald* acknowledged that the Estefans' empire has been dubbed a "mafia." This doesn't mean they're doing anything illegal. It's just a way of describing his control over the South Florida Latin music business.

In fact, when Emilio Estefan was slated to be honored as the Latin Grammys' Person of the Year in 2000, he came under fire by Gilberto Moreno, the head of Fonovisa, the nation's largest independent Latin record company.

Moreno complained the Latin Grammys, which Estefan had championed, failed to include a fair number of Mexican regional acts among the nominees, according to the *Miami Herald.*

Estefan responded that although he had won seven Grammy awards, he also lost 16.

"If I was really the Mafia," Emilio Estefan told the *Herald,* "I would have won those Grammys."

CHAPTER 7

ANTHONY DAVID PARKS

From Welfare to Generous Tycoon

Anthony David Parks, 43, is very concerned about being categorized under the umbrella of dot-com millionaires. It's true that the bulk of his net worth—now some $2 million in total assets—stemmed from an Internet company's stock options. But unlike some dot-com millionaires, Parks says he more than paid his dues.

After growing up in a low-income section of East Oakland, California, he worked for more than half of his life, and previously had been an entrepreneur. So when he had an opportunity to help launch *Webvan Group, Inc.*, an online grocery site, he had vision.

There is at least one other factor that sets Parks, an African American bachelor, apart from other dot-com millionaires. He actually gave more than one-third of his dot-com stock holdings away before the stock went public. While many millionaires typically set up foundations or give to charities, Parks directed his broker to award gifts of Webvan shares along with his own personal letters to some 100 friends, family members, and acquaintances.

Parks says he will never forget the magic moment when he was on the golf course at Pebble Beach. "One of the guys I was playing with was tracking the Nasdaq. He was a broker with a financial institution. He said that Webvan is $34. 'Do you know that puts you over $15 million on paper?' That was kind of a weird feeling. I thought, I've come a long way from East Oakland."

However, the bottom fell out the dot-com marketplace in 2000. Parks left the firm with a few million dollars when he finally was able to cash out his options. Since then, Webvan Group filed for bankruptcy.

"They *call* themselves entrepreneurs," Parks says of many other dot-commers who lost their shirts in the dot-com crash of 2000–2001. "They didn't have any experience in business or as entrepreneurs. Aside from the fact that the bottom fell out of the dot-com thing, there were a lot of business decisions that needed to be made by inexperienced businesspeople. I'm not an inexperienced business person."

Parks's millionaire status came after growing up largely in two-bedroom apartments. His family was on welfare.

"You don't know you're very poor when everybody in your neighborhood is in the same economic situation you're in," he said. "I never lived in a house. We weren't hungry. I don't want to give an impression that we were starving and had rats. My mother worked very hard to make sure we had the things we need."

In his high-crime neighborhood, he said, people moved in the middle of the night, so nobody would see their tempting belongings. His mother, Jacqueline Worley-Kemp, always tried to obtain a second-floor apartment for security reasons.

Parks said his mother had been pregnant with him at age 15 and dropped out of high school to have him, although she ultimately got her equivalency degree. Often, she worked until 10:00 PM in a beauty salon while he took care of his younger brother. To earn extra money, she cut hair on the side in their small 8-foot-by-10-foot kitchen. The added responsibility he had as a child, Parks believes, helped make him a little mature for his age. The children were responsible for keeping the apartment clean. "Today, I can probably iron, sew, wash, or cook better than most men or women."

His mother managed to earn enough money to put him in Catholic elementary school as a way of keeping him out of trouble.

Later on, she managed a beauty salon. Parks at a young age started following her credo: Any honest work is good work. By age 11, he started doing odd jobs—mowing lawns, washing cars, and delivering the early morning newspaper.

"I was embarrassed to be on welfare and have food stamps," Parks said. "I wanted to get a job when I was 12 years old because I wanted to have my own money."

Parks said he remembers that his mother would send him to the store with food stamps. Instead, he would throw the food stamps away and use money he earned from his odd jobs. He feared he might run into kids from school who might see him use the food stamps. "It was not a knock against my mother. It was personal pride," he said.

As he grew up in the early 1970s, the only role models for him and his low-income friends, were athletes and pimps, as they were portrayed in the movies at that time. "Those were the types of people we looked up to. The pimp had a big Cadillac and a diamond ring. I was always a little different."

Parks says he only has seen his biological father a few times. His step-father, Willie Worley, whom he refers to as his father, worked in the restaurant service business. When Parks was young, Worley was in the army and the family traveled to some bases in Texas. "My father [Worley] instilled a thing about money, self-pride, and drive. He's the type of person who would tell me I could do anything I want to do. I always had visions of being more than a pimp. At one point, I thought I was going to be a pro athlete—like everybody else in my neighborhood."

Parks said he has one friend since sixth grade with whom he remains friendly—Ralph Clark, who, much like Parks, had high ideals. "I was going to be president of the United States. Ralph, he'd say 'No. I'll be president and you be vice president.' We'd go back and forth." Clark, he says proudly, went on to get his masters in business administration from Harvard University.

Parks's mother finally moved the family to Larkspur, California, in affluent Marin County during the middle of his junior year of high school. The family still lived in an apartment, but no longer needed to worry so much about crime. The move was a jolt. It took him from a high school of 2,400 blacks and 500 whites to one of 3,000 whites and five blacks. He was crushed, particularly because he was forced to leave a high school sweetheart. "All my friends were in Oakland. As soon as I got my driver's permit, I would beg my mother for the car to drive back to Oakland."

Fortunately, his childhood experience of meeting new people at military bases made it easier for him to blend in. So did the fact that he was on the varsity football team. In addition, he had a very close Italian friend who was affluent, yet was still the subject of slurs about his ethnicity.

Dealing with slurs was something the two teenagers had very much in common. Parks had been dealing with racial slurs his whole life. When it happened, he'd often fight. "I've never accepted being called a nigger. Never. To this day, I can't accept it. It's an ugly word, and a demeaning word."

Something happened in high school that changed his attitude on the sting of prejudice. When he saw his friend, Lenny, being made fun of because he was Italian, he realized non–African Americans also could be picked on.

"The irony was [Lenny] felt he was one of them," Parks said. "That was a catalyst for me."

The experience made Parks realize simply that there are a lot of ignorant people in the world. "I related to Lenny for the fact that he never denied he was Italian and was proud of it."

This new perspective would help him out for years to come. He never would let discrimination stop him from reaching his goals.

Although Parks had earned good grades in East Oakland, his high school performance suffered. "It was a new environment. I wasn't focused. I was out there trying to get comfortable. School became more of a social thing. I played football. I also ran track."

Excelling in sports helped him adjust. Varsity sports can be an entree to social groups that otherwise might not accept you. Nevertheless, his socializing went a bit too far. He began missing classes and failing to complete assignments. Although he finally graduated from Redwood High School in 1977, it had been questionable whether he would make it. "It wasn't until my senior year that my counselor, Eva Turner, an African American woman, pulled me aside to tell me, 'You're not working at your full potential.' I'll never forget, she told me I was 'waddling in mediocrity' and 'you have so much more talent than you're using! You have to turn it around.'" At that point, he said, the light switch went on, and he began applying himself.

Parks always liked to work. He got his first real job at age 14—three months short of his fifteenth birthday—by telling a white lie about his age. He worked at McDonalds, sweeping floors. Through high school, he worked at Round Table Pizza in Marin County. "It was important for me to have my own money."

He got used to giving more than 100 percent to whatever he did.

Initially, Parks wanted to be a police officer and served as a voluntary cadet at the Larkspur Police Department. "I wanted to help people." He would ride around after high school and meet weekly with police officers, discussing procedures.

He attended College of Marin, a community college, studying administrative justice. He paid his way through school, but changed his mind about his career ambitions. "I started to learn that society's view of police officers wasn't positive. Also, it's dangerous. There wasn't a lot of money to be made."

He attended San Jose State College for one semester—until he learned he had gotten a woman pregnant. She went on to have the baby—his daughter, Keiala. "I chose not to be in school and work."

Upon dropping out, he got a job at the Hyatt Regency in San Francisco as a busboy in one of the coffee shops. It was a logical move. Most of his other jobs already had involved the restaurant business—cooking or washing dishes.

At Hyatt, he worked his way up to host and waiter, and was selected employee of the year. As winner of that honor, he earned an opportunity to join Hyatt's acclaimed management training program, which covered the financial, operational, and management aspects of the hotel business.

"I've always been ambitious," Parks noted. "Every position I've ever been in, I started in one position and worked my way up."

By working twice as hard as most others, he said, he was able to get promoted. Parks says he always was willing to work whenever they needed him. "That means sacrificing partying with my friends and hanging out." It also meant spending weekends and holidays on the job.

Parks acknowledged he was not the model father for his daughter. "When I look back on it, I was a 20-year-old kid. I had no idea what to do about being a father. I knew that I wasn't meant to be with the mother of my daughter as far as marriage. We didn't have that kind of relationship. We were both kids."

He often saw his daughter. "I'd take her with me. We'd walk around. I'd buy her ice cream. I was not supporting her financially as much as her mother would have wanted me to. But there wasn't any kind of thing where she was chasing me around for money. She had what she needed. My mother was there. Her mother was there."

With his added financial responsibilities, Parks felt the money wasn't right at Hyatt and that his advancement opportunities were limited. So he quit and returned to his high school employer, Round Table Pizza, as assistant manager. He also was cooking in another restaurant so he could afford the rent on his own apartment.

At one point, he said, he found himself back home, sleeping on his mother's couch. That, he said, might have been about the lowest point in his life. "I was frustrated and didn't have a place to live and didn't like cooking at two different restaurants," he said. "I might have even had three jobs at the time! I've always had this entrepreneurial kind of drive. It all came to a head. I can remember throwing my stuff in my car and never going back."

At that point, he started selling signs for about one year. He was paid on commission, which he only earned if he sold a sign. He sold a mere ten signs. While selling a sign at a shopping center in

Oakland, one business owner mentioned that she was trying to buy a hair salon in another space, but she didn't know the hair business that well. Parks immediately mentioned that his mother was in the hair business. "I remember telling her I know everything you need to know about the hair business and I could be your partner. Who knows why, but she said OK."

Parks found himself managing an eight-chair salon in Oakland when he was 23, for about one year. Suddenly, the salon's accountant, instead of paying quarterly estimated income taxes, pocketed the money. "I came to the salon one day and there was a big chain on the door and the IRS had put a lien on the business." He learned he owed $55,000 in taxes. "I was 23 years old and I was afraid of what that would do to my credit," he said. "I didn't know enough about declaring bankruptcy."

Carrying a terrible debt, Parks was forced to return to waiting tables at yet a different restaurant. Again, he succeeded in getting himself promoted—to general manager.

He later was fired from that job after he beat up an employee who had directed a racial profanity at him. "I threw him out of the place," Parks acknowledged. "Needless to say, [the employee] called the corporate office and complained. Then there was a big meeting. The vice president came up and we were all sitting there—the regional director, vice president, myself, and this guy I got in a fight with. The vice president said, 'I'll never understand why you people get so upset over that little word.' I knew I was in trouble."

Next, he started waiting tables at the Sheraton, and worked his way up to assistant manager after about six months. He became restaurant manager, and, finally, food and beverage manager at the hotel.

Parks was beginning to realize that something was amiss. Even though he had been general manager of a restaurant, he could not seem to get hired as general manager when he went to another restaurant. "No one was giving me a chance, for whatever reason.

"I never blamed the fact that I'm black as the reason I didn't get a job. That might be the case. I don't really care. I'm wasting valuable time and energy worrying about that kind of thing."

Parks always figured he needed to get in at whatever level he could and prove himself after he was in.

Frustrated, he started his own consulting business, Restaurant Solutions, on the side with two other friends while still working at the Sheraton. He maintains that business today.

He worked at the hotel day and night, and when he was not at the hotel, he was doing restaurant consulting. The company, he says, opened a couple of restaurants in Northern California. The first restaurant the three friends opened took six months—from getting an empty building remodeled to having it fully staffed. The company did the whole thing for $5,000, a figure, when shared between the three partners, now draws a laugh. Today, he'd probably charge $100,000. The fee would be paid in thirds—at the beginning, midpoint, and the end of the job—"with all kinds of incentives based on when we got things done."

Also as part of the business, there now are training programs, with an additional fee for each training module. "We were all in our mid or early twenties," he said of those early years. "We were happy to have anybody hire us."

Despite the setbacks, Parks believes that his experience, working in restaurants for an average of 12 hours a day, can be a great foundation for any business. It not only involves serving customers, but there also are decisions that must be made on the spot. "You don't get time to sit back and have meetings and talk about what we are going to do about this like some consultants get to do. You have to make decisions that could mean a whole night's worth of business."

The decisions you make, he adds, also can affect the way your staff operates—not only that night, but for the entire time they are under your direction.

One important lesson he learned as a manager was how critical it is to hire the right people from the beginning. "Never desperation hire," he says.

He learned that lesson the hard way. "I hired bad people when I was young and I didn't have the experience." Once, when looking for a person to fill a supervisory job, Parks related his own experience to that of a prospective hire. That person's only experience had been as a waiter—a job very familiar to Parks. "I projected my hunger and my ambition onto this person," he said. Parks figured the person, like him, would be willing to do whatever it took to advance. He was wrong.

The background of the person to be hired failed to show any ability to manage. "He had been a waiter and did a fine job, but hadn't done much more." Parks's background, by contrast, reflected the fact that he had been employed in virtually all areas of a restaurant—waiter, head trainer, dishwasher, and prep cook.

Although he wound up hiring the person, Parks said he discovered that the employee was totally unlike him. Even worse, when the person didn't work out, "I wound up having to work twice as hard." Not only did Parks have to train the person, but he also had to correct his mistakes. "Eventually, when he had to be terminated, I had to cover his shift." That, he says, doesn't even include the negative impact the poor hire probably had on business.

Parks claims it's possible in the restaurant business to take a good person, who may not have as much experience, if the person is sharp and can use good common sense. But the person also should have experience in the area for which he or she is being recruited. Once you have a good person, he says, even if your training program is bad, the person can succeed by using common sense and working his or her way through the organization. Once you've made a desperation hire and there's a bad training program, that person is doomed to failure.

While Parks was at the Sheraton, the food and beverage director before him, Steve Wiezbowski, left to start a restaurant in San Francisco, and asked if Parks would be assistant manager. The restaurant was the very successful Neptune Palace, located on Pier 39, a heavy tourist section at Fisherman's Wharf. "It still was less money than what I was making at the Sheraton and a lower-level position.

"Once again, I wanted to be general manager of Neptune," he says. "They had a general manager at the time, but after working with him, I could tell he wasn't very good. I could do a better job."

In the restaurant business, Parks reports, there are certain standards that a manager must implement, maintain, and be able to enforce.

"The staff [wasn't] performing at the level of quality service. The food was not at the level standard that I had or that Steve had at that time." When Parks first arrived, the staff's attitude was that service doesn't matter because the patrons were all tourists and wouldn't be returning. Parks vehemently disagreed. "That was not how I viewed the restaurant and neither did Steve."

The general manager at the time, Parks said, lacked the ability to turn the restaurant around. "It takes implementing a program to train staff, things like that."

Yet, Wiezbowski did not wish to replace the manager. Instead, he resolved the situation by having Parks cover the night shift—which included the all-important dinner business.

Finally, Parks says, the general manager left. Parks still failed to get the coveted position of general manager. "I'll never forget. Steve told me he didn't feel I had the experience to run the restaurant. He hired another general manager. That manager didn't last very long."

Even then, Parks didn't get the job. Instead, Wiezbowski called Parks into his office and said, 'Do you have any friends who can general manage this restaurant?'"

"I'm like, 'No. But hey, if I come across somebody I'll certainly tell them about the position.' Leaving, I'm saying to myself, 'he must be crazy! I'm not going to tell anybody about this.'" The restaurant tried yet another general manager and it didn't work out.

Finally, Weizbowski summoned Parks. "OK. I'm going to give you your shot," Parks reported.

Initially, Parks was happy. But the offer came with one seemingly impossible caveat. "If you can't do the job in 90 days, you're fired. You can't go back to the assistant manager job."

Although the ultimatum sounded a bit unfair, Parks was thrilled to get the challenge. "To this day," he said, "this was the best thing he could ever have done for me." (Weizbowski, by the way, later was the recipient of 100 Webvan shares.)

Parks believes that anything that comes easily is not worth having. "I knew I had to earn it. I've actually liked being in a position when my back is against the wall. I work very well under pressure. Now I've got 90 days to turn the thing around and make it happen in his eyes."

As the manager of some 100 employees, Parks began realizing his success. "The greatest thing about it is after I went on to become general manager, we grew the restaurant company. I became director of operations for the whole company [Pier Restaurants, Inc.] and wound up [working] there seven years."

Parks, still lacking a college education, was forced to study hard and has credited Weizbowski with showing him the ropes. "I was responsible for the performance of the company. We were a $12-million-a-year restaurant company." He says he bought books and attended seminars to teach himself the business. "What I would do is get the financial information from our controller, take it home, study it after I'd been working, and then I'd have to be able to speak intelligently about it to my managers. Many times, Steve and I would review it together." In his early 30s, Parks had finally realized his dream. He was making $75,000 to $80,000 annually and had his own office. "Life was good."

While he was at Neptune Palace, Parks explained, the company had grown to five full-service restaurants, a luxury yacht, catering business, and restaurant consulting business. Still, seven years later, he left Neptune Palace to take a job with Starbucks Coffee Co.

"The only reason I left the pier [while] everything was great [was that] I wasn't growing. I had the entrepreneurial itch," he said.

"Any pure entrepreneur will tell you it's not about the money. It's about the challenge and seeing the vision through to reality. I wanted to do something different."

When Parks joined Starbucks in 1994, it still was a small company with 250 stores nationwide. He only received $40,000 annually in salary initially. By the time he left in 1996, he was making $48,000. It marked the first time that he had been introduced to the concept of stock options, which, at the coffee company, were dubbed "bean stock." He got a number of options equal to his annual salary, and was vested, or able to convert his stock options into stock, at the rate of 25 percent annually. Because he was on the job only three years, he was 75 percent vested by the time he left, bringing in an additional $50,000 annually. He was able to use his Starbucks stock to put a down payment on his current home.

Parks opened 20 Starbucks stores in the San Francisco area. "Starbucks probably is the best organization I've ever been part of as far as the corporate culture," he said. He found the company receptive to his idea of creating a diversity awareness program. "We grow up with certain stereotypes about people. We have to let go and reeducate ourselves," he explains.

He believes that companies today are too closed-minded. In hiring practices, they risk failing to hire the most qualified person. "A lot of companies don't recruit in areas where there are people of color," he explains. "They would find serious untapped valuable resources. A lot of companies need to understand that." In his diversity classes, Parks taught employees that just because someone doesn't look you in the eyes or give you a firm handshake does not mean the person is a bad person. Nor does it necessarily mean the person is not self-confident. "It could mean they're from the East and it's not their culture," he says. Parks conducted weekly workshops on such issues, lasting about eight hours each.

By 1995, Parks began watching the advent of the Internet, which had barreled into California like the gold rush. "I could see how technology was going to take its place in our society." He hoped to take advantage of what was happening.

"I didn't have an Internet concept. What I did have is experience." Parks, while at Starbucks, already had started his own company, eCustomer Service, designing customer service strategies and systems. "No one was really interested. I wasn't making any money."

As Starbucks grew into a major national company, it became more corporate. "I didn't really see my place." He really had hoped to be part of the Internet boom. In 1996, he was contacted by Louis Borders, the magnate from Borders Books, about starting an Internet business. For Starbucks, the busiest time of year was the Christmas holidays. He stayed at Starbucks through the holiday, still running his consulting business, and then quit.

"I'll never forget when Louis told me he wanted to have people order groceries over the Internet and deliver them to their homes. I said I don't know if people are going to go for that."

Parks, though, truly admired Borders's vision. "The first concept that we designed is not what Webvan is today. Initially, we were going to have gourmet grocery stores that people could go into."

The investors convinced Borders that wasn't the way to go. Rather, he should design a huge automated distribution center which would revolutionize the warehousing fulfillment business.

Parks, the fifth to be hired for the venture, directed customer service and earned about $60,000 to $65,000 annually in the new job. He still had bills to pay. By 1998, he was putting his daughter through college and still paying off his debt from the beauty salon. He burned the candle at both ends, working the night shift as a bartender in a hotel until 2:00 AM to help make ends meet.

Webvan was planning to go public. To position the company for the public offering, the board felt it needed to have high-profile executives. "In my opinion, as one of the people credited with the design of the delivery and the customer service operational strategy, I didn't feel these people knew what the hell they were doing!" Parks said. "They were being brought on because of their reputations."

There was a recruit from the prestigious Andersen Consulting firm, as well as executives recruited from Federal Express. "They felt they needed to follow the Federal Express model of delivery," Parks said. "I didn't agree. That's why I wanted to leave. I spent a lot of time studying the emotional aspects of grocery shopping. Grocery shopping is a generational thing. We can all look fondly back to riding in the cart with our mother or father as they went up and down aisles of grocery stores. Those were good memories. They mark a time I don't think we want to completely forget. You don't want to mess with that.

"My whole thing with Webvan had always been [that] we want to replicate the grocery shopping experience as closely as we can, but we want to offer the convenience of not having to leave your home. You can get quality and you can get service—just like you can from a grocery store. A big part of that is how you educate one person—the Webvan courier.

"I felt the training needed to be thorough. A courier needs to understand how to answer some basic questions someone may have. Like, if someone pulled some produce out of their tote, which is what we put groceries in and says, 'Is this romaine or bibb lettuce?'"

"These executives from Federal Express didn't think this was necessary. The Federal Express model was just delivering a business letter. Personal groceries are not a business letter." Parks believed every courier needed a minimum 30 days' worth of training, while the new executives felt they didn't need more than a week.

"I'm not the type of person that can operate doing something I don't believe in." So Parks quit in 1999. Later that year, the company went public and Parks left with 500,000 shares.

"Part of the package was I got accelerated vesting. I had the ability to buy shares that I had coming to me."

Everybody who had options in the company, he says, got a certain strike price at which they could buy shares. Because he was a founding member of the company, his strike price was a mere one-quarter of one penny. "It was a cashless transaction." After leaving Webvan, he joined another dot-com, BigBow.com, which, he says, did not make it.

Meanwhile, he had given much of his wealth away. Many recipients of his Webvan wealth were old high school chums and single parents. Other were restaurant buddies—including cooks and dishwashers—he worked with over the years. Even his biological father, who left before he was born, was awarded 500 shares.

"Some people got 1,000 shares. Some got 500. One friend had four kids. So I gave 100 for each kid," Parks reflected. The gifts were based on the recipient's situation, the role they played in his life and how they had helped him in the past. The personalized generosity, along with the mentoring foundation he created, R.E.A.L. (Real Examples of Actual Life) Role Models, Inc., San Rafael, California, garnered him national media attention.

Today, Parks feels that he has some unfinished business when it comes to giving gifts. He has helplessly watched Webvan's share prices plunge from a high of $34 a share, which might have made his holdings worth $17 million on paper. Unfortunately, when the shares were at their peak, his shares, because he was a founding member of the company, were "locked up." In other words, he was prohibited from selling. By the time he and his other share recipients were able to sell, the share price had dropped to $10 and continued to spiral downward. He still has some $500,000 in cash, some other investments, businesses, a luxury house in Marinwood, California, and three cars, including a Mercedes.

He regrets that the shares, distributed from the 500,000 he finally walked away with, could not do as much for his friends and family as he had hoped they would. He would like to do more. "It's like I gave the gift of a diamond to people who were close to me," he said. "They wound up getting them appraised and they were glass. I gave with the full expectation that they were diamonds, and it hurt. Although 99 percent of the people that I gifted understand, it bothers me."

After spending much of his life just making enough to get by, Parks now lives in a four-bedroom house with a hot tub and sauna. He has a sports utility vehicle for driving with his dog and a Mercedes, from which the dog is banned.

If there is one downside to his wealth, however, Parks reports it is the quarter-million-dollars in loans he has issued on top of those outright gifts. If he had it to do again, he would start saying no much sooner to those who would ask him to borrow money. Many of the loans, incidentally, were made without promissory notes.

Parks wants to make one thing perfectly clear about those loans. It's not the fact that the loans are going 95 percent unpaid that bothers him. What upsets him is "it instantly strained the friendship once I lent them money. They treated me differently."

He wants to know why these people don't come over or call him anymore.

"The disappointing part about it is how it affects the relationship when you lend somebody money and they can't pay it back," he says. "It's not a problem with me. It's not like I'm calling them and saying, 'Where's the money?'"

Parks's media exposure also made life more difficult. After an appearance on Oprah's television show, he says, he received about 100 e-mails weekly, most blatantly asking him for money. "Oprah made me an angel," he said. "Everybody wanted me to be their angel. It's very hard. People write and share their whole life problems with you and say, 'if only I had $20,000.' That bothered me. If I hadn't had the notoriety, it wouldn't have been so tough." Parks said he wound up denying all the e-mail requests. He said he prefers instead to put his money into R.E.A.L. Role Models Inc., which brings role models into public schools. He hopes the program will, by giving young people ideals to emulate, help eliminate the causes of many of those e-mailed problems he received.

"There are just too many hustlers out there," he explained of his decision to deny the requests. "There's no way I can take the time to separate who is honest and who isn't."

Even some of the honest requests were of questionable merit. Take the long-winded one he received from a woman seeking $40,000 because she was going to lose her house, which was the only thing she had left in life. In case he didn't believe her, she advised him to make a check out directly to the bank. "Then, her last sentence was, 'So if you could, just send $39,000 to the bank in this bank's name and send me $1,000 so I can get some things for myself,'" he recounted.

"I just said, 'God bless.'"

Nevertheless, he wouldn't change one thing about his idea to give outright gifts to people who are important to him. The idea of giving back, he said, was drummed into him first as a child by his late grandmother, Naomi Crump, with whom he was very close. Perhaps, he speculates, their closeness was due to the fact that his mother had him at such a young age—16—leaving his grand mother to care for him much of the time.

"[My grandmother] would talk about how we have to do things for other people—the importance of giving back."

He also cites the wisdom of Rev. Martin Luther King, Jr.

"[King] talked about [how] in the final analysis, the question won't be how many cars did you have, how much money did you make, or how big was your house. The question would be what did you do for others. That is a true way a person can gauge their success. That's always been very important to me."

Parks believes part of his success stems from the fact that he always knew he was going to share his good fortune with his friends. "That was always my goal. I was able to do that." Exactly how he did it didn't really matter. "It could have been that I wound up owning a chain of restaurants across the country and friends would be able to eat free.

"A real upside was that some of my friends shared feelings for me that I never really knew. That's what I want everybody to take away from this. It's not about the gift. It was about the act."

Parks battled a long and hard life to get where he is today. In fact, his brother, Godfrey, who is five years younger and shared a similar upbringing, so far has met with a very different fate. Although hailed as a talented chef, he has been waging a constant battle with drug abuse. Parks initially held back a gift of stock shares to his brother, uncertain whether it would be a prudent move. Finally he gave in. "As I thought, he immediately cashed it in." Subsequently, it was reported that his brother had given up his drug habit and the sale of his shares was prudent, given the fate of Webvan Group.

When we interviewed Parks in 2001, he was involved in many businesses. The thrust of his effort was an Internet-based start-up. "I'm hoping by the time this comes out that we're in business."

The company, *Quikzone,* he says, is similar to Webvan, but, he claims, better. "We're in the process of getting funding. "I studied all the concepts out there that are failing and figured what they did wrong." The new company, he says, will let people order products—including groceries, dry cleaning, videos, prepared meals, gifts, books, and CDs, over the Internet from local businesses.

His for-profit ventures, he says, operate under the name, ADP Enterprises, Inc. Among the businesses it includes is a majority ownership of the Savannah Grill in Marin County. There also is a film and television screenplay writing company. "I'm trying to get a teen show produced locally, and eventually have it national." His goal, he says, is to target teenagers with round-table discussions on tough issues—such as peer pressure to take drugs, drinking, or date rape.

He owns ADP Management Group, an agency that handles the business end for musical artists, actors, athletes, models, sculptors, and photographers. He still has his restaurant consulting business, his eCustomer Service business, and Restaurant Solutions consulting firm. There also is a limousine company, Newpark Transportation, serving the bay area from Marin County.

He operates all his businesses out of his building in San Rafael, with a staff of five employees.

Parks enjoys playing golf. "I wish I could play more," he admits. "You have to play a lot to play good." Plus, he works with his R.E.A.L. Role Models program in schools nationwide.

With that program, he says, he targets eighth and ninth graders. "Young people get an unrealistic view of what's going on," he said. "I don't think it's healthy. They need to see and meet more small business owners—even people in the corporate world."

Shortly before we talked to him, he had taken a friend, Patty Monge, a Larkspur police officer, with him into schools. When she attended grade school, she was just five-foot tall and never grew beyond that. You might think that her height would be a handicap in her effort to achieve her life-long dream—to be a police officer. Yet, it didn't stop her. Not only did she join the force, but she since was selected Marin County Police Officer of the Year.

Parks says he remains spiritual. "I believe in God. I'm very comfortable with my relationship with God and I don't have a need to go to church to solidify it."

Anyone looking to advance from a job, he suggests, can follow a few simple rules. The first rule is to do your job first. "You have to do it better than anyone else. Parks says too many people think they can advance from a busboy to a waiter by starting to do things a waiter does. "What they're being is a pain in the ass to the manager," he said. You're better off doing your job 110 percent. Then, find out what is needed for the position you desire. If, for example, a restaurant manager wanted the wait staff to clearly communicate the specials on the menu, Parks says he would be able to do it. "I would have waiters coming to me for help. Management staff would see that."

Always understand what management is trying to do, he advises. Parks says he realized when he was at Neptune Palace, that the objective was to grow the company. His goal was to figure out how to grow it and increase revenue. "I looked at the one little restaurant I was responsible for and we had a banquet room that was used only 100-some days a year." Largely, it was a storage area. "I figured we could utilize this room for a cafe concept that would complement our full-service restaurant. I did the research, I figured out that for a $100,000 investment, we could blow out a wall, make a door that could be a separate entrance, and we could use the same kitchen [used] for fine dining and attract families with small children. We'd capture that market as well as the fine dining market.

"That first year, that cafe wound up doing $1 million in sales on a $100,000 remodel. As a result of that, I was promoted to director of operations and we began to build other restaurants."

Parks admits that saving money never has been a major priority of his, though he does use a stock broker. He also does not necessarily recommend his entrepreneurial way of life as the correct way. In fact, he says, meeting the risk-taking challenges of entrepreneurship can be downright stressful. "I grew up watching my mother survive," he said. "She hustled. She worked hard. I learned and adopted that attitude.

"I think I grew up with a mentality not about saving, but about earning and making a way—dealing with every day."

That mentality, he says, might have helped make him a risk taker. In fact, he says, he is having problems with one of the companies he's running due to a chance he took on someone. "That's the way I like to live my life. I pride myself in making a way out of no way—coming back from a situation when people say, 'Gee, I can't believe that happened to you. What are you going to do?' I thrive on that type of challenge.

"Where it becomes a problem as I get older, [is that] I have employees, and my daughter's involved. So I don't want to have them live their life that way. That's not fair. They may not be that type of person."

He admits his risk-taking personality might have made his daughter's life harder, but he believes that simply is one of the hands she has been dealt in life. He is who he is.

"Maybe, when I get too comfortable, I want to push myself where I have a challenge. I've been in positions that were cush jobs and put myself out there to be challenged with new opportunities. I try to stay aware of how my actions affect my daughter. Being that I'm a bachelor, there's not one particular woman that my actions affect—probably my mother, sometimes."

Some might call him a workaholic. He rises 6:00 AM to exercise. "I know I can get caught up in a project—in my office all day. I can come home and be on the computer. My daughter might try to talk to me and I'm into what I'm doing right now. A lot of people would view that as a sickness in itself." His rationale: He figures he has all summer to be with his daughter. Until then, "it's about the next thing I want to conquer."

He says he'd like to be married, but admits it would be hard due to the fact that most other women already have kids. "I don't know if I'm up to stepping in as some other kid's father. Or, maybe, with women, the clock is ticking now and they want to have a child immediately."

Money, he agrees, does not buy happiness. "I'm happy because I was able to do something I always wanted to do. I'm not satisfied though." He'd like to do more for those close to him.

"I'm happy I've got a great daughter who's smart and will be graduated from college next year [2002]. She seems to be happy. I have people in my life I love. I've got stuff and things—three cars. I sold one to a friend. There was no money transacted. When he gets the money, he'll pay me back."

One thing he also is grateful for is the unique education he received by giving so much of his fortune away.

"I wouldn't have changed a thing," he stresses. "The most disappointing thing was that people I thought were friends didn't think they got enough. That was very hurtful. Some people actually said, 'Is this all you're giving me?'" One friend rejected the shares because he claimed "the stock market makes people crazy."

"I thought that was pretty wild—especially at that time," Parks said. "The truth is it probably does. But at the time, everyone was just cashing in.

"Some people were very touched and moved by the act. I never knew they felt that way about me and I didn't think I felt that deeply about them. It's good to find out how greedy and how insensitive some people are. That experience is something I would never trade. I needed to know that. The gifting of shares I would not do differently."

CHAPTER 8

PAUL E. KIEFFER

*Childhood Money
Discussions Pay Off*

Paul E. Kieffer, 46, the oldest of six children in a middle-class Minnesota family, has two things going for him when it comes to making money. Money was discussed quite a bit around the dinner table when he was growing up. He actually enjoys working hard. It has paid off handsomely into an attractive net worth of slightly over $3 million.

Kieffer owns and operates a Red Wing shoe store in Rochester, Minnesota. He also owns six manufactured housing communities with 225 lots. He rents the lots for an average of $165 a month.

Before one interview with us, Kieffer had just returned from a meeting that he said could lead to his purchase of yet another manufactured home park. He had called the owner cold. "I described who I was and asked if he was interested in selling." Kieffer says he typically puts feelers out rather than searching through newspapers. "You truly don't ever want to pay a middleman to be involved," he says. Why give them an 8 to 10 percent commission? He also believes he gets along well with people and can negotiate better deals on his own.

"I don't know that I feel that wealthy," Kieffer says. "I feel just comfortable." Kieffer says he can afford to buy his two children what he wants. He also is comfortable taking a vacation if he needs one and lives in a comfortable home, for which he was about to build an addition. He has a nice pickup truck and his wife, Jeanette, drives a Chevy Tahoe sports utility vehicle. He has a big screen television.

Kieffer, though, believes that net worth truly doesn't mean much until everything is paid for and you have a nice cash flow. "If I pay off one manufactured community, I will take the same amount of money of the old payment and apply it to another one. I'm very, very conservative. I've never borrowed money for a car. I've always saved until I can afford a car."

Some might consider Kieffer a workaholic. He is very focused and goal-oriented. He loves his work and relies on his wife to help out with business. He characterizes himself as self-motivated. It's a trait, in part, he learned from being the oldest member of a large, competitive family. But he's not just a numbers guy. He is friendly and likes dealing with people. Although he must keep tabs on several businesses at once, he still finds time to help out at his church and tackle the next new business venture.

He has learned quite a bit by asking other successful people how they did things to get ahead. So, he doesn't mind passing along his knowledge to others. He even self-published a book once. His secret, grounded in the midwestern work ethic, is to work for yourself, live within your means, and be conservative. Never pay credit card interest. If you fail in business, move forward and don't dwell on past mistakes. Also, do your homework before venturing into an investment or business venture.

Kieffer credits his grandfather, Paul J. Kieffer, who was 99 years old at this writing, for teaching him the significance of avoiding debt. That's because his grandfather went so far as to provide Kieffer with calculations to illustrate the amount of savings he could accumulate if he avoided succumbing to the average American's custom of buying a new car every four years.

Here's Kieffer's adaptation of that advice.

Say you buy a $20,000 car at 10 percent interest for four years. You're talking a monthly payment of $507.26. If instead, you had put that same $507.26 monthly payment to work for you in a savings account at a mere 5 percent interest for four years and let it compound, you'd have $26,892.33. That's more than the price of your $20,000 car!

Figuring the average person might own 12 cars in a lifetime, you automatically could accumulate $134,889.72 merely, he says, by saving up the money to buy a car instead of borrowing money.

Add in more savings if you buy a used car that is at least two years old, and avoid borrowing money for items that don't offer you any income in return, such as boats, snowmobiles, and motorcycles.

As often is typical of an oldest child, Kieffer rebelled against his parents. But he became extremely close to his grandparents. "I had an admiration for my grandfather's ability to keep finding ways of making money," he said. "He'd have anything from a mink farm to an implement dealership business [which sold farm equipment such as tractors and plows], farming, buying or selling real estate, or just being a REALTOR®. He worked as a REALTOR® until he was 95 years old. He also bought and sold antiques all his life." Kieffer fondly remembers his grandfather driving a 20-year-old rusted out car. To anyone who gave him grief about the condition of his car, he'd flippantly respond that he simply took the same amount that others were using to buy new cars and bought municipal bonds.

His father, Charles, who also worked hard, took an early re-tirement from IBM and got into the apartment business.

"I always thought about money," Kieffer said. "It was drilled into us by both my grandparents and parents. Save that dollar a day." Athletics were big in the Kieffer household. Kieffer's younger brother, Mark, was a star athlete.

Kieffer, too, played baseball, basketball, and football through tenth grade in high school. "The only sport I could start in was baseball," he said. "I didn't like sitting on the bench in eleventh grade, so I went to work full-time." Kieffer accepted a 40-hour-a-week job at the Holiday Inn South in Rochester. He worked as a busboy, bartender, front-desk clerk, and also drove a van. It was a fun job and paid well, he said. "I was always fairly good at getting tips. I tend to tease people." Kieffer, however, wasn't very studious.

Largely, he got Bs and Cs in high school. Perhaps, he acknowledges, that was because his job often had him working until 1:00 AM. So he'd catch up on his sleep in classes. Although he managed to get average grades, he remarks, "I didn't put an ounce of effort into it."

When asked about the influence of school on his good fortune, Kieffer scoffs. Catholic elementary school, which he attended for six years, was "about the limit of my education." Beyond that, he believes his education was not beneficial. "I could have started work at 14 and would have been talking to you, doing the same thing right now." The job he held during high school started him on the road to financial security. When he graduated from high school in 1973, he already had built a comfortable savings of $2,500. He also had completely paid for a motorcycle and car. He admitted he initially borrowed money at age 16 to buy that motorcycle. The thought of paying extra interest to the bank irritated him to no end. Yet, his hard work to pay it off impressed both his father and grandfather.

Despite his distaste for school, Kieffer had a boyhood dream of becoming an FBI agent. So he continued his education and graduated from Rochester Community College, obtaining an associate degree in law enforcement. His parents had paid for part of the education, but books and tuition were covered through a program in which he worked, policing a small town on weekends. "[I] carried a gun," he said. "I had full authority to arrest. I enjoyed law enforcement."

His law enforcement dream took a detour, though, when another opportunity came his way. His great uncle had a small men's clothing store in St. Charles, Minnesota, a community of about 2,000. The town is 20 miles from his birthplace, Winona, and 20 miles from Rochester, headquarters of the Mayo Clinic. Kieffer was able to convince his grandfather to cosign a $60,000 loan for the business, which he later renamed Town & Country Men's Wear. He rented the building from his uncle. The free-standing store was an old-fashioned one, with clothes piled to the ceiling and ladders scattered around the store. Kieffer put in long hours at the 1,000-square-foot shop to make it a success.

His idea had been to run the business for a year or two. Then, he planned to let his future wife run it while he obtained an additional two years of college education to become an FBI agent. It was 1975. The economy was doing well and Kieffer enjoyed the retail business. He still had his sights set on law enforcement. "Where else could you drive fast and get into bar fights and get paid for it?" he chuckled. While working in the clothing business, he frequently ran into law enforcement officers, including small town patrolmen, highway patrolmen, and sheriffs. He'd tell them that he had a degree in law enforcement and asked how they felt about their jobs. Most were positive. But the story seemed to change whenever he directly asked whether they thought he should pursue a career in law enforcement. "They all said absolutely not. Stay in your business," he said. Kieffer finally decided to take those words to heart.

Kieffer's store was small, and lacked room to properly display clothes. "We knew we had to expand or die." After he was in business for three years, he borrowed about $100,000 to build a new 4,800-square-foot building next door to the existing location. "I used clothing inventory for equity on the loan," he said. "The business was doing well."

While it might have been risky to borrow money for the venture, he believes strongly that debt is fine as long as you've thoroughly done your homework and you borrow for a business or a home in which you're building equity.

Although Kieffer's career path had diverted from the law enforcement career he once dreamed about, he was bound to be successful. One chief reason, he says, is that he sets goals for himself—generally every ten years. (When he was in his early 20s, for example, he had resolved to become a millionaire by age 30.) These are not just pipe dreams either. He actually writes down his goals and the amount of money he plans to have. He didn't quite achieve his early goal of becoming a millionaire by age 30, he admitted, largely due to the economy. He blames inflation and high interest rates. However, he still firmly believes that by setting high goals, even if you experience failures, you'll be much further along in life than the majority of the population.

Kieffer had taken some added steps to build his wealth. He bought a small triplex property. He rented out two units and lived in one. "I paid $38,000 for it [in 1976] and I sold it for $63,000 in 1989," he said.

Kieffer paid the whole building off in eight years. He was able to live inexpensively and use income from the other units to help build equity. It also was a great way to learn landlording, he said. Once the building is paid for, you can accumulate enough savings that you can use it to buy another business or a home.

In the meantime, his father had bought an 18-lot manufactured housing community in St. Charles. "He had it for one year and didn't want it." Kieffer was able to convince his father to sell it to him for the price he paid for it. To finance the deal, Kieffer again borrowed from the bank. Once he paid off about one-third of the loan, he was able to use the equity for the down payment on his next manufactured housing community. He repeated that process again and again.

Kieffer's men's clothing store, in business for 16 years, was successful, he believes, because he was very careful to stay on top of the latest fashions. He carried everything from bib overalls to Red Wing shoes and very nice suits. Also, he advertised quite a bit. "We had to draw people out of Rochester to make the business survive." His promotion largely was through direct mail, he said, noting he was one of the first in town with a computer in his store.

Despite a grueling schedule, Kieffer often relieved his stress by working out regularly and playing racquetball three times a week. He also played softball, but stopped after age 30. He continues his workouts today, but his activities are limited due to a heel injury.

With his wife also working at the store, he was able to go out on the road during his store's slowest months—January, February and March—and sell Lauer gloves. He says he broke sales records for that company in Iowa, Wisconsin, and Minnesota. "I think in my life I've been very fortunate to have a wife that can pick up the pieces when I run hard," he said.

But by 1987, after a divorce and subsequent second marriage, he realized that he and his new wife were both working 60 hours a week in the men's clothing store, yet the business was netting a mere $20,000 annually. That wasn't much for two to live on. It also was a poor return on his investment of over $200,000, he reasoned. "We were open seven days a week." The business never actually lost money, he says, but he wasn't making very much at the end either.

"I would say at that point in my life I was overdoing it," he admitted. "I did not have children." He subsequently adopted the first of his two adopted children in 1991. But the writing was on the wall. He felt it was time to sell the business.

He already had bought another property in 1987. After paying off his triplex early, he was able to use savings from his rental income to buy ten acres of vacant wooded land at a cost of $11,000. He was attracted to the location that joined the main entrance to St. Charles on the south because he was able to obtain permission to put a billboard on his own land promoting the clothing store. Today his Red Wing shoe store is too far away to make the advertisement worthwhile, so he rents not only that billboard, but a second one on his property for an average income of $250 a month.

Meanwhile, he kept four acres of the land for himself and sold 4½ acres to the builder who went on to build his current home. The remaining acre was used to build a city road, which, he admits, is named after him.

Closing Town & Country Men's Wear, Kieffer says, probably was the lowest point in his life. "It wasn't like I was desperate," he said. "It's like a person realizing that their family farm is no longer making them money. You put your heart and soul in it for seven days a week and a lot of evenings. Not stretching it, we worked 70 hours each a week during the last years."

Kieffer's far-sighted thinking helped ease the blow. Two years prior to closing the men's store, he had been contacted by the Red

Wing Shoe Co. in Red Wing, Minnesota. Kieffer was selling 1,500 pairs of Red Wing shoes a year through his men's store. The company wanted to open a store in Rochester, but did not want to step on the toes of the area's largest seller. "So they asked me if I wanted to get it cooking." He not only got that store going in 1990, but also had opened a store in Montgomery, Alabama, with his brother, Jeff, using equity from his manufactured housing communities to purchase inventory. His brother since has bought him out.

He moved his own Red Wing shoe business from his clothing store to the new location. After he had been renting the Rochester Red Wing shoe store location for about six years, he wanted to buy a property. Fortunately, he had paid off his house by age 40. He was able to take a loan against his house to build his own 1,800-square-foot facility at the store's existing location. "Being a landlord owning manufactured housing communities, I understood the game and certainly didn't want to make someone else money by leasing. So I built my own building. It was one of the better moves I've ever made." When leasing, he says he had been paying $2,000 monthly. By owning the building, loan payments and taxes add up to the same amount. It had taken a few years for him to make his move. He was waiting for the ideal location to open up. It finally came. The store sticks out like a sore thumb from the main highway, he says. Not only do nearly 6,000 employees have to pass it to get to IBM, but he says a Home Depot and Target just opened nearby. IBM employees, as well as virtually anyone headed north, must exit right near his store.

When he was selling Red Wing shoes at Town & Country Men's Wear, he says, he sold about 1,500 pairs annually. "The whole town's population was 2,000." At his rented location in the more heavily populated Rochester, he had increased to 2,500 pairs annually. At the new location, he says, "right off the bat, we did 4,300 pairs [annually]." Most Red Wing shoe stores, he says, average 2,000 pairs annually.

One chief reason his shoe store is successful, he notes, is that he never waits for people to come into the store. He personally went out and aggressively sold safety boots to all the factories within 30 miles of Rochester. "That's about half of our business," he said.

Here's how he does it. Kieffer gives the factory a 15 percent discount on the shoes. The factory may elect to pay $25 or so toward the safety shoes. The balance—about $100—is payroll-deducted out of employee paychecks. "Most CEOs who are running the factories realize the benefit of our shoes," he said. "Their employees are less injury prone if they have correct[ly] fitted shoes." Kieffer says the business also has succeeded because he carries a wide variety of shoe sizes and styles. Each customer order is recorded in a computer. "We have a 95 percent repeat rate," he says. "Once somebody comes into our store, we put their name, address, style, and size into a computer. Working guys hate to shop. They can get on the phone, call us and we'll FedEx [Federal Express] them another pair."

Kieffer says his lifestyle now gives him total freedom and flexibility. "I don't have to be anywhere at any time." I do go to my store most mornings, but just to do the book work." The store, he says, is overseen by a manager and four or five employees. The manufactured housing community business also has changed dramatically for the better, he says. "When we first had a mobile home park, I would rent it with a handshake," he says. "Today, the rules and regulations are 12 pages. The lease, 10 pages." There are criminal checks and credit checks. "It is much easier keeping somebody out than it is kicking them out," he said.

Kieffer says his taxes now show an income of around $200,000 annually. It is split between the Red Wing shoe store and his manufactured housing parks. He expects the scales will tilt more toward the manufactured housing parks as he pays off more of his loans. "But I don't feel like I make that kind of income," he admits. "So much goes toward the government. I'm making $13,000-a-month payments [on his manufactured housing parks and shoe store]. I don't think I have enough money to comfortably retire. I'm going to follow my grandfather's footsteps. I may slow down, but I'm never going to retire."

Not all Kieffer's business ventures have been successful.

Kieffer says he tried to open a Town & Country Men's Wear branch in Plainview, Minnesota, in 1982. The economy turned against him. Interest rates soared to 21 percent. Our business was totally dependent on farmers. They were all going broke."

His Plainview business only lasted one year. It was not a terrible financial blow. "I probably washed on the going out of business sale. I lost $15,000 on the building." But, he said, the fact that he never had any frivolous debt and had a comfortable house payment helped ease the blow. "If you don't have debt, you can get by. Now I'm pretty secure because I don't have that much debt left."

He said he was able to take all his Red Wing shoe business from his old clothing store to his new business.

"A lot of people wonder why businesses in small towns fail. If you go to most little towns anywhere in the United States, they have no Main Streets or businesses left. Everybody's gone to shopping hubs."

Part of the reason, he strongly believes, is that the tax burden is so heavy that both spouses have to work. "Even 20 years ago, there were more stay-at-home moms. When they needed clothes for dad, they would shop for him at local clothing stores." Now, he says, the moms are shopping at the big city stores, near their jobs. I sell more Red Wing shoes today while I'm in Rochester to people who live in St. Charles than when I was in business in St. Charles selling to St. Charles people!"

After his Town & Country Men's Wear going-out-of-business sale, Kieffer began looking for a new venture. His Red Wing shoe store was running smoothly under a good manager. Already familiar with the direct mail business, he bought a Money Mailer franchise, which was to be in Rochester. The business mailed out a host of coupons promoting area businesses. "I did really good because I worked 80 hours a week," he said. "I made it work. I was so competitive I wanted to beat the other franchise owners in sales. I worked so hard I burned myself out." One day, he visited a REAL-TOR® to sell a Money Mailer ad. However, after three no-show appointments that day, he decided to tell the REALTOR® to sell the Money Mailer business. Although he only had paid $20,000 for the franchise, he sold it for $117,000.

After he sold that business, he attempted to invest in another franchise that sold used clothes, toys, and furniture. "I sold out of that at a $30,000 loss," he admitted. To this day, he angrily blames the franchise, and warns that if you're ever considering buying a franchise, you had better not rely on the figures you're given by franchise promoters. "They said it would cost $80,000. Well, it cost $120,000," he declared. Besides that, he says, the franchise also misinformed him on its business projections.

From that experience, Kieffer provides one piece of advice that he claims is worth three times the price of this book. Anyone considering a franchise should not only call the *existing* franchises, but they should also call the ones that *failed*. "What I'd really call is the ten franchises that sold out or left and ask them why," he says. When you buy, of course, the salespeople are going to give you other franchise names. Franchise owners need more franchises to be successful. The more notoriety they get, the more successful they are. They're going to tell you they're doing great!"

Red Wing Shoes, he says, is not a franchise. Although Kieffer says he uses the company's fixtures, carpet colors, and computer system, he does not pay royalties. They make their money by selling him their shoes.

Kieffer says he also initially "lost his butt" in the purchase of the land on which he built his home. Never buy undeveloped land, he advises, unless you have a substantial net worth.

Kieffer says that to develop the land, he had to build a street and bring water and sewers from the city to his piece of land in the country. "We had the city engineer actually figure out what it would cost to the penny," he said. That wasn't good enough. Although he thought he had done adequate homework, the actual costs wound up being three times higher than the engineer's estimated cost. The engineer failed to realize all the rock he would need to dynamite.

"[Buying land is] not something I would advise—until you [are] affluent enough that if you mess up a little on your first one, you will recover."

After Kieffer conducted a going-out-of-business sale for Town & Country Men's Wear, he also privately published a book in 1993 about how to conduct a going-out-of-business sale. He sold about 120 copies at $30 apiece. "I did all right," he said. "I didn't get rich. It gave me something to do."

Kieffer says there are many scam artists who will offer to conduct your going-out-of-business sales. "They take so much of your money. They spend it all on advertising." Fortunately, he said, he had a very honest person who handled his sale and also helped him write the book.

If you are going to go into business, Kieffer advises you first contact other successful people. "You'll find these developers and the CEOs of most any type of company are most cordial. They're always willing to help anybody."

That's what Kieffer did when he went into the manufactured housing community business. He contacted a major park owner, and was surprised at how helpful he was. The stereotype is that big-hitters are like J.R. Ewing of the old television show, *Dallas*, he says. "It's just not that way." They bend over backward to help someone out and give advice. "Do not be afraid of contacting somebody in a field you're considering entering." If you have to pay an accountant or lawyer for advice, he adds, do it!

Kieffer even carries that concept into his personal life. He is very concerned about bringing up his two daughters to spend money wisely. At one point, he was considering the prospect of buying an eight-plex building in his daughters' names. He had just finished reading *The Millionaire Next Door* (Andrews McNeel) which makes the point that giving money to children actually could hinder their efforts to build wealth. After reading the book, Kieffer worried that buying the eight-plex would be doing exactly what the authors had suggested not to do.

Concerned, he called one of the book's authors, Tom Stanley, and left his name on Stanley's voice mail. Stanley actually returned the call. "We chatted for one hour." Stanley liked the idea of Kieffer buying the eight-plex for his daughters. Kieffer's daughters, Stanley reasoned, would not necessarily get cash. Yet they would be able to get a great education by learning management skills if he bought the property. They'd also learn how to build equity using other people's money.

"As it turned out," Kieffer said, "I never did buy it, but anyway, he was such a nice guy." It goes to prove, he says, that successful people are within reach, and can sometimes be the best sources of information.

Kieffer learned that if you fail at something, it's not the end of the world—especially if you don't have much to lose. Keep going, he advises. Do something that has fewer startup costs that you can build easily.

Although Kieffer's first marriage failed, he says he now is happily married for 18 years. "It's very critical that you find a spouse who is on the same page as you as far as workability," he says. "My second wife works as hard as me—harder probably."

She also has been very supportive, he notes, backing him on every business venture—except the failed franchise venture in which he feels he was bilked. "It did turn out she was absolutely right," he acknowledges.

Most of his close friends are happy about his success. "A lot of my friends are successful as well—a lot more successful than me. They're all doing very well."

He continues setting goals. He is careful to pencil out his plan for reaching each goal. He even uses spread sheets to determine what his IRAs will be worth and the value of all his real estate. This helps him see what his next investment should be. He anticipates being totally out of debt within ten years at age 55. "In reality, that's not true because I'll keep buying more properties," he says. For one mobile park in St. Charles, he plans to add 12 lots every other year.

Kieffer says he never plays lotteries. When he shops, he still only buys bargains. "Being that I was in the clothing business, I still have access to getting most of my stuff at cost." Recently, he said, he bought a snowmobile on sale at the end of the season.

He is careful to put $1,000 a month into a SIMPLE plan, a type of retirement program for employers with 100 or fewer employees. He has mutual funds and lets his stockbroker, Don Charlson of Edward Jones, worry about them. We interviewed Kieffer as the stock market plummeted into negative territory, and he was unconcerned. "I'm not all excited now because the stock market took a big nosedive," he said. "That's a position you can get in if your debt load is low."

Kieffer says he doesn't travel much, but intends to do more traveling in the future. His family recently bought skis and they go skiing locally. They also took a trip in the summer of 2000, he says, to Branson, Missouri, and Amarillo, Texas, where they picked up friends and went to Santa Fe, New Mexico, and Breckenridge, Colorado.

Kieffer is a Catholic church-goer and sits on the financial board of his parish. "I'm one of ten people who get to give my input." He also is a generous donor. Although he attends church every Sunday, he does not necessarily credit religion for his business success. Success, he believes, comes entirely from self-motivation. "I have a deep faith, but I never pray for success," he says. "You have to make success happen for yourself. I am very good buddies with our priest."

He reads a lot, although he admits he doesn't read as much as he once did. He finds books on tape are more beneficial and make the time go quickly while he's on the road.

Kieffer says he never paid interest on credit cards, and keeps just one. "I have to use credit cards to keep track of business expenses." Also, he gets free airline miles, so he figures he'd be crazy not to use credit cards.

He considers debt, however, the downfall of most of the people he knows when it comes to building wealth.

"I have friends who have been up to $20,000 in credit card debt for the last 20 years," he says. "They just cannot escape it. People in general say they make $4,000 a month. They figure out a way for them to make their interest payments add up to $4,000 a month. They never allow themselves to get ahead. That is not a way to live. I don't think a lot of the people are very comfortable, and they will never be financially independent."

Kieffer puts the blame squarely on the American educational system. "Most people don't have a clue how an amortization schedule [a schedule showing principal and interest payments needed to pay down a loan] works. They can't figure out that over 30 years, if they add $100 a month, they can pay it off in half the time."

Despite Kieffer's aversion to the American educational system, he is sending his children to a local public school. "It seems to be a good school," he says. He also is teaching them at home. "I just hired a tutor to teach my nine-year-old Spanish." He believes that by teaching his daughter the language at a young age she will find it easier to get the correct dialect. "You're going to see Mexico and the United States almost have an open border shortly." Knowing the language, he believes, will give her an added opportunity.

As for his own success, he credits the fact that he truly enjoys his work. "I've always been independent. I've never had to punch a clock. I never had anybody telling me what to do. My work is truly fun. I'm happiest when I've got a pile of stuff in front of me to get done. If I run out of stuff to get done, I will look for another venture."

CHAPTER 9

RILEY B. "B.B." KING

Sharecropper to King of Blues

Riley B. "B.B." King stuttered and was diagnosed with diabetes as a child. He lost his mother at the age of nine and his grandmother about five years later. He dropped out of school after tenth grade. Although his life seems to have started with the deck stacked heavily against him, he now is a millionaire blues star. He credits his success to a passion for blues and his decision to finally hire the right manager—an accountant. But it didn't all happen for him until he was in his 60s.

B.B. King, 76, hasn't slowed down much despite his newfound wealth. He still is reported to perform 250 concerts annually. Perhaps one reason is the fact that he claims to have 15 children by 15 different women—none of which happens to be by either of his two ex-wives—and he swears he provides for them all.

It was a long tortuous haul for King, who calls a 3,100-square-foot, four-bedroom house with two fireplaces in Las Vegas his home, and a luxury tour bus his home away from home. He says he owns a Mercedes and a Rolls Royce, as well as a GM low-rider truck. While good management finally got King where he wanted to be, King's rise to success was built slowly through many of King's own efforts. He expanded his exposure dramatically by performing in concerts with the popular musicians of the times. He made time to meet with the press, and he paid and treated his employees well.

King was born on a cotton plantation in Itta Bena, Mississippi. After the deaths of his beloved mother and grandmother within just a few short years of each other, he lived and worked alone on the plantation that had employed his mother. Finally, his father came to get him. As a child, he claims he lived alone for three years, and spent time in the sharecropper's home of his aunt, uncle, and cousins near Indianola, Mississippi. Located in the heart of the Mississippi Delta, the home had no lights. King initially worked on a cotton plantation where he earned at most $1.75 a day. One of his early jobs was to follow a mule as it plowed the land.

"The mule will shit, piss, and fart in my face . . ." he wrote in his autobiography, *Blues All Around Me* (Avon Books). Later on, he said those memories made him truly appreciate earning a living through music.

In King's early years, however, he didn't really mind the hard work. It served to provide a refuge from dealing with the deaths of his beloved mother and grandmother that had so traumatized him as a child. Both had been religious. King says the greatest influence in his life was his late mother, Nora Ella King. The first time he experienced the blues, he claims, was when she died.

"I don't have a picture of her," King says. "I just have an image of her in my mind."

When he was a child, she told him that even though he was young and couldn't do much to defend himself, he should always be nice to people. His mother's words, suggesting that if he were nice to people, people would be nice to him, stayed with him throughout his life and carried him through some of the toughest times.

Music was his refuge from the painfully hard work. He taught himself to play music on a homemade guitar—a strand of wire tied to a broom handle. He got his first real guitar when he was 12, with money advanced to him by a plantation owner. Then, he began listening to music on the radio. He learned to bend notes to express feelings, a style typical of blues music.

He began playing in some gospel groups. He watched early music movies, dubbed "soundies," and enjoyed movie shorts, which sometimes featured black performers.

But King grew up with some strikes against him. As an African American, he felt like an inferior citizen in the heavily segregated South. He wrote about going to the theater and sitting in a certain section where white boys would throw popcorn at him.

African Americans had to sit in the back of the bus, use black-only bathrooms, and drink from black-only water fountains. He experienced firsthand a couple of lynchings.

"If you see a sign that says white and colored and you don't want problems, so you don't drink out of the one that says white," he reported on CNN's *Pinnacle*.

"I couldn't believe it," he said the first time he saw a young man lynched. Of another, he reported: "They castrated him and he was already dead. They had him lying out near the courthouse and that was sad to me and hurting."

While traveling, King often was stopped for speeding, particularly while driving a fancy car. Once, he was followed by a police officer in Texas while driving with his second wife Sue Carol Hall— a white woman—and her son. Even though he was extra-careful to keep to the speed limit, he was pulled over and informed there had been a kidnapping in the area and police were stopping suspicious people. His wife had to assure the officer that everything was all right before they could continue their drive. Needless to say, King was humiliated. "Inside I felt so little," he said in his book. "There's nothing I could do, no complaint I could file."

King just got used to such incidents. He didn't let the poverty and discrimination get him down. Instead, he used it as fuel to achieve a better life. The hurt actually helped him express himself through music.

As a teenager, King would walk eight miles from his plantation to sneak a peak in local nightclubs. At the time, jazz was starting to take hold. King moved on from his gospel to a solo singing career when he began belting out gospel music on an Indianola, Mississippi, street corner.

It is on that street corner that, he writes, he learned his first major marketing lesson. His music would draw only a few kind words from passersby until he substituted the words *my baby* for *my*

Lord. After making that switch, he began attracting tips. He found that people would give him a few dimes and an occasional beer once he concentrated more heavily on songs that conveyed the intense emotions between men and women.

King's salary on the plantation had climbed to $22.50 a week, which he said was good pay at the time in the Mississippi Delta. He became a tractor driver and married his first wife, Martha, just before getting called to serve in the then-segregated army during World War II. He went through basic training at Camp Shelby in Hattiesburg, Mississippi, in 1944. However, due to the need for farm workers, King never was called to active duty and ruefully returned to his farm work. He truly regretted missing out on the unique opportunity the army would have provided for him to see the world. He also regrets—to this day—being unable to receive the great benefits the GI bill might have afforded him in furthering his education.

Turned off by the lynchings in Mississippi and still feeling a need to expand his horizons, King decided to leave Indianola in 1947. He left behind his young wife, hitchhiking with his guitar and $2.50 in his pocket to Memphis, Tennessee. He was determined to pursue his musical career.

Beale Street in Memphis, home of Elvis Presley, was a hub for black musicians in the 1940s and 1950s. That's where King wanted to be. He stayed with his cousin, Booker T. Washington "Bukka" White, a highly regarded blues musician of his time. White taught King how to really play blues. Beale Street, King has reported, became his college education.

King has said that although he liked Bukka White and enjoyed hearing his music, he didn't want to play like him. King recounted to New Jersey's *Asbury Park Press* the advice from White that really sunk in: "If you're gonna be a blues singer, you've gotta dress every day like you're goin' to the bank to borrow money."

He also never forgot his childhood trip to Parchman Penitentiary to visit White, who once served time for shooting a man. "After that, I knew I wanted to stay far away from the place," King said. Parchman Penitentiary, known for being more concerned about profits than rehabilitation, is considered a blues musicians' hall of fame, having lodged White, and other landmark blues musicians.

King got his first break when he performed on Sonny Boy Williamson's radio show on KWEM in West Memphis. His playing went over well on the radio and he was offered a job playing at the Sixteenth Avenue Grill in West Memphis. Afterward, he got a ten-minute spot on the black-managed radio station, WDIA. His show, called *King Spot,* was sponsored by a health tonic, Pepticon. It became so popular that the time was expanded and the show was called *Sepia Swing Club.* He was able to promote his local performances on his radio show.

King needed a catchy performer's name. He'd been calling himself Beale Street Blues Boy. He shortened it to Blues Boy King and then to B.B. King.

Anyone familiar with B.B. King knows he calls his Gibson guitar Lucille. King says Lucille is the love of his life. It is his trademark. Why Lucille? When he began playing weekend engagements outside of Memphis, King was performing in Twist, Arkansas. It was a stop on what was called the chitlin circuit—a series of black clubs, cafés, dance halls, and roadside jazz joints in the deep South. Two men got into a fight and knocked over a kerosene stove which set fire to the club. King ran to safety outside, when he realized he left his $30 guitar inside. Risking his life, he ran back into the building to get his beloved guitar. Later, he learned that the fight had been over a woman name Lucille. He decided to name his guitar Lucille, and each one of the Gibson guitars he has used since have been named Lucille.

While in his 20s, King's popularity grew and, in 1949, he started cutting records for the Memphis label, Bullet Records. Initially, he earned a mere $100 per side. While that doesn't seem like much today, King was pleased at how his life had improved from his early days on plantations. King noticed that even though he was writing the words and music for almost all the tunes, someone else's name always seemed to appear on the label next to his. Nevertheless, he was undaunted.

151

"I love what I do—and I get paid for it," he told the *San Francisco Chronicle* in 1991. "I would have done it for nothing. A lot of times my pay has been the faces of the people smiling up at me."

The next year, he signed with another record company, Kent/RPM/Modern, and went on to have a number one blues hit, "Three O'Clock Blues." It remained on *Billboard*'s rhythm and blues chart for three months, making him a national name. He began touring the country, playing more than 340 one-night stands annually in the 1950s. He was reported to have played on stages ranging from crates stacked on concrete blocks to New York's elegant Apollo Theatre. In his travels, he had many affairs. One time, he shot up drugs with one of the women and went to work ill, he wrote. From then on, he took a hardline stance against the drugs that have ruined so many musicians. Not only did he never do drugs again, he says, but he also fired his band members if he learned they were using drugs.

Steadily, his popularity grew. Aiming to follow in the successful footsteps of singer Ray Charles, he signed with ABC Records in the early sixties. He had seen his salary rise—from $1,000 to $2,500 weekly—and King began splurging. He bought a white Cadillac. King also loved to gamble.

In retrospect, King now admits that he was a bit too lax about business in his earlier years. While jazz greats like Louis Armstrong cut major deals for royalties with record companies, King received flat fees, which were unusually low for black musicians. For some reason, he had noted, his records always wound up in the 99-cent pile in stores.

A major blow came in 1958, when a tour bus carrying B.B. King's crew of at least 15 people was involved in a crash—just after its insurance had lapsed the previous weekend. King was stuck with a $100,000 liability that haunted him for years to come.

Less than a decade later, his bus was stolen in Atlanta—once again, after he had halted his theft insurance. Then, his second ex-wife sued him for a divorce and the IRS hit him with a $78,000 lien on his income. King's financial struggles continued through the

1960s despite his rising popularity. Today, he blames not the IRS, but his poor money management skills.

Originally, he felt he was being persecuted for being a black entertainer, but subsequently, he realized he had made some mistakes. Chief among them, he revealed in his book, is not realizing that you can hire a tax attorney to work out a deal with the IRS. King has complained that the IRS always has been a noose around his neck. Even at this writing in mid-2001, after King had revealed he was a millionaire, an IRS lien of $112,145.23 continued unreleased in his name. It was filed against him in 1985, according to the Clark County, Nevada, recorder's online records.

In the 1960s, King stayed on the road, traveling from one gig to another, barely getting by.

He had a legendary relationship with his musicians, whom he reports work without contracts. He is known for paying for them to fly home to their families and generously giving each a separate hotel room while touring.

"Most of us who came up through the ranks know what it was like to be a sideman," he explained to the *San Francisco Chronicle*. "Those memories stay with me."

King also reported that he understood how hard touring was on family life. "One of the things that makes me work like I do is that I've got to keep them working so they can take care of their families."

"Nobody [his band members] has ever let me down, and I don't let them down," King told *Guitar Player* magazine. "There have been times when I've paid them a month in advance, but they have always been there when I needed them. I've got the greatest bunch of guys you could find.

"Every household has some rules, though, and I have a few. You don't smoke, drink, or swear on the bandstand—I don't, so you don't. If you want to get drunk, do it in your own room or someplace, but don't miss work. You don't fight either. If you fight, you get fired. Another rule has to do with wives and girlfriends. A guy has to treat a lady like his lady when she is around us. It has been that way for 50 years."

King said he always is receptive when his musicians suggest a new sound.

Although King worked hard in his early years to build a following, he had not been paid very well. As rock music started gaining popularity in the 1950s, rhythm and blues took a back seat. It simply was not respected by many mainstream whites, who believed the "jungle sounds" corrupted the morals of young whites. Meanwhile, some blacks considered rhythm and blues "devil's music," played by uneducated black sharecroppers who drank moonshine whisky and gambled.

"I was never real lucky like James Brown or Jackie Wilson, who had the young kids liking what they did," King once told the *Seattle Post-Intelligencer.*

Even as late as 1985, the *Financial Times* reported that a media interviewer had asked King why he didn't play in a certain style. "Well," King replied, "I guess I got stupid fingers!"

King, though, was a good promoter and had jazzed up his wardrobe to help create a stage presence. But the prejudice that humiliated him through most of his life also seemed to be hurting his career. As a result of the Civil Rights Movement in the 1960s, his music became more popular with white people. But it still was not played much on the radio. To this day, he laments the fact that young black children don't know about the blues.

"In general, when I'm signing autographs for kids, it's rare to meet a black one who doesn't want it for his mother, grandmother, or grandfather," he told *Ebony* magazine. "But the whites usually ask for themselves.

"I don't altogether blame them. I blame us for not making a better effort to let them know their roots."

King was determined to cure the lack of interest in his music. He believed that traveling was a way to build a following. He admits his life on the road didn't do much to prolong his marriages, but it paid off handsomely for his career.

First, his touring attracted press coverage wherever he went. After his shows, he'd meet with his admirers and refuse to leave until they went home. The next time he would revisit the area, he noticed that the crowds would get bigger and his record sales would increase.

Even later in life, King's music drew mixed reactions. In 1990, it was reported that his radio show, *The B.B. King Blues Hour,* had been canceled by its syndicator, Bullet Productions of Burbank, California. The show had been carried on 112 primarily black-oriented radio stations. The company cited a lack of national advertising support for its demise. "We didn't know it was being canceled until it had already happened," Sidney Seidenberg, King's long-time manager reported in the *Chicago Tribune.* "We only found out about it when I called the syndicator about another matter and then they mentioned they were canceling the show."

In Chicago, WXRT-FM's program director, Norm Winer, was angry and urged fans to write to the syndicator in care of the radio station to vent their feelings. By the end of the first week, the station had received more than 100 letters. A spokeswoman for King told us he never resurrected his radio show due to lack of time.

King also had difficulties being a traveling father. It left many children and grandchildren with lonely lives. One of his daughters, Patty Elizabeth, attracted media attention due to her problems with the law. She was the product of an affair King had with Essie Williams, who had owned the Blue Note, in Gainesville, Florida, where King played. The two never married, said *People* magazine.

Patty, the third child of the already divorced Williams, had been in and out of trouble with the law. The Florida Department of Corrections reports she finally was released after serving a 13-year prison term at Lowell Correctional Institution, near Ocala, in 1995. Her latest prison term resulted from convictions on forgery and cocaine trafficking charges. King purposely performed before her in prison while she was incarcerated.

On the road, it was not uncommon for King to make remarks while on stage to his children, who would go to hear him when he was in their areas.

"They've all gone their separate ways," King told *People.* "I've always told them, individually, that they're special, that they're my favorite. I was there for them and I tried to help them. That's no excuse for having children, but if you have them, it's your responsibility to take care of them. That's why I'm still working." Two of his daughters, Shirley and Claudette, were reported to have tried singing careers. Even though Shirley King, went so far as to bill herself as "The Daughter of the Blues," she expressed regret that King never invited her up on stage or to do a record with him. King cited restrictions placed upon him by his record contracts as the reason.

Shrewd representation over the years by King's manager, Sidney A. Seidenberg, is one of the major reasons King is a multimillionaire today.

Back in 1968, at age 43, King dreamed of being a major hit. Not quite making it was getting him down.

His road manager, Lou Zito, recommended that King talk with Seidenberg, who came up with a five-year plan for King. First, though, King had to give up gambling and pay back the IRS. Seidenberg negotiated a tax settlement and made certain that King made his payments on time.

He lined King up with Associated Booking, one of the nation's top booking agencies. Associated represented such great stars as Louis Armstrong and Fats Domino. The year after King signed with Seidenberg, he recorded one of his greatest hits, "The Thrill is Gone."

Good bookings were key to building business. Associated would team him up with rock musicians in key cities. B.B. King, who once shunned rock music in favor of the blues, wound up playing the San Francisco Fillmore West with the Grateful Dead and Jefferson Airplane. Audiences went crazy when King sang "Rock Me Baby" and "Sweet Little Angel."

In addition to frequently meeting with the press and his admirers, King further aligned himself with popular rock musicians of the 1960s. He attributes the burgeoning interest in the blues to rock stars like Eric Clapton and the Rolling Stones. When Mick Jagger told the audience he was influenced by B.B. King and other blues greats, young audiences began to seek out King's music. King was in even greater demand.

King especially credits Eric Clapton, the rock and roll and blues guitarist, for the growing interest in blues.

Clapton's music is played on popular radio stations. His videos are on MTV and VH1. A number of his songs have been number-one hits over the years.

King found that associating with popular rock musicians, and opening his sound to their influence, boosted his career. In fact, the B.B. King and Eric Clapton album, *Riding with the King,* released in 2000, went double platinum in the United States. In other words, it sold 2 million copies. It sold an additional 2.3 million copies internationally, making it the biggest-selling album in his career.

King more recently has served as a mentor to young up-and-coming blues prodigy Kenny Wayne Shepherd, of Louisiana. His jam sessions with the young Shepherd on stage and photos with him in the media helped endear King to the younger set.

He has teamed up with great jazz and blues musicians like Etta James, Albert Collins, John Lee Hooker, and Bonnie Raitt.

King, Muddy Waters, and Bobby Bland were the only blues musicians to record on a major record label. That's important because his MCA label at the time was the nation's largest record company. It put lots of money into promoting its artists' records. Seidenberg also moved King into other areas of business that were lucrative. He arranged for Gibson guitars to begin their retail line of Lucilles, B.B. King's signature guitars that sell for as much as $3,500 apiece.

Seidenberg also helped establish the B.B. King Blues Clubs in Memphis, Hollywood, and New York. He set up the merchandising of B.B. King jewelry, belt buckles, postcards, baseball caps, casual clothing, barbecue sauce, salad dressing, salsa, and bean spreads.

How do the blues club deals work?

Under the first contract in Memphis, *The Commercial Appeal* reported that King's business arm signed a licensing agreement to use "the mark" "B.B. King," for food, beverage, paper goods, printed matter, clothing, toys, and souvenirs for live entertainment.

In return, King's business arm would receive:

- Five percent of the gross proceeds from the sale of food and merchandise

- A three-year lease on an apartment primarily for the use of King and his manager while they were in town

- Up to $1,000 worth of free food and beverage per quarter for King and his guests whenever he dines at the club

King's responsibility was to make no fewer than four free performances annually at the club.

At this writing, B.B. King was coming into his own. Seidenberg had retired and King had a new manager, Floyd Lieberman, former president of Sidney A. Seidenberg, Inc. In his 70s, King now makes between $70,000 and $130,000 per show. King developed a mini-conglomerate of income-producing businesses. He has appeared in a number of films, received 11 grammy awards, and obtained honorary degrees from four universities, including Yale.

He had advertising deals with XM Satellite Radio, Lifescan-One Touch, Northwest Airlines, Wendy's, M&M's, Greyhound, Texaco, Budweiser, and Sears.

King likes to wear $1,400 silk suits. His concerts gross at least $17.5 million annually. He pays his band top wages. He recently gave out sterling silver monogrammed cuff links to people who helped him become a success over the years. The links have a musical note on one side and a guitar on the other.

At his concerts, he routinely hands his fans items, such as personalized guitar picks or pins, which he says he orders by the thousands.

Two albums, *Best of B.B. King,* and *Deuces Wild* became gold records, selling at least 500,000 units each. *Deuces Wild* and *Riding with the King* became platinum records with sales over 1 million.

He has received numerous music awards, including a fistful of W.C. Handy Awards for best blues musician. He is in the Rock and

Roll Hall of Fame, as well as the NAACP Image Awards Hall of Fame. He has received the B'nai B'rith Humanitarian Award.

"I have to pinch myself sometimes, King told CNN. "I've met the pope. I played for the president. It is all very important to me. Also getting honorary degrees from some great universities like Yale, OLE Miss, Robes College, Berkeley School of Music. . . . All of that to me. I'd pinch myself sometimes and you know, is this really B.B. King."

King is capitalizing on his name and the recent surge in interest for blues music. His newest B.B. King Blues Club in Times Square is expected to be a profitable venture. Times Square has been revitalized, and the demand for good jazz and blues clubs is strong.

Danny Bensusan, a New York restaraunteur, saw that blues was becoming popular. Bensusan owns the famous Blue Note, a Greenwich Village jazz club where the world's top jazz musicians have played over the years. Bensusan got King, who already had blues clubs in Memphis and Los Angeles, to agree to a deal to open a club in New York. He is the majority owner of the Times Square B.B. King Blues Club, which has 500 seats, a $350,000 sound system, huge video screens, and big dressing rooms for the acts. There also is a separate 150-seat restaurant named *Lucille* after B.B. King's famed Gibson guitar.

Faith in God is one thing that has helped King as he's run the gauntlet to become successful. Although as a child he went to church regularly, now his travels interrupt his visits. But he has some favorite preachers he goes to see if he is performing in their areas. "I believe God created everything and I'm awed by his handiwork," said King in his autobiography.

As a young man, when he was feeling "serious heartache" and wanted to go to church, he often found help from singer Aretha Franklin's late father, Rev. C.L. Franklin of the New Bethel Baptist Church of Detroit.

Franklin often talked about racial pride. "Whenever I was in Detroit, I'd make it a point to get myself up on Sunday morning to hear him," King said in his book. "He inspired me."

King bought cassette tapes of Franklin's sermons and played them when he was on the road.

Traveling also made it hard to have long-lasting romantic relationships. "I've been in love many times," King told CNNfn. "I've had affairs with ladies that I thought wouldn't last and they didn't. But the music was one of the things it seems like I could depend on. Music was there like a crutch. I get my love from my music."

King says in his book that if there is anything he could change, he would have finished high school and gone to college. Plus, he would have waited longer to get married—until age 40. He reported that he is requiring his children and grandchildren to go to college as a condition to receiving an inheritance.

He advises aspiring musicians to stay in school and go to college if possible. "Major in business of some kind, computers or something that leads to that, and minor in music, if you will. And practice," he suggested in *The Commercial Appeal.*

King could retire. However, he's supporting his 15 children and at least another 15 grandchildren. "My family is sort of like a factory," he told CNN.

King has some unusual attitudes. You get the feeling he would be on the road playing great music for the world even if he didn't make money.

At the opening of the B.B. King Blues Club on 42nd Street in New York, King was asked about money. His love of his work and his natural promotion skills shined through in his answer. "Let the good times roll," King said. "Yes, we want to make money. You can't pay your bills if you don't make money, but it's not only that. We feel that New York is a city of culture and blues is part of our culture and we think there is a place for it. And New York, being the great city it is, some of my friends tell me it was such a great city they named it twice. So we want to be part of that and we think a lot of people are glad we are."

King is modest. As recently as 2001, he told the *Florida-Times Union* in Jacksonville that he didn't consider himself a star.

"I know that I'm popular, but I'm not a star." When asked what it would take to be a star," King responded: "I don't know." I guess I will when it happens. Eric Clapton is a star. Stevie Ray Vaughan was a star. Ray Charles is a star. Bing Crosby was a star. There's a lot of them out there, but I'm not one of them."

When asked when he was going to stop touring, King told *Guitar Player* in 1998: "At age 73, I feel the need for [playing] now more than ever before. It's the urge of going around the world playing and meeting people that keeps me out there. It's still fun and exciting. When people ask me if I'm going to retire, I say, 'Yeah five or ten years after I'm dead.'"

Three years later he still was cranking out the hits. In June 2000, his album with Eric Clapton, *Riding with the King*, debuted at number three on the *Billboard 200* list. VH1.com reported that the album was a surprise hit.

In February 2001, King received his tenth and eleventh Grammy awards for best traditional blues album *(Riding with the King)* and best pop collaboration with vocals for the song "Is You Is or Is You Ain't (My Baby)."

"It is still exciting," King said when he accepted his awards. "I've never won two in one day. It's something we put our hearts in. I do that every time, but every day is different. And if I play each day as I feel, sometimes it's better."

King said that although many didn't want to hear the blues, he loved to play it.

"How could it be the devil's music if it made people happy," King always believed. "That is when I got the idea that I could make a living in music rather than driving a tractor."

CHAPTER 10

J. PETER UYS

Steel Worker to High-Powered Money Manager

J. Peter Uys, 49, knows hard work. He worked summers as a laborer at steel mills around Youngstown, Ohio, during college. Sometimes it was backbreaking, involving heavy lifting in the heat for eight hours straight. Even though he was young, he couldn't move when he got home from work. But the experience taught him a great lesson: Save money, get an education, and make a good living.

Today, with impressive business degrees under his belt, Uys runs a small hedge fund, the Peter Uys Partnership Ltd., out of the bedroom of his Atlanta home. Hedge funds are privately managed investments, typically available only to wealthy investors. They are similar to mutual funds, but they are largely unregulated and are allowed to make certain riskier investments that mutual funds can't.

He pegs his net worth at $2.1 million, although he admits it fluctuates quite a bit based on the direction of the stock market. We interviewed him in early 2001, just after the stock market had suffered its worst year since 1994. Prior to the market's nosedive in March 2000, his net worth was more than $3 million, he says.

Born white in South Africa, Uys and his family moved to this country when he was three so that his father could attend graduate school at Massachusetts Institute of Technology (MIT).

It proved to be a good move. In those days, South Africa still adhered to apartheid. With black Africans poor and segregated from society, it was politically dangerous and volatile.

The Uys family, which came to the United States on a grant that had to be repaid, might have been the poorest family at MIT. In fact, Uys can remember his mother slicing a banana three ways between family members. "That would be a treat," he said.

Uys's high net worth might not seem surprising when you consider he obtained his undergraduate degree from the Wharton School of University of Pennsylvania, one of the nation's top business schools. Plus, he has a master's degree in finance from Columbia Business School, New York. However, Uys doesn't necessarily believe those schools deserve complete credit for his success.

The chief catalyst, he believes, is the fact that he started saving massive amounts of money very early in life—perhaps because he felt a bit disadvantaged as a child when compared with his friends.

"I've thought about that," Uys says, referring to the role of his education. "It's very expensive going to those schools. I wondered if I had taken that same money and gotten less education or a less expensive education, what the difference would have been." All that money, he muses, might have been invested in a largely rising stock market during that period.

The higher education experience, though, definitely gave him a few advantages. For one thing, it expanded his horizons. "I'd grown up in a very small town," he said. "At those schools, you have a lot of people who are very, very rich."

Also, it gave him exposure to the investment industry, which has since become the principal source of his success.

Uys's family left a deteriorating political situation in South Africa. His father, whose own father had died during the Depression, was attracted to the career opportunities in the United States. Hoping to improve his family's plight, he went on to get his Ph.D. and subsequently became a metallurgical engineer. He landed some attractive jobs, starting in research at Allegheny Ludlum in Pittsburgh. He moved from job to job throughout the Midwest, finally winding up in quality control, where he retired from an executive position at Wheeling Pittsburgh in West Virginia. His father, Uys reports, worked very hard to establish financial security for his family and made certain Uys and his sister and brother lacked for nothing. However, growing up, Uys always wanted to have some money. "I grew up wanting financial security and a little bit more," he said.

Uys moved with his family from Boston to Pittsburgh and then Youngstown, Ohio. "I was a fairly typical kid," he said. "I didn't have a whole lot of interest in school. I didn't have the motivation to study. My mind often wandered in classes." By the time he was in the middle of high school, though, there was a great deal of emphasis on education. "I reached the conclusion that just to get a decent job, you had to get a really good education." He was not a very good student until the last few years of high school, when he realized how important learning was. He also was "mildly" athletic, once taking a local breast stroke swimming championship.

Even now, Uys can't forget the two years his family spent in Natrona Heights, a small town outside of Pittsburgh. The family had first rented an apartment, which became too small when his mother was expecting her third child. They came upon a home owned by an elderly couple that had moved to a nursing home. The couple had willed the home to charity, but the charity was prevented from selling it until the couple died. So Uys's family was able to rent it. "It was a palatial home on the fanciest street in town," Uys said. His family was the poorest on the street in a very rich neighborhood. "I always felt less economically well-off than the other kids."

The feeling of not having as much as his friends when he was young never left. While living in the Midwest, Uys initially entered college at University of Pennsylvania thinking he wanted to go to medical school. "When I looked further into medicine, I realized it was not the right field." He enjoyed economics, though, and decided to major in it.

Having spent much of his life in Youngstown, Uys had learned the importance of saving money. One well-known area resident, the late Edward J. DeBartolo, had started with nothing only to become a very wealthy shopping center magnate. DeBartolo's son was three years ahead of Uys in high school and the family was the talk of that small town. "He was notoriously frugal," Uys says of the older De-Bartolo. "You'd hear from people in town how cheap he was. He lived in a home that was extremely modest relative to what he might have lived in."

The DeBartolo home actually had been across the street from the junior high school. Often Uys saw DeBartolo outside. "It was a nice home," Uys said. "It was very, very modest—sort of the home a prosperous physician or dentist would have." Although the stories about DeBartolo's frugality were not necessarily favorable, the message was clear. As wealthy as he was, he definitely was more frugal than most people.

The stories stayed with Uys and sparked his awareness of the role frugality can play in building wealth. After all, you can't accumulate a lot of money if you spend it all. Uys enjoyed reading biographies, and often took them out of the library. The message of frugality sank in deeper as Uys read about Warren Buffett. "He's notorious with his penny pinching. That's a theme you see with a lot of people who accumulate money. It's a theme I've picked up on."

As Uys grew older, he watched his father go from job to job at various steel mills. The steel industry began to deteriorate in the late 1960s. Most of the factories were located in what was called the Rust Belt—a string of factory towns in Western Pennsylvania, Eastern Ohio, and West Virginia. The factories were old, inefficient, and labor costs were high, and as a result, U.S. steel producers could not compete with foreign producers. In the early 1970s, many Rust Belt factories shut down. By the late 1970s, Youngstown, Ohio, once a prosperous mid-size city in Eastern Ohio, looked like a ghost town. American steel producers built new and more efficient factories in the South.

Seeing his father move around from one economically depressed area to another left an indelible impression on Uys. He wanted to have a better life. He wanted to be in charge of his own destiny rather than taking orders from a big corporation.

Although his father was successful, Uys says he did not necessarily hold the same view as his father when it came to financial security. Having grown up very poor in South Africa, Uys's father frequently aimed for financial security by hooking up with a solid corporation. Although he didn't spend money lavishly, he enjoyed going out to dinner and was fairly generous with his money.

Uys had a different perspective on financial security. "I didn't grow up with the idea that a job in a big company was a source of security or comfort."

As Uys got older, life became a bit easier. Uys's family paid for his college education, and Uys worked in the steel mills in the summer. "It paid very well." But it was grueling. Uys filled in all types of jobs. Although the job taught him respect for blue collar workers, it also reinforced his idea that he'd definitely prefer working in an office.

His desire to be self-employed gained more ground in college. He remembers hearing about a psychologist's survey that polled a group of 45-year-old Harvard Business School graduates to see if they were happy in their lives. The results showed that almost all those who were self-employed were happy, while all but one of those employed at large corporations were unhappy. Uys was becoming increasingly convinced that self-employment was the way to go. He went on to graduate school, borrowing some money for tuition, but paying for much of it himself. "I also had a little help from my parents there," he admitted.

He worked for two years as a securities analyst and portfolio manager in the trust department at Equibank, a Pittsburgh-based bank that at this writing was called National City Corp. After graduate school, he joined the small Greenwich, Connecticut, office of a company called Amax, commuting by train from New York. He also worked for five years as an analyst for Swiss American Securities, a tiny brokerage firm in New York, owned by Credit Suisse. Despite his impressive degrees, the salary at his highest paying job was only $65,000 a year in 1991—not very much considering the enormous cost of living in New York.

Fortunately, Uys's early lessons about frugality paid off handsomely and provided a way out. He started being careful with his money in college. While going to school in Philadelphia, he would take a Greyhound bus home, when most of his classmates would fly. When he graduated from college in 1974, he didn't have much money. But afterward, he started saving. His efforts had a great impact as he watched his investments zoom.

Uys got into the stock market after the great bear markets during 1973 and 1974, when stock prices dropped almost 50 percent. The early 1970s were characterized by high unemployment and an economic recession. The late 1970s were a period of superhigh inflation and interest rates—not a healthy environment for stocks. From 1969 through 1979, the stock market grew at a measly 5.8 percent annual rate. Meanwhile U.S. Treasury bills earned 6.4 percent annually. It was a good time for Uys to learn his craft. He was able to buy beaten-down stocks and profit when stocks rebounded with a vengeance in the early 1980s.

Recognizing that frugality had been a common theme among those who had built large net worths, Uys looked very hard for an inexpensive place to live in New York. He settled in an apartment that was tiny—a mere 12 feet by 14 feet. But he was careful to confine his search to desirable neighborhoods, and wound up at Tudor City Place. "I carried pinching pennies to an extreme," he said. "A lot of my friends would joke about it. I didn't eat in restaurants terribly often."

Nevertheless, he was not as deprived as it sounds. His jobs often took him abroad and to some very fancy restaurants. So he didn't really need to eat out often. He furnished his apartment with furniture he bought used, often seeking bargains from those moving out of town. Later on, he bought his furniture at estate sales and auctions. He found that if he liked a piece of furniture he often could shop for bargains and get it for one-third of the retail price, or less. In New York, he didn't need a car, but he had to dress well at work. "I certainly didn't have a wardrobe anything like some of my friends."

Vacations were booked as inexpensively as possible. He would go to Europe, but would struggle to get the cheapest rate he could. Sometimes he brought backpacks and stayed at youth hostels.

He would save as much as he could in his 401(k) plan, particularly if the company matched funds. "That didn't make a big difference," he admitted. The total he had accumulated in such retirement programs was only about $60,000. He simply didn't earn enough to gain a very large matching contribution from his employers, he said. But there is one technique that Uys did find effective. Every year, he would set a savings goal and try to save as much as he possibly could. In his first year at work, for example, when he made $18,000, his goal was to save $2,000. When he was making $65,000, he aimed to save $10,000 after taxes. Typically, the savings would average on the order of 10 percent of his annual salary, and he was successful in meeting his goals. By comparison, the average American savings rate at this writing was less than 1 percent.

Uys never seemed to have a problem making good investments either.

After five years at his last job, "I felt like I was saving and investing carefully and living rather miserably," he said. But his frugality had paid off well. He had accumulated a nice cushion—a comfortable $450,000.

Uys actually had the idea of starting a hedge fund as far back as 1985, when he left his job at Equitable Bank.

At that time, his savings were not nearly as high. "I couldn't raise as much money as I had hoped," he added. Besides that, he said, the market looked extremely high, so he decided to return to the brokerage world. Originally, he had hoped to keep the fund on the side and run it, but because of the demands of his job as a securities analyst, that didn't work out. He abandoned the plan. However, he kept the fund's legal structure intact.

By 1991, he was ready to try again.

Hedge funds typically are restricted to wealthy or what is known on Wall Street as "accredited" investors. In other words, its investors must have a net worth of at least $1 million or an income of at least $200,000 in each of the two most recent years. Under the structure that Uys had set up, Securities and Exchange Commission rules permitted him to have 35 nonaccredited investors.

He had no close friends who had started a hedge fund, but he knew that Warren Buffett had a very similar type of fund. He also was on friendly terms with two people in New York who had set up funds. "They gave me some help in setting up mine. They had done reasonably well."

Uys figured out his startup costs, which were pretty modest, and adopted a cost-conscious business model. "I did have a portfolio of stocks built up over time," he said. "I did do better than average. My accountant and I, to help me raise money, calculated the returns on that portfolio and they were well above average."

Armed with that information, he was able to convince some friends to invest as little as $5,000 apiece. "What I did was approach everybody I knew and ask if they'd be interested," he said. "I approached my parents." They invested. Many of his friends did not have much money. But he found a friend who, with a death in the family, had received $75,000 from an insurance policy and invested. Another received an inheritance from his mother a long time ago and invested $15,000. "I was always surprised by who would invest and who wouldn't," Uys said. There was one person, for example, that he didn't know well at all and whom he didn't think would have any spare money. He was very tight. Although he lived in New York, he never took taxis. "His home is in pretty bad shape. He dresses very modestly. You'd never think he had money." Today, he said, this man is in his 80s and still invests with Uys.

Initially, Uys attracted $180,000 to start his hedge fund. A decade later, the fund has assets of $10 million.

"My plan was to focus on getting returns as high as possible and to attempt to turn the small size into an advantage," he said.

He started with five investors. Now he has 35, with an average account size of $250,000.

He realized his customers live everywhere. Friends he had in New York and Ohio would move. So the location of the fund was unimportant—as long as he was in an area with reliable telephone and mail service. New York has one of the nation's highest costs of living. Some friends had transferred to Atlanta, which has a cost of living equal to half of New York's. Atlanta had a large airport and attractive climate. He moved to Atlanta in 1993, originally retaining his New York apartment for two years just in case he wished to return.

There are strict rules prohibiting advertising of hedge funds. So Uys says he largely has grown the fund by word of mouth. "I was amazed that I would get checks of $100,000 from someone halfway around the world who would get word." Of course, he says, he also tries to spread the word where possible. "Like any businessperson, when you meet someone you think might be a prospective client, you bring up the subject of what you do."

For running his fund, Uys earns a fee based on its profits. Here's how it works. His accountants at year-end calculate the year's profit. "If we earn 6 percent or anything less, I'm not paid anything." But if he earns more, the fees can be lucrative. He earns one-quarter of any profits over 6 percent. So if his fund earned 10 percent, which is slightly less than the average return of stocks over the past 70 years, he'd earn one-quarter of 4 percent, or 1 percent of the fund's assets. On $10 million, that translates to $100,000 annually. Most years have been good to him. His annual salary has ranged from zero—in the year 2000—to $300,000 the year prior. "The last several years have been pretty good," he said. For at least the prior five years, he has earned more than $100,000 annually.

The year 2000, though, was his only bad year as of this writing. Despite all his hard work, the value of his fund was down, so he earned nothing. "As a result, I worked all year for free for my investors. It's unpleasant," he admits.

Because he has been so frugal, though, Uys says he is not as stressed out as he otherwise might be during a bad year for the market, nor is he turned off toward stocks. If you look at most people who have made a lot of money, he says, you'll see that they did it by investing in companies—stocks—not bonds.

He says he keeps about 20 percent of his assets in government-guaranteed Treasury securities with a term of seven years or less. This ultrasafe money acts as a cushion in the event of a market downturn. If the bad market of 2001 were to continue, he figures in the back of his mind that he could live comfortably on that cushion for about another 10 years. He admits, as the market was souring, that he had a bit more in Treasury securities than usual. Generally, he says, he keeps 8 to 10 percent of his money in Treasury issues.

Uys says he has one part-time employee, a student. "I'll go to local schools like Georgia State or Georgia Tech," he says. He seeks someone who is good at math. Rather than have a bookkeeper, he contracts out with an accounting firm. He also uses a part-time computer consultant.

Uys is a value investor, buying out-of-favor stocks. "What I always try to do most importantly is be a contrarian. That really pays off more than anything else," he said.

He and his employee recently completed research that indicated in the late '80s, stocks had a great return on equity. In other words, there was a high return on the value of the shareholders' stocks due to excellent net income from corporate profits. At that time, if you had bought stocks with a high return on equity, you would have had greater returns. But if you bought stocks with a high return on equity ten years ago and looked at how they did, you'd be disappointed. They did worse than stocks that had a low return on equity.

"The common theme from all the work that we've done and what I've seen consistently in my whole career is to do pretty much the opposite of what everyone else is doing.

"Our most recent acquisition was Berkshire Hathaway—when it was doing very badly." Uys says he also does as little trading as possible. "That's something that contributes to getting good returns." By not trading heavily, investors typically can save both on brokerage commissions and, possibly, capital gains taxes. At this writing in early 2001, when technology stock prices have been hammered, Uys was looking at some potentially "good buys" in the technology sector. "When people are panicking and writing the area off, that's where you get really good buys," he believes. Uys had not yet bought the technology stocks because his fund already was heavily invested in technology. "But I'm certainly looking around. I bought a lot of tech stocks in the early '90s when you had a similar period when they were not well liked. I bought Intel at 10 times earnings back then. We still have some of those companies."

At this writing, he said, his fund's total technology holdings were similar to the proportion in the S&P 500 index, a measure of the stock market based on the performance of 500 common stocks.

When the market turns sour, as it did in 2000—particularly for tech stocks—Uys does a lot of positive thinking exercises. Instead of thinking what can go wrong, he forces himself to think of ways they can go right. "Over time, the future is so unpredictable, often nice things happen."

Fortunately, he says, his clients are long-term investors and in fact were pleased that his hedge fund lost less than the S&P 500 during that down period. It also lost less than many of their other investments.

Although he is a millionaire, Uys continues his frugal habits. His office is in the bedroom of a 1950s ranch-style, 1,800-square-foot house. The house actually belongs to his roommate, and Uys pays rent. He estimates that his total living expenses run $30,000 to $40,000 annually. "I'm very comfortable living that way." Somebody making $50,000 annually probably could live the way he does. Though the house is in a nice neighborhood, "I don't know most of the neighbors. It doesn't make any difference."

Although most financial planners likely would recommend that he own his house and take out the largest mortgage he could afford, Uys prefers to keep his investments in stocks. "I think if you have any confidence in your ability to invest in stocks, you're better off putting your money there," he says. "My impression of owning a house is you can get some appreciation. But you throw in taxes, maintenance, and the time you spend taking care of a house . . . I've never seen anybody get rich by buying a house."

On the other hand, he says, he has seen property turn into a burden. In fact, he had one friend who bought a house and an apartment building in Pittsburgh as a first investment. He lost money on both. The same friend, he said, came to New York and bought another property—exactly at the wrong time. "My feeling is that if you want to accumulate a nest egg, you're better off to buy stocks directly."

Uys never has been married and has no children. "I'd love to marry and raise a family," he said. "I love kids." It's a matter of finding the right person. In the meantime, he rises at 5:00 AM to work out at a gym and estimates he works 50 to 60 hours weekly. He doesn't mind the hard work. He dresses casually. During one interview, he was wearing jeans, moccasins, and a flannel shirt. Often, he's on the telephone, so it doesn't get lonely. Plus, being on his own, he has the freedom to take a midmorning break, say, to get a haircut. This way he gets out, yet avoids the rush. Working at home, he figures, also saves him the need to buy expensive clothes and gas or pay for parking. He lives a quiet life and says nobody has ever asked him for money—neither family members nor charities.

He still buys used furniture. He bought an upholstered chair at an estate sale for $250 that would have retailed for more than $1,000. He also bought some little nightstands for $300 apiece at auctions. He estimates they would retail for three times that. He admits that he has loosened up a bit. He has upgraded his used Ford Taurus for a used Volvo. There are no big-screen televisions. "I'm not a big television watcher," he explains, although he usually watches *Wall Street Week* or rents a movie now and then. Although he is Episcopalian, he says he is not very active with his religion, and does not believe it has played a role in his business success.

Even though Uys seems comfortable financially, he doesn't feel wealthy. He never has. "What happens is you often end up socializing with people whose financial situation is about the same as your own," he says. "You almost feel poorer now because so many

Steel Worker to High-Powered Money Manager

more people have so much more than you. I run into people with $100 million and $500 million so I don't feel affluent at all."

If you're at the bottom of the top 1 or 2 percent of the wealthy segment of the population, sometimes you can feel even poorer than if you're a little further down.

"I have a nice social life, a circle of friends. I get out occasionally. I do everything. I do sculpture work and take classes. I lead a pleasant life."

In retrospect, Uys says that the one mistake he made, perhaps, is not making more of the opportunities available in the corporate world. For example, if he had stayed at Equibank's trust department a few more years and built up a client base before he started his money management business, perhaps he would be in a better position. Because he lacked a built-in client base, he was very worried when he started. "I had so little money to start out with in the fund, and didn't know how well I'd do." He feared that clients might leave and he wouldn't get more. "I just worked as hard as I could and things have turned out OK."

Uys notes that his money management business, while smaller than those of some friends, probably is more profitable. One friend, he says, manages $40 million—$30 million more than he does. Another manages $80 million—$70 million more. Both, he says, started five years earlier than he did. "All started with nothing other than savings." Yet, Uys says his net worth is higher than theirs. Neither, he says, has a net worth of more than $1 million.

He credits his more impressive performance to the savings he realizes by working out of the house and his frugality.

However, he has noticed that his perspective on money has changed as he earned more. "Twenty years ago, if you had said, would you have felt comfortable with $2 million, I would have said yes. But there's a ratcheting up of expectations as you make more." A client of his is going through the same thing, he says. "His net worth is going up along with mine."

First, he says, you figure that if you get $1 million, you'll retire. The figure rises to $2 million. "Now it's $5 million."

Steel Worker to High-Powered Money Manager

Uys says he has no intention of retiring any time soon. "Having a little set aside does give you a feeling of independence," he says. "That was the thing I wanted more than anything else. I never wanted to put up my feet and relax. I have no desire to retire now or at any particular point, but I like the idea that I could do it if I wanted to."

From his current financial position, he now sees where people who have not succeeded financially have failed. "I have seen friends who have been careless about buying habits and end up paying much more for something than they need to," he says. "That definitely is a mistake. I have one friend who graduated from college when I did—a person I respect and admire very much. He's always earned more than I have and his net worth is a little bit less than mine. He would go out to dinner at nice restaurants every night. I would go home and make something at home. If he had it to do over again, he might do what I did. If you want to accumulate a nice financial reserve like that, the thing to do is save money and look at ways to enjoy yourself at a lower cost."

Uys says that in Atlanta, there is an auction house that all the furniture and antique dealers visit. He has a choice. He can buy from a dealer or take the trouble to go to the auction and get something for one-third of what his friends pay.

Such simple decisions, he believes, are what truly make the difference.

CHAPTER 11

DONNA M. AUGUSTE

Humble Beginnings
Breed Science Whiz

Donna M. Auguste, 43, grew up in a two-bedroom home, one of five daughters of a mother who worked as many as three jobs at a time to support them and pay for Catholic school. Auguste is African American, with Native American ties to the Choctow nation. With nobody around during the day to watch the children, Auguste and her four sisters diligently looked after one another. They rounded each other up daily after school to receive the phone call their working mom would place to the house to check up on them. Auguste never even thought about becoming a millionaire!

Yet, she has become one. She pegs her net worth at $40 million. The bulk of Auguste's wealth came after she barreled into the white-male-dominated field of computer services to help start the company Freshwater Software in Boulder, Colorado. In May 2001, while technology-related companies were experiencing closures and layoffs, that company was sold for $147 million in cash to Mercury Interactive Corp. of Sunnyvale, California.

Nevertheless, a question about the luxuries Auguste's wealth has allowed her to enjoy brings chuckles. She lives in a small rustic house near ranchers in the wilderness of an unincorporated area of Larimer County outside of Boulder, Colorado. Her furnishings are left over from college. She is a vegetarian and drives a Jeep.

"I'm not very much into owning a lot of stuff," she told us. "It's not part of my personality. The kinds of things I do spend time and money on are things that further any task that I'm called to. I'm a gospel musician. I play for choirs at my church. I own very good quality musical instruments." She reports that she has a bass guitar and synthesizer. She became very interested in gospel music in around 1993 and was involved in a CD released a few years ago by a gospel music workshop.

Auguste, who stands just five-foot-two, remembers her mother working various jobs—waitress, telephone operator, clerk in a liquor store. It was difficult for her mother to juggle her hard work while taking care of her children and paying bills. The children slept in bunk beds in the crowded house. Yet, Auguste says that she personally always felt financially secure—despite her mother's struggles to make ends meet. Now, whether Auguste admits it or not, she definitely is much more financially secure than she was then.

Since leaving Freshwater Software, of which she had been president and CEO, Auguste has been running her private Leave A Little Room Foundation from a one-room office building in Boulder.

The goal of the five-employee foundation is two-pronged: to blend her strong faith in the gospel with her love of technology. One goal, for example, is to bring technology to remote rural areas.

Prior to our interview with Auguste, she had just returned from a two-week trip to Tanzania, cosponsored both by the Leave A Little Room Foundation and the Cure d'Ars Catholic Church of Denver. "It was a fantastic trip!" she said. Auguste was one of three emissaries from Colorado who met up with two friars. They drove two days by Jeep to a remote village in Northern Tanzania. The group's task was to help set up a clinic so that the Masai population, which largely raises cattle, would have significantly better access to medical care. The group outfitted the clinic or *dispensary* with lighting, a vaccine refrigerator, and e-mail communications via satellite.

Besides using her technological know-how to help the needy, Auguste also hopes to more aggressively develop her love of gospel music. Her foundation sells gospel CDs, including her own.

Auguste credits much of her success to the basic foundation of spirituality with which her mother, Willie Mae Prudhomme, raised her. Having grown up primarily in Berkeley, California, Auguste was actively involved in church activities. Her mother always stressed the importance of being resourceful and innovative, as well as how to pray.

She and her sisters were extremely close. "We were always each other's friends," she said. "We studied together, solved problems together, and resolved issues as a set of sisters." They also were each other's greatest supporters. All, she said, loved school, enjoyed studying and liked learning about new things.

Yet, each was significantly different.

Auguste was the introvert. "I've always been really comfortable with the fact," she said. It was her sister, Karen, who taught her how to read at the age of four. When she did, they'd get stacks of books from the library. Karen, Auguste says, also would explain that she needs to get out and talk to some people. "I'd say, 'OK. If you think I should.' It was never a situation where I felt like there was anything wrong with being introverted."

However, she admits now that she truly appreciates her sister's effort to draw her out. The social skills Karen helped her develop were a great help to her once she finally became a CEO.

She also credits her grammar school, St. Joseph's Elementary School in Berkeley, California, with using an innovative curriculum that allowed her to study at her own pace. By sixth grade, Donna Auguste was doing tenth grade math.

She acknowledges that money was very tight in her household. Yet, her mother realized how critical it was for her children to have a set of encyclopedias to assist them in their school work. Her mother negotiated a deal so that the family could obtain a set of World Book encyclopedias that she would pay for over time. Auguste and her sisters truly appreciated those books and their mother's resolve to obtain them.

"Maybe the other kids went to the amusement park on Saturdays," Auguste admitted. "But we had our encyclopedias!" Any time one sister got interested in something, the other sisters supported that interest. In fact, the girls actually taught themselves how to play chess by reading the encyclopedia. Auguste says she was fascinated by the logic surrounding the game.

By age eight, Auguste became interested in taking things apart. She disassembled a toaster, a doorbell, and radio. Then, she'd try to put them back together. Auguste had just one tool to her name—a butter knife. She also had an empty cigar box that a friend of her mother's had given her. Whenever she would have leftover parts after she put something back together, those extra parts would go in her cigar box, which became her own personal tool box.

Then, the Apollo 11 mission, the first in which a man walked on the moon, began consuming her attention in 1969. "That was an amazing thing for me," she said. "I was riveted to the television set!"

There was only one television in a household of five children, but it didn't matter. Whenever Apollo was on television, her sisters knew they must relinquish it. By the same token, she says, when one of her sisters became a cheerleader, the family would go to cheerleading events. Auguste had little interest in cheerleading, but "if my sister was there, that was reason enough for me to be there!" To this day, she adds, the unique bond between Auguste and her sisters continues. Her older sister, Karen, is vice president of marketing for the Leave A Little Room Foundation.

Donna Auguste went on to participate in math and science fairs. At John F. Kennedy High School in Richmond, California, she was involved in a math, engineering, and science achievement program. The program specifically was aimed at encouraging black and Hispanic high school students. Through it, there were field trips which allowed the students to meet and talk with professionals in math, science, and medicine. Auguste loved being able to fire away at these professionals all the questions that came to her mind. It provided her with her first opportunity ever to talk with an engineer. Prior to that meeting, she said, she thought engineers strictly drove trains.

Auguste says her grades in high school averaged 4.0—the equivalent of As. She applied for and obtained scholarships to college. She graduated with a bachelor's degree in electrical engineering and computer science from University of California at Berkeley. She worked as a computer programmer during her summers at Bell Labs in Murray Hill, New Jersey, and drove a bus 20 hours weekly on campus as part of a work-study program. Auguste says she found that she loved driving the bus. Not only was she able to sign up for hours when she needed the work, but the totally unrelated job also presented her with a refreshingly different perspective from her studies.

The experience was an example of the diversity in life Auguste had come to relish. It is diversity, she strongly believes, that has been a significant factor in her success. It started with her home life. Each sister was totally different, yet each was extremely valued in the family. It wouldn't have been nearly as much fun if they were exactly the same, she believes.

"Fast-forward to me in the professional world," she says. She began to realize how important it was to have different types of people on a job.

At both Freshwater Software and the Leave A Little Room Foundation, she purposely cultivated a varied group of employees. "Each person brings a perspective," she firmly believes. "It broadens your ability to solve a problem."

This belief also has been a major factor in some of her landmark accomplishments. Perhaps the most notable was that she was the key engineering manager in the development of Apple Computer's Newton Personal Digital Assistant—a handheld computer.

She joined the Apple team after working at Intellicorp, a company she says had been very diverse. The core team at Apple was different. Everyone in the group already knew people on the team. Because her role was to grow the project, she immediately set about hiring people from more diverse backgrounds—including minorities and women.

Diversity, she stresses, does not strictly mean hiring minorities or women either. "Diversity is background—perspective, diversity of life experiences," she says.

Her belief in this concept was substantiated once again when she started Freshwater Software. Initially, there were just five employees. Four were technical people, but fortunately, the fifth was an artist. The artist, she said, played a significant role. He was the lone employee who was able to visually create what the others were trying to present. An engineer's job is to make products functional, she explained. But the artist was capable of creating art and a logo around the concept so that the group actually could sell its product on the company's Web site. "Lots of people came to the Web site and remembered it," she said. "The Web site was our storefront. We made 100 percent of our sales through that gateway!"

Being a black woman interested in a predominantly white male field wasn't always easy. She received tremendous encouragement in high school, and was encouraged to attend science fairs. But in college, she says, a faculty member in the physics department emphatically told black and Hispanic engineering students that they were diluting the quality of education.

"There were people around who had those kinds of opinions," Auguste said. "The physics professor had a view that blacks and Hispanics should not be there. My view is that we are as smart, talented, and blessed, and if it's God's will, we can achieve it. My greatest inspiration comes from Jesus Christ—the life he led and the lessons he taught." Her strong faith has helped her overcome virtually all the challenges she has had in life.

After college, Auguste went on to become the first black woman to enter the computer science program at Carnegie Mellon University. She was a fellow in the Xerox fellowship program in Palo Alto, and the company sponsored her three years of graduate school work. She had been working at the renown Xerox Parc, when she met some people leaving to create another start-up, Intellicorp. She dropped out of Carnegie Mellon to join them and work on artificial intelligence programs. She never did obtain her Ph.D., but she says she has no regrets about that move.

Her different job experiences proved invaluable. The experiences of working at Bell Labs and Xerox Parc had presented her with two entirely different perspectives on her passion—inventing.

By sampling the business world, she also learned an important lesson. The only inventions that add value are those that have business value.

"It's a concept that emerges at a place where engineering and business converge," she said. "With engineering alone, you and I can invent lots of things that nobody wants and needs. There are lots of little inventions on the workbench of my garage." Only when the engineering idea solves a very real problem do you have something you can take to the market that people want to buy.

Bell Labs, she notes, is where transistors were invented. Her experience there allowed her creativity to be "wonderfully flavored" by the notion that you can create the smallest item and use it as a building block to other things. She learned from inventors how to carry a concept to a patent and through the complex process of commercial development.

At Xerox Parc, she worked on artificial intelligence—which closes the gap between how a human being thinks about using the computer and how the computer responds. Technology developed at Xerox Parc included items that are widely used in computer mouses and keyboards.

After working at Apple Computer, she became senior director for U.S. West Advanced Technologies, where she worked on a broadband multimedia application. While there, she moved to Colorado and was working with an old friend, John Meier, who also had been a coworker at Apple. As they completed their project, they met for lunch a few times. "We knew we wanted to start a company together because we had recognized that we had complementary skills," she said. The two came up with a list of ideas for which they both thought they had expertise. Then, they devised a second list of ideas that they believed had a definite market need.

"We put the two lists together and picked one of the items that was on both lists," she said. The idea resulted in the formation of Freshwater Software in 1996.

At the time, companies had begun to build 24-hour Web sites or online stores. Those sites, though, often crashed. As a result, the company lost money and risked having its reputation, as well as the customer relationship, damaged. Freshwater Software helped cure that problem.

Customers were able to download software from Freshwater Software's Web site. The software automatically pages and e-mails the site administrator at the first sign of trouble. It also notifies the administrator whether the problem has been fixed.

"We could see that the Internet had begun to emerge as an important commerce platform," Auguste said. "If folks were going to do home banking online, there couldn't be any mistakes."

The two decided to seek venture capital and wrote a business plan. Auguste contacted the former president of Intellicorp, her prior employer, seeking the names of venture capitalists. She found three prospects.

"I felt very confident," she said. "I was very certain that we had a good team and a good concept for a business. It was a situation that if investors were to choose to invest with us, they would get a good return."

Auguste had been used to public speaking. She already had spoken to numerous organizations about her work and projects. So the presentations went smoothly.

"One of the three said yes, they're interested." Mayfield Fund provided capital in May 1996. But she needed more venture capital. "I just did some networking and figured who was likely to be interested in the type of company we were proposing," she said. She stayed in touch with many people around the country via breakfast meetings and e-mail. Finally, she made a second presentation before Mohr, Davidow Ventures in July 1996. They agreed to invest in the company the same day.

By September 30, 1996, Freshwater Software had closed $1.25 million in funding. The following year, the company was profitable and didn't need any more venture capital.

Whenever you seek venture capital, it is important to understand the type of deal the company is looking for. Some venture capital companies look for software deals and others look for services. Venture capitalists also might seek to invest in companies at various stages of development. "In the case of Mayfield, they were looking for a deal with certain attributes and the leadership component was extremely important to them," she said. "In a large part, they make investment decisions based on the executives and the leadership of the company."

Every new company is an extremely risky investment and more likely to fail than more established companies. So it is crucial that potential investors make certain the leadership is resourceful. The investors want to know that there were problem-solving people on board who don't take no for an answer, she says.

Auguste notes that the business plans a company creates when it is starting out are subject to change at any given moment. Nobody knows what's going to happen with a concept that has never been tried before. So the resourcefulness of the company's leadership is more important than a business plan to those seeking to loan money.

Auguste said she typically invites the venture capital prospect to ask her some questions so that she can learn exactly what the prospect wants to know. Questions she has been asked include: "What will you do when you run into problems?" and "How will you handle situations when the company runs into competition that hadn't been anticipated."

If you can make your business profitable, you don't need venture capital, she believes. Also, some venture capitalists generally like to have a hand in running the business—a factor that turns off many entrepreneurs.

Auguste says, however, that there are different types of venture capital deals you can negotiate. "[Venture capitalists] can be helpful—especially as board members." In the case of Freshwater Software, the venture capitalists were minority shareholders, so they did not have primary control over the company.

Auguste says Freshwater Software could have considered obtaining a second or third round of venture capital funding, but decided against it because the company already was profitable.

At Freshwater Software, Auguste became revered for some unique strategies. When you call most companies and are put on hold, you typically hear music. At Freshwater Software, you hear running water. Employee offices are separated by aquariums rather than traditional office partitions or walls. The aquariums, which are soothing and transparent, foster collaboration, she believes. "The culture of the company is lots of fresh water," she explained.

The company also takes employees and some customers white water rafting on the Colorado River annually. The employees also have a gym, which they helped outfit and design.

She admits that between 1996 and 1997, the company was "hanging by a thread to get sales going." The market hadn't yet recognized the problems it had. "By mid-1997, that had all changed."

At the merger in 2001, Freshwater Software was reported to have 60 employees and 3,000 clients, including Merrill Lynch and Barnes & Noble. But initially, Freshwater Software had no salespeople. It didn't have its first professional salesperson until July 1999. Freshwater Software's first employees also did some consulting work. "Other companies needed our expertise," she said. "We helped them on a short-term basis. They were delighted, and we were delighted that it covered our payroll."

The company focused its culture heavily on customer service. "That keeps everybody really clear about priorities and decision making," she said. "The customer comes first."

Freshwater Software developed a database using the Filemaker Pro data program. The database tracked specifically why the company lost a sale and why it made one. The information, she said, proved invaluable and was examined many times daily.

The database offered some important insight. Early on, for example, clients were able to download software for a 30-day trial period from the company's Web site. In analyzing the company's database, though, it was determined that if the customer hadn't made a decision to buy the software within the first ten days, the decision usually wasn't favorable. So Auguste says her company quickly slashed the evaluation period to ten days. The shortened period, she explained, created a greater sense of urgency and actually may have prompted some clients to make purchases when they otherwise might not have.

Each Freshwater Software employee had full responsibility over a customer relationship and had complete authority to do what the customer needed. All employees were taken offsite quarterly for team building, which Auguste would lead. The goal was to make sure the company was performing as well as it could. If there were any problems, they would be discussed and tackled.

There also were exercises aimed at getting people to look at problems from a new perspective. One time, for example, employees split into five different groups and built mobile robots. The robots then navigated an obstacle course in a prizeless contest to see whose robot could finish first. The exercise was designed to enhance the employees' ability to work as a team and foster creativity.

"One of the things I encourage when I talk with entrepreneurs is [that] the value and importance of the culture of a company is extremely high," she said. "Everyone throughout the company owns, embraces it, and lives it. It comes through with the customers and with the day-to-day interaction."

Each employee was given six weeks worth of working days as holidays and was required to take those days off. "We made sure people's time was valued and appreciated. We had lots of athletes. Adapting to their training schedule was important, so we would encourage them not just by word but by actions—giving them time."

She purposely avoided making a lot of rules. "I didn't feel there was a reason to make rules for exceptions," she said. She'd rather have everybody cooperating and collaborating all the time.

Since 1997, there were annual bonuses for employees, and there was a stock option plan.

Auguste admits things at Freshwater Software didn't always go smoothly.

When she started the company and needed to set up the accounting and financial tracking, she heeded an accountant's advice that she needed a very complex high-end accounting package.

Thinking that her business would grow quickly, she wanted to make certain the system could handle a large business. "For a year, we used this accounting package," she said. Not only was it difficult to use, but it required the expensive services of a Certified Public Accountant to work with them on a regular basis.

Dissatisfied with the system, she finally switched to Quickbooks, which is very easy to use and designed for a small business that grows. "I wish I had chosen it a year earlier," she said. With the new program, the company was able to do its own accounting, and use a Certified Public Accountant only to check the entries every few months.

She also was greatly challenged in March 2000. The company was bursting at the seams and it was time to move from its 2,800-square-foot office to a much larger space.

The company planned to move March 1, only to learn two days before the move that the phone company had not hooked up the company's Internet access, and would not be able to hook it up for three months!

Auguste logically rationalized what some might have considered an insurmountable problem. There were three possible solutions, she figured. The company would not move on time. The company would move and not have Internet access. Or, the company would find another way to get Internet access.

Auguste determined that the building next to her space had a hi-speed T1 line in its office. Because the occupants were moving, they were ready to turn the line off. She was able to arrange to have holes drilled in the roof of the neighboring building as well as the roof of her company's new building. A heavy-duty coaxial cable connected the two buildings' routers. "[The former occupants of the neighboring building] agreed they would leave the T1 line and we would pay the bill."

The arrangement took all night to work out, but served to further prove her steadfast belief that virtually any problem has a solution. "If you have strong faith and a strong relationship with God, these are the kinds of things that are within your reach," she said.

Auguste believes that there are three important ingredients required to succeed.

"It is important to have a spiritual base from which to draw. While everyone's spiritual base might be unique—a Christian approach or a Jewish approach—it's more a matter of having a foundation that you can draw on at any time. It means, I'm never going to run out of faith. I'm never going to run out of courage or access to knowledge."

"Be passionate about what you do. If you are passionate, people will follow you because they want to be part of that passion too. With a diverse and blended team, you can draw accomplishment that's unmatched from anything that those individuals can achieve alone.

"Be tenacious. I'm a very tenacious person myself. I'm very persistent. If the door is closed, I'll find an open window. There's a way to get where you want to get to. You may have to step back from a problem and think about it in a different way. The obvious solution is not always the best solution."

Auguste shies away from topics that deal with her personal money. She does not want to discuss how much she contributed to start Freshwater Software. She also does not like to talk much about her investments. She uses independent advisors. "They are people I have respect for in terms of financial decision making," she said. "I enact the decisions myself, but I like to have good advisors around."

When she invests, she pays attention to things like impact on the environment and ecology. She also believes that global companies have challenges that are different than those of U.S. companies. She suggests that anyone investing in global businesses do their homework on the implication of the business in developing countries.

"Without that background, I'd be making a decision without enough information."

She also provides a few words of wisdom on the issue of money management. People pay so much attention to the type of yields they can get. "Maybe they can work their way to 6 percent or 10 percent using certain kinds of investment paradigms," she says. "But with good careful study of the laws around taxes as well as the responsibilities we have as citizens—understanding where the tax savings may be can give you saving in excess of 30 percent."

By setting up a private tax-exempt foundation, for example, the charitable contributions you give may be tax-deductible. The Leave A Little Room Foundation, founded by Auguste, is tax-exempt.

Today, Auguste goes to church at least three or four days a week. She is a musician and teaches a computer class at her church.

She says she likes to read children's books and just read the Harry Potter series. "That was a great thing to read and talk about to the kids at church," she said. "The kids were really into it." She likes the idea of staying current on the nomenclature in the books.

She says she also reads the Bible daily. "One of my favorite books is the Bible." She particularly likes Deuteronomy 8. "It speaks to the importance of each of us who have been blessed to remember where we came from and the hardships and adversity that God brought us through to the point where we can realize our blessings," she said.

She never has married and has no children. Yet, she is unconcerned. She considers marriage optional.

Auguste still gets excited about the prospects of technology, which she believes ultimately will form a universal network—in homes, vehicles, and workplaces.

For those who would like to succeed in the technology field, she advises they do what they're passionate about and be passionate about what they do. "Each of us is called to different roles," she said. "Passion is linked to that calling."

She and her team can create and invent, she says. Suddenly, she will be called to see what another person is doing in another area. "I would look at it and say, 'That's amazing. I never would have thought about it!'

"Pursue your passion," she advised. "You will find that we are uniquely suited to invent, innovate, and create."

CHAPTER 12

HARLYN AND KAREN RIEKENA

Couple Builds Wealth
Buying Farmland

When Harlyn Riekena's father died of a brain tumor at age 48, Riekena gave up a career teaching science. He and his wife, Karen, moved back to the farm with his family. Then, the farm was 280 rented acres. Today, Harlyn, 62, and Karen, 61, live on the same farm. They own 750 acres outright, worth just under $2 million. Riekena estimates that his income from the farmland is about $100,000 annually. His net worth stands at about $2.3 million. Karen Riekena says their farm equipment alone is worth about a quarter million dollars.

Farming isn't an easy business. Supply and demand dictate prices. You've got mother nature to contend with. Estimating when to sell your crops for the best profits is more an art than a science. Livestock get sick and machinery needs to be repaired. There are bank loans to pay off. Plus, in today's world, small farmers have to compete with corporate agribusinesses that are more cost efficient and can buy supplies at lower prices.

When we talked to Harlyn Riekena, he was planning a ten-day trip to Germany to research his family tree. He had been abroad previously only to visit his daughter when she was stationed in Germany. His wife was staying home. "I don't want to go to Germany and walk around on cemeteries," Karen Riekena said.

Couple Builds Wealth Buying Farmland

"Being a millionaire today is not the same as it was 50 years ago by a long shot," Riekena muses. "I don't feel that we're struggling. Probably, until a few years ago we were. Your attitude changes when you get older.

"We've quit trying to grow. More or less, the feeling is hopefully, [the wealth] will grow by itself at this point. Hopefully, by not changing our lifestyle and doing things foolishly, we should be at a point where [the wealth] grows on its own. Land is always like the stock market. It goes up. It goes down. Hopefully, it stays stable. We are at the point where we don't spend what we earn in a year. There should be things left over for savings.

"Before, if we didn't spend what we earned, we put it into paying off debt."

The Riekenas have three grown daughters and live in the small town of Wellsburg, a central Iowa farmtown of about 850 people. "We were just like everybody else," he said of his childhood. "I can't say that we were poorer than the rest of the people. If we were poor, we never noticed."

Riekena's late father, Emery, had been a farmer, and often had expressed disappointment that he never went to college. He had grown up during the Depression, and when he had finished high school, there was no money. "He talked about the tremendous scarcity of money—not food, shelter, or things like that. He just stayed home and helped his dad farm."

But growing up in the Depression, Riekena said, led his father to be very conservative. Yes, Riekena remembers having a bicycle that he was given by either his parents or grandparents. He also remembers that as a child, he wasn't permitted to have a whole stick of gum. His father didn't think it was necessary.

His father worked hard. There was manure hauling. He'd build his own buildings rather than hire a carpenter. However, he always encouraged his children to go to college, and made certain that when Riekena, his older brother, and younger sister were children, they were earning money so that they could meet that goal.

The chores on the farm started when Riekena was six or seven. He and his older brother would have to go to the shed and get corn cobs, which the family would burn in their cook stove. The corn had been shelled off and used for feed and the cobs stored in the small dry building in the summer so that they could be used later on. The two would load the cobs in a basket and carry them from the shed to the house. "They weren't too heavy," he said.

When he was about ten, he, his brother, and father bought hogs and cattle when they were small. They would show them at county fairs and 4-H camps. At the fairs, they would earn ribbons, which made the animals more valuable. Riekena would bring them back home, milk the cows, and keep his own separate records to make sure that when the animals were sold, he got profits.

He says he got the most profit from selling a dairy herd. He sold the cows and their offspring, which yielded money for college. He kept the herd from when he was about 10 to age 18. "My dad had his herd of cattle longer."

By age 12, Riekena was getting up at 6:00 AM—before school—to feed cattle and hogs. He also had to feed the chickens and gather eggs. "It wasn't hard work," he said. "I don't think we liked it. We were just kids. You always complain when they made you work."

Riekena was a B student. Generally, he says, he made honor role, although he was not at the very top of the class. "I kind of liked chemistry when I was in high school," Riekena remembers. He attended Iowa State Teachers College, now University of Northern Iowa, Cedar Falls. The four-year school was just 30 miles away—the closest college he could attend. He was able to commute. "At that time, almost everyone who went there were teachers," he said.

He met Karen in high school. She was a junior and he, a senior. She did not attend college, but worked in a grocery store. Karen Riekena also had grown up on a farm, one of seven children. "I had a sister who was 15 months older. She was Mother's helper. I was Dad's helper," she recalled, noting that she milked cows and took care of chickens. "I liked to be outside." Karen never had an allowance. If she needed spending money from her parents, she got some. She grew up, though, carefully watching pricetags. With seven children in the family, she had no choice but to watch every penny.

The two were married in 1959—two years before Riekena graduated from college. They moved into an apartment that cost about $50 a month. Because Karen Riekena had worked two years out of high school, she had succeeded in saving money. In fact, she purposely saved because the two had planned to marry. Riekena also worked some nights in a gas station to help out. But 15 months after they were married, they had a child and the money started running out. He had to borrow money from his brother to get him through the rest of school.

The growing family moved into a two-bedroom house in Eldora, Iowa. Riekena started working as a science teacher, earning about $4,500 annually. The couple also had a second child. One year after he began teaching, the couple's first child, a daughter, suddenly was killed in a head-on collision at the age of 13 months. Karen, too, was seriously injured in the same collision. A man was believed to have entered into a diabetic coma and had lost control of his car. In fact, only the couple's six-week-old son was uninjured. The family had no health insurance. "I only know from when I start remembering things," Karen Riekena says of the crash today. "I was in the hospital for seven months. Nowadays, that wouldn't happen. I had both legs broken and one arm broken. I was in traction.

"It's almost like it really didn't happen," she said. "Our son was just a baby at the time. He was staying with Harlyn's parents for several months after I got home. They would bring him over for me to see." Harlyn Riekena would get home from school at noon and she would get up on the couch.

To this day, Karen Riekena says, the accident has left her unable to bend her elbow. She also is missing a knee cap. As it turned out, the other driver's insurance company covered the family's hospital bills. "The really interesting thing about that is our doctor was very upset with us," she said. "He wanted us to sue." The couple, though, decided against a lawsuit. Instead, they settled and obtained just $2,500 for their daughter's loss of life. "We put it in a savings account and gave it to our other children as they got older," she said. "We just didn't feel right about using that money for anything. Your firstborn is just something that's not replace-able. We wouldn't want to use money that [we received] for the death of our child."

After the accident, the family did get health insurance. How-ever, shortly after Karen finally recovered, Riekena's father was taken ill with a brain tumor. His parents had moved off the farm into a better house, and had hired help that lived in the farmhouse. While Riekena was teaching, the hired help quit. "The hired man didn't like to take suggestions from me, like he did from my dad," Riekena explained. The two had a falling out.

Riekena's father died in 1963. With no one left to mind to farm, Riekena, his wife, and his family were forced to move back into the farmhouse the following year—sooner than they might have liked.

Karen Riekena actually was happy about the move. "I did not like living in town," she said. "I always wanted to be on a farm."

Harlyn Riekena says that although he liked teaching science, "looking back, I probably wouldn't have stayed with it all my life. I probably would have done something else. I think maybe it would have gotten boring."

He has no regrets about attending college either, and enthu-siastically endorses "the whole college experience. We lived here in a small town," he says. "If you didn't go to the college or the army, some of those people never saw the outside world at all!"

The only thing Karen didn't like about her move back to the farm was the house they were forced to live in. It was the very house that her late father-in-law had left before he died. "It was very old. It had a kerosene stove. It was awful. You had a tank on the outside of the house that kept the stove going. The fuel tank truck would stop by and fill it."

The house had a basement that Karen Riekena would not ven-ture into. "It was just too dark," she said. "It was a big, old bad house."

Any work that needed to be done around the house had been done by Emery Riekena when he was alive. That was it. "That was why, as young as [Harlyn's] parents were, they built a house in town," she said. They had lived in the farmhouse and they, too, thought it was awful. Harlyn and Karen Riekena stayed in that house for two years, and saved money to build a house right next to it. They have not moved since. Of the new house, Karen says, "It's just a pretty common one-story house with three bedrooms. It's not a large home. It's just great!"

Karen says she is different from many women. She doesn't need anything fancy. In fact, if she had a lot of things in her home, she figures she'd merely have to dust more. "If you look at my decorating, it's just awful." But her home has a large kitchen—quite nice for a farm. "You could say we don't have a living room. Our living room is our family room. We use it."

Upon returning to the farm on which he had grown up, Harlyn had to make some adjustments.

"I'd never planted corn, which is kind of the last thing your dad lets a boy do," Riekena said. "So I didn't do too well. I didn't drive very straight. The rows were crooked. It didn't hurt too much, but it didn't look too good." His uncle helped teach him what he needed to know about farming, he says.

Initially, Riekena farmed on shares rented from his mother. The way it works, he explained, is you get half of the proceeds from everything that is sold. "We had to buy the equipment and bought half the livestock." His mother had owned 200 acres and his grandmother, 80 acres.

"Prices were very low when my father died," he said. "This was both an advantage and a disadvantage. It made the prices we had to pay for things to get started low too. You might say it was a better time to get started than when prices were high." But it also negatively affected the prices you could get for your crops.

Karen was back to milking the cows twice a day. "She helped do everything," Harlyn said. "She particularly liked to help—and still does—driving the tractors and doing the fieldwork."

"The equipment and machinery they have now is so trouble-free and it's so comfortable," Karen explains. "It's a lot easier. Men think it's very hard work, but I know better."

Couple Builds Wealth Buying Farmland

Unfortunately, however, the tragedies in the Riekena family had not yet ended. In 1973, their only son, having miraculously survived the crash that killed his sister, was killed at age 12. "I know Harlyn didn't mention this to you," Karen said. "To this day, we can barely talk about it—he, moreso than myself. He was our only son.

"Our son went across the road. A trucker left him off on the other side of the road. He was talking to me and didn't look and walked right in front of a car."

That, she says, was by far the absolute worst experience of her entire life.

At least when her daughter died, Karen never actually saw it happen, and even lost most of her memory of the experience. The death of her son, though, occurred right in front of her eyes. It was a tragic experience she never could forget.

The family continued their hard work and grew. Although the couple's three daughters helped out on the farm, "they never did much in the way of tractors," Harlyn said.

Harlyn started growing his fortune when he acquired his first land from his grandmother's estate in 1966. She had 80 acres, worth about $600 an acre. She left it to her four children, which included his father. "I inherited six acres of it," Harlyn reports. "The rest, we bought for about $48,000. We had to finance it with as much [of] a loan as we could get." He, his brother, and sister, together had inherited 20 acres. His brother and sister helped Harlyn so he could borrow most of the money from the Federal Land Bank. He paid about 6.5 percent interest on the loan to buy the 80 acres, and continued to rent the other 200 acres from his mother.

In 1974, a neighboring farm of 160 acres came up for sale. Riekena bought it. "We had to borrow for it, but had some money at that time." Fortunately, he always had a pretty steady income from the dairy herd.

Why buy so much land?

"It's just what you have to do in today's farming," Riekena responds. "In order to have any efficiency, you have to have some size. It takes about this size farm for a family to live on and be fully employed."

In 1980, he bought another 60 acres, when land prices were high and interest rates were more than 13 percent. "Everybody was crazy to buy land at that time," he said. "All farmers were on a buying binge. Prices had been pretty good. Land values were just skyrocketing and everybody wanted some of it, it seems. We did all right, being it was only 60 acres, but a lot of people at that time got into a lot of financial difficulty by buying bigger quantities with those high interest rates. A lot of the rates at that time weren't fixed. They were variable."

Riekena said many farmers took out variable-rate loans at 9 percent. Some jumped as high as 17 or 18 percent. Riekena was careful to lock in a fixed rate. "We probably paid a little bit more than you could have gotten a loan for at a nonfixed rate. But I was afraid of variable rates." Fortunately, the dairy herd provided a fairly steady income—even when other prices were down. "We milked about 70 cows. At that time, he said, there were no other sources of income. "We tried to pay our loans down as fast as we could."

Four years later, he bought another 120 acres. "That was for about 60 percent of the price that we paid in 1980," he said. "It just happened. It came up close to us. It was an estate, with heirs selling it." Then, in 1986, he said, they bought another farm. "That was about rock-bottom price," he said. "Down to 40 percent of peak value. This was a friend of ours who had lost a farm. It was kind of a forced sale." All the land, he said, is within a few miles of where he lives.

It's not hard to hear about these sales in a small town. Riekena served on the school board, community betterment board, and at this writing, served on the county board of supervisors. "It's kind of interesting," he believes. "It's important in a small community to have people do this. Somebody has to do it."

Riekena says he has served on several boards, taking his turn, just like everybody else. He doesn't travel much, he says. He visited Florida for a week and visited people in Arizona. Karen Riekena says she particularly enjoys spending the weekend on gambling boats. "We're not like high rollers," she stresses. She also likes going shopping with their six grandchildren.

In her spare time, she enjoys reading mystery novels and dabbling on her computer. Harlyn, she says, subscribes to numerous farming magazines.

"We have a few mutual funds," he said. "One is a Keogh fund. It used to be worth $100,000 prior to last year [2000]." He has another small mutual fund and a few mutual funds in his granddaughters' names.

"We don't live high. We don't live low," he said. "We live like everybody."

He credits his current success with the fact that he "kind of bought [land] gradually—never going overboard in debt." Before buying a piece of land, he'd make sure the previous purchase was "pretty paid down." It was "a whole series of medium-size steps."

"We knew exactly what we would get and what we could spend," Karen says. In their early years together, they initially aimed to save $100 monthly. "We really didn't have any debt to speak of—except [the loan] from his brother. The first thing was [to get] that paid off. Then we decided we had to save."

Afterward, saving regularly became more difficult as more purchases were needed for the farm. Today, though, Harlyn Riekena says the couple finally is able to start putting away some money again.

The couple never argued about money, Karen says. In fact, it was something her husband always appreciated. "He'd come home and say there's something for sale coming up here. A lot of wives around would say no, no, no. I always wanted to expand. I love farming."

Karen said she generally left most of the financial decisions to him. "He had this fear of maybe going broke when that was happening to different people. He could absolutely not handle that. He was overly cautious. Then, when we did get something, our whole goal was to get it paid down.

Couple Builds Wealth Buying Farmland

"We were very fortunate that things came up at different times. We didn't buy large. That's where people got into trouble a lot. The biggest thing we ever bought once was 160 acres. That was one where friends were losing their farm to the bank. They were very kind to us."

Karen said that a relative also had been trying to get the farm from the bank and the owner really didn't want that person to have it. "The bank," on the other hand, "wanted to sell it to him—not us." It took a little finagling, she said. "We talked to the guy who owned it."

Their typical land purchases were between 60 and 120 acres. "It wasn't like some people who would buy 300 or 400 acres," she noted.

Karen says there is at least one other strategy the family has used to help maximize their income. The Riekenas try to store their crop longer "hoping for better prices before we have to get ready to put in the new crop." In May 2001, for example, Karen reported that she has not yet sold the 2000 crop. "It seems like many people are the other way around. Everything is sold in the fall."

Historically, the strategy has worked well, Harlyn Riekena said. "You'd get a little more for it. This year, it probably took about a 30-cent-a-bushel jump, but it didn't hold long enough for me to get rid of it all." Of the 50 or 60 percent of the crop he sold, he says, he probably made 30 cents a bushel. But he continued to hold the rest in the hope prices would continue upward. "Then it went the other way again. By holding, if you have a lot of notes or bills to pay, you're losing out on interest, so it's costing you something too. You have to get quite a bit more for it to really pay. This year, I held it three or four months and did pretty well on it. A lot of times, May or June is your best market. This year [2001], it doesn't look like it's going to be that way."

Harlyn Riekena doesn't feel wealthy at all. "I'm still pretty cheap, everybody says," he says. "I'm just slow to reach in my pockets."

Karen Riekena says her husband's bark is worse than his bite. It's true that she uses a credit card, and he doesn't. She also likes nice cars. "About certain things he's a tightwad," she said. At other times, though, "he'll just go and do things, like, say for instance, there's one fellow in town he saw walking with no shoes. Harlyn goes to the store and gets him boots and puts 'em in his car."

Harlyn declined to talk about the incident or provide other examples of his quiet charity. "If you talk about them, they don't mean anything anymore," he says.

Harlyn, Karen says, always wanted to buy the cheapest possible car. "Our first nice car was an Oldsmobile." Now, she says, she drives a Volvo. "We have sitting in our other garage a Honda CRV—a sports utility vehicle. He got that for running around."

Those, though, are not the cars Harlyn typically drives. "He has a '91 Plymouth Dodge Colt with 200,000 miles on it. That's what he drives all the time. That thing gets gas mileage like you wouldn't believe. So that's what he uses."

There's also a four-wheel-drive Dodge pickup, she says. "That mostly sits there for some farmwork."

Although the livestock succeeded in putting Riekena through college and providing the family with good income over the years, he has gotten rid of most of it. "That makes a lot less work," Harlyn explains. "We're strictly grain farmers, now that we're older. That has probably reduced our income." The couple farms corn and soybeans. If he still raised cattle, he says, his income would be quite a bit higher. With the livestock gone, Karen says she feels like she is retired. Instead of getting up at 5:00 AM, she rises at 6:00 AM.

Although Riekena thinks about retiring, there are no concrete plans. "I'd like to keep it in the family," he says of the farm, "but none of our children will follow it."

His oldest daughter works in a bookstore and her husband is in the service, he says. His middle daughter works as a nurse in a hospital, and the youngest daughter works as a receptionist in New York City.

"They can own it and carry it as an investment even if they don't live there. Plenty of people are willing to rent it from you."

It's true. The value of farmland has risen, and they certainly could realize a nice profit if they sold the land. They also could rent it, and not have to work so hard. Ultimately, as they get older, they admit they might have to rent their land. If they did, Karen says she'd probably have to go away during the warmer months. "I'd feel so bad about not going out in the field," she says. "It's so enjoyable to be out there in the open!"

The couple, though, aims to hold onto their land as long as possible. "We hope we can get it through to our kids to never sell," Karen says. "Hang on. That's what our goal is. We don't want a big corporation to be farming [our land]."

She is concerned about renting it out to large corporations. "There is someone about 20 miles from us—a fellow who sits behind a desk and has all guys working for him. He's probably in charge of 20,000 acres. We'd leave it [sit] and not [have] it farmed if we had to rent to someone like that!"

Such corporate farming, she says, may profit them if they sell or rent their land, but it hurts everyone else around them. "It's so much harder for any younger person to get started on their own, because they would just be working for the corporation. It's harmful to the whole industry.

"It's really hurting the smaller guys financially. They have to pay more for fertilizer, seed, and when it comes to renting the ground, they will have to pay more rent which they can't afford.

"There are a couple of people like that driving prices up.

The advent of corporate farms, Harlyn says, makes it difficult for some of his nieces and nephews who would like to farm.

The past two years, Riekena admits that had the couple just rented their land out to the highest bidder, they probably could have done better than they did actually farming it.

The problem: "I wouldn't want to rent to the highest bidder because that would be one of those corporations," he said.

He admits that his only other option, if the couple wishes to retire, is to rent the farm "at somewhat of a discount to top dollar to some of your neighbors—younger people."

Right now, that's what he would prefer to do when the time comes, but "you never know. You can't blame people either." Some, who have a limited amount of land, may need top dollar to live comfortably.

Fortunately, Harlyn said that by attending insurance seminars, he learned about the bite estate taxes threatened to take from his estate. In 2001, estates worth more than $675,000 are subject to estate taxes, which, without proper planning, can take as much as a 50 percent bite out of an estate. The couple had consulted an attorney. Due to a legislative change after our interview with the Riekena's, though, estate taxes are slated to be phased out, starting in 2002 to be eliminated entirely in 2010. Analysts were warning that due to a sunset provision in the new law, the tax still could be reinstated the following year.

Riekena says he purchased quite a bit of life insurance for the express purpose of paying estate taxes. "We have some life estates for passing on some of the property."

Prior to the passage of tax cut legislation, Riekena was featured in a *New York Times* article as one of the family farmers who already had protected his large estate.

Karen was surprised at the response she received from the article in her small town. The article detailed how much their land was worth. "There are some people that aren't happy for you," she said ruefully. "Everybody knows everyone too well. The one thing I could say about this is when we had these tragedies happen to us, people were great! They are not nearly as kind when good things happen to you. I feel a little bad about that. I thought I had some very good friends who I know saw the article and never mentioned it.

"There are people who are just very comfortable. They like it. We're so common, ordinary, that they were a little bit shocked to know what we might really have. They like you to be not above them. That's the way it is."

She said she was trying to ignore the reaction. "I'm also sort of a recluse. I don't go out much," she said. "I used to go. We had this group. We called it a happy hour group. I got tired of it. We talked about the same old things all the time."

The Riekenas are Lutherans, and go to church regularly. "That's the way we grew up," he said. "We're trying to increase our charity. Our major charity is the church, but then we try to have others."

Harlyn reflects on the one mistake he has seen friends make that he didn't. About 20 years ago, when rates were high, many friends were too highly leveraged. "I've just been a natural born tightwad," he said. "There've been times when debt is terrific. In general for us, we never got too deeply in debt."

Riekena says that things were a bit easier for him when he started than it is for farmers today. At this writing, prices were just way too low.

Indeed, prices have been weak since 1997 due to productivity increases, testifies Bruce A. Babcock of the Center for Agricultural and Rural Development of Iowa State University. Low prices for crops make it difficult for farmers to profit.

"I would hate to be in the position of these young farmers who were trying to get a leg up," Riekena said. "A lot of them do a really good job. It doesn't make any difference. There just is not enough income. Farm prices are just awful, really. That shows up in what the income is compared with the net worth. I don't have the answer."

Riekena says we could be on the verge of another crisis like the one farmers experienced 17 years ago. "It wouldn't take us much to get over the edge. That's when, you know, the farmland prices crashed and banks didn't have enough collateral. It got to be a vicious circle. That could happen again."

The couple says that to help cut costs they have invested $35,000 recently in a new "no-till" drill. In fact, Karen Riekena reported she would have been out using it to plant beans the day we spoke to her had it not been raining outside. "You don't have to work your fields as often and use as much fuel," Harlyn explains of the drill. "It also makes your soil less subject to water and wind erosion."

The couple, Karen says, has an employee who helped with some farmwork. "He helped with milking, too. Now, since we have just a few livestock and I take care of those, he has another job. He's mostly here for spring work and fall work."

Harlyn notes that the farm business is tough and he has made some mistakes.

"There are commodities dealers who like to have you buy hedges," he says. "I've tried that. About the most you get out of that is margin calls. That's what I've learned.

"I've told the story that by hedging my grain, I put three kids through college. Unfortunately, it was my broker's kids—not mine."

CHAPTER 13

TONY HAWK

Skateboard Millionaire

Sometimes you actually can turn a behavioral problem into a money-making opportunity. In Tony Hawk's case, the behavioral problem that caused him to turn to skateboarding was hyperactivity. It led him to become a professional skateboarder at age 14. By the time he was in high school he was making $70,000 a year and had appeared in a Mountain Dew commercial.

Today Hawk, credited with inventing more than 50 skateboard tricks, is enjoying compounded success. He and his wife, Erin, also were expecting their third child as we wrote this profile, and declined, through his publicist, to be interviewed. Unlike other team sports, which have leagues that take a cut of royalties through licensing agreements with its members, skateboarding has no such organization. So Hawk, whose Pro Skater video games have been selling out, gets to keep a larger share of his royalties. In addition, a skateboard company Hawk co-owns, Birdhouse Projects, Inc., of Huntington Valley, California, is reported to have annual sales of $10 million. Hawk also gets an estimated $1 to $1.5 million a year from product endorsements and he has a contract as a commentator for ESPN. Needless to say, the 33-year-old is a millionaire.

Tony Hawk, known for his tall 6-foot-3, lanky stature, started out as a surprise birth. He was born when his parents were in their

40s. Both spouses worked to support their family in Serra Mesa, California.

His parents just about made ends meet. In fact, he never realized until later on in life how close they were to financial insolvency, he notes in his autobiography, *Hawk Occupation: Skateboarder* (ReganBooks). His father worked as an importer and his mother, a receptionist. But they managed to raise four children.

When Hawk was born, his father had a heart attack. His mother used to joke that he had the attack when she told him she was pregnant at age 45.

Hawk's father, Frank, had been a decorated navy pilot who flew bombing missions in World War II and Korea. His mom, Nancy, worked full time. She raised the kids and took college classes at night school. By the time she was in her 50s, she had earned a master's degree on her own. She earned her doctorate in education when she was 62.

Hawk was a handful. As a child, he decided he wanted to teach math, so he set up school in his backyard. He had an IQ of 144 and a mind of his own. He reported that he threw temper tantrums, and often went into a rage when he did not get what he wanted. He even was expelled from preschool.

His parents obtained a psychological evaluation of Hawk because of his problem behavior. The results: at 8 years old he had the mind of a 12-year-old. His young body could not keep up with what his mind wanted him to do, which made him highly frustrated and angry.

Sometimes the little things in life can make all the difference in how a child develops mentally and physically. One small event changed Tony's life forever.

In 1977, when Hawk was 9 years old, his older brother, Steve, gave him an old blue Bahne fiberglass skateboard. Hawk's dad had built a small ramp in the driveway, and Hawk had finally found an outlet for his pent-up energy. He loved skateboarding and spent all his time practicing.

Because all his energy went into skateboarding, Hawk's personality started to improve. But it wasn't easy. He was a small skinny child. The other kids at school made fun of him. Although he was a top student, he felt like an outsider and didn't talk to anyone.

Many high-strung children can calm down once they find an outlet. But in Hawk's case, skateboarding became a passion that drove his life. Successful people often find role models to inspire them. In Hawk's case, his role models were the big kids at the skate park.

Hawk began skateboarding at a local park and made friends. He admired the big kids who were doing tricks on their skateboards. He learned skateboard tricks, like flips and spins, and taught himself new ones.

Vertical skateboarding is done on a U-shaped concrete or plywood ramp, called a half-pipe. Skaters gain momentum by riding up and down the curved sides of the ramp, and then launch themselves into the air where they can do flips, twists, and aerial maneuvers.

The first tricks Hawk learned as a child were called "fakies" and "rock and rolls." In a rock and roll, a skater reaches the top of the U-shaped ramp, slips the skateboard on the lip of the ramp, turns 180 degrees, and skates back down the ramp. When a skater slides the skateboard across the top of the ramp and then skates back down, it's called a fakie. In another trick called "Airs," a skater shoots up the ramp, becomes airborne, and lands at the bottom of the ramp.

It took many hours—and bumps and bruises—to learn those basic tricks. Skateboarding is not like golf. If you miss and land on the concrete or wood ramp you can cut yourself, sprain an ankle, or break bones.

Hawk says his parents, nevertheless, were very supportive of his efforts in the sport, which helped him excel. Hawk's father, initially a Little League baseball coach, was a major influence on his life. When Hawk took to skateboarding, his father shifted gears from Little League to skateboarding. He supported his son completely and ultimately founded the National Skateboarding Association. Every day his father drove him to the now-defunct Oasis SkatePark in Mission Valley, the local skateboarding park where Hawk learned many of his skills.

His father also began driving him to amateur contests throughout California. At age 12 he was considered one of the best amateur skaters in the state and was sponsored by Dogtown Skateboards. Two years later, he became a professional.

Skateboarding, due to its high risk, is not exactly a mainstream sport. In fact, it often was banned in public places. Hawk is reported to have received at least a dozen tickets for endangering public safety in the San Diego area. When Hawk attended San Dieguito High School Academy in Encinitas, it was reported that teachers regularly confiscated his skateboard. His father even was summoned to a lecture on the evils of skateboarding. Today, that very same school offers its students a rare course in skateboarding.

Hawk has admitted the stiff price he has paid for developing his unusual skill. He has had several fractured ribs, a broken elbow, teeth knocked out three times, compressed vertebrae, popped bursas, more than 50 stitches on his shins, torn cartilage, a bruised tailbone, sprains, and torn ligaments. He also has been knocked unconscious at least ten times.

But Hawk, who passed a high school equivalency exam in his freshman year, did not buy the bad rap that had been given to his favorite sport. Although he heeded his parents' wishes and finished high school, he put all his energy into skateboarding. In fact, by the time he was 16, he was considered one of the best skateboarders in the world. In his senior year at Torrey Pines High School in Del Mar, California, he paid $124,000 for his own home with funds he earned from his tournaments, product endorsements, and royalties. A couple of years later, he rented out his house and bought a larger home on five acres near Fallbrook, California.

Hawk had calmed down dramatically once he devoted himself to skateboarding. "Spending all my time at the park changed my perspective on life," Hawk wrote in his book. "I was a skater, and inside the Oasis gates age didn't matter as much as in the outer world. Older skaters who were a bit on the rowdy side became my friends. I never had problems with any of them."

Hawk also was greatly influenced by *Skateboarder* magazine. What inspired him was the magazine's pictures of amateur kids from around the world doing skateboard tricks.

All his practice paid off. Over his entire 18-year professional career, Hawk won 73 of 103 contests. He had 19 second place finishes.

In the 1980s, he became the first person to do the "720" trick, in which he shot off the ramp and did two somersaults on the skateboard before landing. He also did the "540 McTwist," which is a 1½ rotation flying off the skateboard ramp, with a flip which occurs in the middle of the rotation. In 1999, he was the first to do the "900 trick," which is 2½ somersaults on a skateboard.

Hawk's professional skating career blossomed in the 1980s. He was the National Skateboard Association's championship skateboarder year in and year out for more than a decade. He was part of the Powell Corporation skateboard team. At the time, Powell was the top manufacturer of skateboards and accessories. Hawk traveled the world competing in tournaments and giving skateboard exhibitions. He made a number of videos. In his senior year of high school, he was collecting $7,000 a month in royalties. He also had his own skateboard brand.

Hawk attributes a large part of his success to the support of his parents. Skateboarders in the 1980s were a motley rebellious crew. But Hawk's parents always had his skateboard friends over to his house. His father's National Skateboard Association sponsored skateboard competitions nationwide.

"My parents helped skaters out whenever they could," Hawk said in his book. "They'd pick them up at airports and give them rides to contests. They would let them stay at our house and feed them. Skaters slept in bathtubs, closets, the garage . . ."

Being young with plenty of money, though, was a recipe for disaster. Hawk built a humongous skate ramp in his backyard. The house was full of skaters and there were plenty of parties. People were coming and going at all hours. When he went on elaborate vacations he often paid for his friends to join him. He bought a

Lexus. He would spend thousands of dollars at electronic stores. At age 19, he was getting royalties from skateboard videos and money from winning tournaments. By the end of 1988, at age 20, he was making $100,000 a year and had a steady girlfriend, Cindy.

The events that followed would turn Hawk into a man. He married Cindy in 1990—just when an economic recession hit. The skateboard industry was hit particularly hard. The skate park business began to slow, while insurance premiums rose through the roof. Hawk began to worry about money.

He had two mortgages and never had been thrifty. He frequently ate meals out, and was known to spend as much as one month's worth of royalties on gadgets at The Sharper Image.

The reckless spending caught up with him. By mid-1990, the skateboard business had died. Hawk's royalty checks were cut in half. There were fewer tournaments. Plus, demos and touring stopped. Skateboard companies that sponsored skaters and events were losing money. When he did demonstrations, only about 30 or 40 people would show up. In the past, he had been drawing crowds of 2,000.

Skateboarding's reputation became even more tarnished when Mark Anthony "Gator" Rogowski, one of skateboarding's biggest stars, was convicted of murdering a woman in his Carlsbad, California, condominium. The case fostered the perception that skateboarding is antisocial and marketing that targets young male skateboarders encourages bad behavior.

Hawk said he made $70,000 in 1990. He and Cindy started living on a tight budget. It got worse in 1991, the year after he married Cindy, a manicurist. She became the breadwinner in the family, and gave Hawk an allowance of $5 a day so he could eat at Taco Bell—one of his favorite restaurants. He sold his Fallbrook house because he could not afford the $3,000-a-month mortgage.

He moved into his Carlsbad home and refinanced the property. He also downsized his Lexus.

Although Hawk was down, he was not completely out. Although money was tight, he kept on promoting to keep his name in the public eye. It was a smart strategy because once the economy improved, he was fresh in the public's mind and ready to take advantage of opportunities.

In 1992, the couple had a child, Riley. Although Hawk skipped college, he formed a company, Birdhouse Projects, with Per Welinder, a former skateboarder who had a master's degree in business administration. By refinancing his Carlsbad home, Hawk had freed up $40,000, which he invested in his fledgling business. But he was worried. If it didn't work, he'd have to declare bankruptcy.

"It was definitely a risk, but if there was ever a time to start a company, it was then," he later told Skateboard.com. "It didn't take as much money. . . . It was also easier to advertise because most of the magazines were hurting for money."

The goal had been to "start a skateboard company with a positive image and [one that] was based on skateboarding and good skateboarding products and not on imagery or shock value," he told the *Morning Call* (Allentown, Pennsylvania).

Hawk was then 24. Most of his endorsement money had dried up. His company was paying him $30,000 annually, which only covered the mortgage and utility bills. His wife Cindy had to pick up the slack.

Business got so bad that Powell Corp. stopped sponsoring skateboard tours. So Hawk formed his own low-budget tour—aimed at keeping his name in the public eye—and earned money freelance-editing videos.

He rented a cheap van and toured the east coast and Midwest. In hotels, he would sneak as many as seven other skaters into the room. They lived on fast food—mostly Taco Bell. Half of the time they did shows, they did not get paid. Later, he and Cindy rented a minivan and did another tour. They lived on fast food and performed before sparse crowds. Both tours lost money.

Hawk has admitted to the *Orange County Register* that his major mistake was that he didn't save enough money. Also, "I lent my name to some bad companies."

Hawk went though financial hardships in the early '90s before things improved. But his life story is not a fairytale. He learned to live with major disappointments.

The hardships had put a tremendous strain on his marriage and he and his wife divorced in 1994. Just as things started to turn around, he was dealt another devastating blow. His father was diagnosed with terminal cancer. He passed away three years later at age 68.

Hawk still was doing a lot of free work when he met his second wife, Erin, at a paid event sponsored by Charles Schultz, the creator of Peanuts. But what really triggered a renaissance in skateboarding was a series of ESPN sports events called the "Extreme Games."

Extreme Games was a new concept in sports. Unlike the traditional team sports of baseball, basketball, and football, extreme sports include those with high risk, such as skateboarding, snowboarding, stunt biking, and mountain biking.

In the show that featured skateboarding, Hawk won the vertical skating contest. ESPN focused on him as the star of the event.

Right after the Extreme Games, Hawk spent some time with his dying father. He wanted to cancel his next tour, but he obeyed his father, who had encouraged him to go. That had been the last time he saw his beloved father alive.

It's not easy for a son to lose a father who has helped him succeed. All of a sudden he isn't around to give you advice and support when you need it. You have to go it alone based on what he taught you and what you've learned from life.

What Hawk learned was to fight and compete. His tenacity finally started paying off. His company's business picked up dramatically after the ESPN event in 1995. Business grew and, in 1996, Hawk married Erin, a former professional skater. Three years later, their son, Spencer, was born.

Disney's ESPN continued broadcasting what it now calls the "X Games," which has helped to dramatically boost the popularity of skateboarding. Hawk was so busy with promotions, interviews, and competition that he hired his sister, Pat, as his manager.

His company, Birdhouse, began to sponsor more elaborate tours because business was booming again. Hawk handled the marketing, skateboarding, and media, while his partner, Per Wielander, managed the business end. The company often sponsored skateboard events. Hawk became so popular and was being offered so many deals, that he signed up with the William Morris Agency, Inc. of New York. He attained national attention when he became the first person to perform the 900 skateboard trick at ESPN's 1999 X Games.

Activison produced a Tony Hawk Pro Skater video game which became the bestselling game the Christmas of 1999. He started a clothing company called Hawk Clothing which was purchased by Quicksilver in 2000. Meanwhile his book, *Hawk Occupation: Skateboarder,* hit the *New York Times* bestseller list.

Hawk retired from skateboard competition in 1999 to spend more time with his family. He still does exhibitions and demos, and he signed a three-year contract with ESPN in 2000 to be a commentator for skateboard competitions. The deal, reported to have garnered him at least $1 million, makes him a commentator, an online reporter, and creator of a 12-city televised tour of the nation's skateboard parks, according to *USA Today.* It also restricts Hawk's skating to ESPN events.

Hawk is particularly proud of the fact that he has turned skateboarding, which to this day is prohibited in many areas, into his career.

As we wrote this chapter, Hawk was on a major roll. *American Demographics* reported that the growth of skateboarding was outpacing team sports. "Skateboarding increased by 49 percent to 12 million enthusiasts, far outpacing tackle football, which grew by only 15 percent to 6 million players in 2000," the publication said.

Generation Y males, it added, "are driving much of the growth in extreme sports, which appeal to individuals with a need for speed."

Hawk has been capitalizing big time on this trend. In 1998, he signed a $120,000 deal with the shoemaker Adio. The world's first Hawk Skate Shop also opened in New Jersey. The shop was opened by Quiksilver, Inc., the company that, in 2000, acquired Hawk Designs, Inc., the maker of signature skateboard apparel bearing the name of Tony Hawk.

Activision continues to release new versions of the Tony Hawk Pro Skater video games, and Swatch issued a Tony Hawk watch.

He has appeared in a "Got Milk" magazine ad, and in a Gap TV commercial.

"I have to credit my agents for creating the financial situation I enjoy right now," Hawk said in his autobiography. "There are numerous times I receive substantial money for something I would have previously done for free or a minimal charge."

Skateboarding, though, remains a bit different from most other sports. Apart from its riskiness and the lack of an organized league structure, it also has an antiestablishment air. It is not uncommon to see "no skateboarding" signs in public places.

Yet, it is regarded as an honest sport, in that, without any organized leagues, it is open to virtually anyone who wants to participate. Hawk has received some criticism for making it a bit commercial.

In fact, *USA Today* noted that in 1998 and 1999, readers of *Big Brother* skateboarding magazine picked Hawk as their "most hated skater." To those who believe he has sold out, Hawk responds that he hasn't. Rather, mainstream media has bought in, the newspaper reports.

He also has come under fire for photos of him in the media in which he appears without a helmet. *People* magazine responded to one such letter, explaining that Hawk actually does wear a helmet, but did not happen to have it on for the photo shoot.

He is reported to be extremely loyal to friends, and he claims that he is very picky about his causes. He has appeared in a "Wipe Out" commercial, which is sponsored by the California office of the Secretary of Education, aimed at getting young boys to read. "I wanted to get involved in READ California because it's important to encourage kids to read," he said.

He says he is a logical spokesman for the campaign because it was the reading of *Skateboarder* magazine at age 9, he claimed, that changed his life.

He also has said that he is very careful about the use of his name, although he's not concerned about getting big money for events related to skateboarding. His agent, Brian Dubin of the William Morris Agency, told the *Orange County Register* in 2000 that "the vast majority [of deals] are turned down, such as a recent offer from a pasta manufacturer interested in making Tony-shaped pasta."

It also was reported that he turned down a tour of the Far East because the sponsor would have been a tobacco company.

But although Hawk declined the deal for Tony-shaped pasta, he did agree, according to *Advertising Age,* to be featured in a $6 million TV campaign for H. J. Heinz Co.'s new line of Ore-Ida Hot Bites frozen snacks.

In the early 1990s, Tony Hawk was in financially sad shape. Nevertheless, he had the insight to hire the right people and managers to capitalize on the growing interest in skateboarding. He publicly stated in mid-2001 that his video games were his most lucrative project. Activision reports that Hawk had developed Pro Skater games for a number of platforms, and was about to launch Pro Skater 3. Hawk consulted in the making of the games. "Tony plays the game throughout the development cycle and makes comments/ suggestions where he likes," the company reported. His franchise, Activision reports, has sold close to eight million copies of the game on various platforms worldwide.

Hawk was planning on doing more behind-the-scenes work in the video world by developing skate instructional videos through a film production company he formed with some friends, 900 Films.

CHAPTER 14

VENUS AND SERENA WILLIAMS

Young Tennis Stars Make Millions

Practice to perfection coupled with the signing of a good management company has been instrumental in allowing sisters Venus, 21, and Serena Williams, 20, to rake in millions at a young age.

The African American tennis star sisters, while still students at the Art Institute of Fort Lauderdale, became the two highest-paid female athletes in the world. In 2001, *Business Week* reported that six-foot-two-inch Venus, who won Wimbledon for the second year in a row in 2001, would earn $20 million annually over the next few years. Five-foot-ten-inch Serena, who stunned the world by winning the U.S. Open singles title in 1999, was slated to bring in $16 million annually.

Starting the high-stakes money race was a record-breaking $40 million contract Venus Williams signed with Reebok. The deal, for at least three years, was hailed as a gargantuan step in women's quest to catch up with the financial success male athletes already have enjoyed. Golf star Tiger Woods, by comparison, had a $100 million deal with rival Nike. Basketball star Michael Jordan's three-year income after retirement was reported to be $40 million.

Serena Williams has a five-year $15 million contract with Puma and the two together have a $10 million pact with the Wrigley Co. The two girls also were promoting Nortel Networks Corp., a Sega video game, and Avon Products, Inc.

All this was on top of their tournament winnings, which tallied $8 million for Venus Williams and $4.7 million for Serena Williams through July 2001. The two sisters moved from their parents' home into a home they built on a half-million-dollar lot in the plush gated community of Ballen Isles in Palm Beach Gardens, Florida. The sisters have had the good fortune of building their wealth at a young age. Financial planners often advise that the earlier you start investing money, the more time you have for it to grow exponentially. However, the Williams sisters have come a long way to obtain their riches.

Venus and Serena are the youngest of five children of Richard and Oracene Williams. They grew up living in a grafitti-strewn neighborhood in the predominantly black Los Angeles suburb of Compton, California. They began hitting tennis balls on broken-down tennis courts over patched-up nets.

Their father, Richard, was one of five children of a Shreveport, Louisiana, single mother. He owned a security company, Samson Security, and was a former basketball player. Published reports indicated he was a high school dropout. Others say he had enrolled at Southwest College and later L.A. City School of Business. The girls' mother, the former Oracene Price, of Saginaw, Michigan, a nurse, had obtained degrees in education and nursing from Eastern Michigan University.

It's hard to distinguish, though, what is fact and what is fiction in the upbringing of the two sisters, who have attracted worldwide attention for their style, independence, and intelligence.

One thing is clear. Their father, Richard, is the most outspoken of the Williams sisters' parents. He took control of their careers at a very young age. In fact, he has said that he went so far as to deliberately get his wife pregnant with two more daughters after he saw the whopping $30,000 check won in a tennis tournament by a player named Virginia Ruzici. Piquing his interest was the fact that the tennis pro won the money for playing a mere four days. The check, he said, dwarfed his own annual earnings. He reports that he went so far as to hide his wife's birth control pills to get her pregnant with

Serena. He subscribed to tennis magazines and rented videos to teach himself the game he once had labeled a sissy sport.

Richard Williams has reported that the girls played in an area where gangs created trouble. In fact, published reports have said, a round of shots actually was fired while they were playing near a street gang, known as the Bloods. The girls had to take cover on the ground. Other reports were that Richard Williams got gang members to stand guard over his daughters while they played.

The girls, though, have denied any reports of violence in a more recent interview with *Essence* magazine.

Then, there is information that indicates the opposite extreme about the Williams family. "Most people thought we were living in Compton because we couldn't do any better," *Women's Sports* and *Fitness* claims Richard Williams told that publication in 1998. "Everyone thought we were poor, that tennis was our way out. It was not . . . I wanted to give the Weinsteins, the Rubensteins, the I-forget-the-other-Steins, competition. So I went there and bought a few hundred, about a hundred homes."

The conflicting and sometimes outlandish stories told by Richard Williams actually prompted *Time* magazine to call Williams "a piece of work" and an "odd duck."

One thing seems clear, though. Both Venus and Serena truly loved the game of tennis. Venus started playing when she was four. Her father reported that she would hit 1,000 balls across the net and immediately demand 1,000 more—even though she might miss some. He also talks about how much she complained at age five when he took away her tennis racket for one year.

The move was part of an effort to make certain his daughter kept tennis in its proper perspective. "When someone loves something to much," he told *People* magazine, "it's more detrimental than a person who doesn't love it at all."

Serena started joining her sister on the courts at age five. Both Venus and Serena, Richard Williams later told the *Los Angles Times,* practiced with flat tennis balls in Compton. "If they would get to the dead balls, it would make them faster than anybody else."

Young Tennis Stars Make Millions

Although Venus excelled at tennis, that was not the only sport at which she excelled. She also was reported at one point to be undefeated in track. At age ten, she opted to focus on tennis because she reported that she thought she could be the best at the game.

The public grew especially fond of the Williams family when published reports seemed to indicate how well the girls were brought up. For one thing, the family was raised staunchly in the faith of Jehovah's Witnesses.

Jehovah's Witnesses have no churches. Instead they meet in buildings, called Kingdom Halls. All Jehovah's Witnesses are considered ministers of the gospel, so there are no ministers in the faith. In fact, Serena Williams once was reported to be handing out Jehovah's Witnesses literature to her classmates at the Art Institute of Fort Lauderdale.

The religious sect refuses to bear arms in war or to participate in government. Members won't salute the flag and they refuse blood transfusions. In fact, the Jehovah's Witnesses, who believe the second coming of Christ has started, are considered pioneers in paving the way to freedom of speech. They fiercely fought in court the many challenges that their activities have drawn over the years.

While a Jehovah's Witness, Richard Williams has been reported to smoke cigarettes. The faith was reported to be primarily that of the girls' mother.

Besides their religious faith, the Williams family became revered for their family values. No one was permitted to answer the phone before 10:00 AM, so that the family could be together at breakfast. Bedtime was reported to be 9:00 PM.

Venus Williams hit the *New York Times* in 1990 slightly more than one month past her tenth birthday. She had just won her seventeenth singles title in less than a year. The tournament had attracted 1,900 entries.

To raise money for the tournaments, the *New York Times* reported, Richard Williams and his wife had distributed a brochure to potential sponsors outlining long-range goals.

The following year, Venus Williams was on the front page of the *New York Times*. Dubbed a prodigy and as "ghetto Cinderella," she had been shutting out others her own age on California's junior tennis circuit.

Richard Williams, despite certain exaggerations about his young five-foot-four-inch prodigy, made his priorities for his children clear to the media early on. "We put God first, then comes the family, her education, and her tennis," he brazenly told the *New York Times*. The newspaper had been questioning the ethics of all the agents who were courting the young Venus Williams. Among them, it said, were International Management Group, ProServe, and Advantage International.

That *New York Times* article was to be the earliest of a series that questioned the wisdom of dangling millions of dollars in checks before such young tennis prodigies. The courtships came as the game of tennis desperately sought new young blood to revitalize interest in the sport. The controversy intensified after fast-rising tennis star Jennifer Capriati, who won the French and Australian Opens in 2001, turned pro at age 14. During her early years, before her recent success on the tennis circuit, she was reported to have been suspended from the tour and arrested on a charge of possession of marijuana. Observers had cited the tremendous pressures that turning professional can place on a young teenager. Richard Williams himself reported he had noticed that Capriati's smile had disappeared by age 15.

Stan Smith, the former Wimbledon champion and U.S. Tennis Association's head coach for junior-play development, criticized four hours a day of training for children between the ages of 10 and 12. Such a grueling schedule, he said, risks injury as well as a loss of balance in their lives.

The drain of early competition on the parents' pocketbooks also was attacked. In 1992, entry fees were reported to be $16 to $20 per tournament. Expenses, the *New York Times* indicated, could run $10,000 to $35,000 annually.

Despite all the criticism and a proclamation by Richard Williams early on that promoters were sharks that deserve to be shot, Venus Williams appeared to have endorsements at an early age. Reebok claims it has had a relationship with Venus Williams since she was 11. She had been in the Reebok Jr. Tennis Program, which provides athletic footwear and apparel to underprivileged and promising youths who possess a passion for tennis. By the time Venus was 13, the U.S. Tennis Association had offered the Williams family "unconditional assistance."

The family moved to Florida—initially, Pompano Beach—so the girls could get better training. Williams family lawyer, Keven Davis, told the *New York Times* that the Williamses had a "personal services contract" that paid back Venus's Delray Beach, Florida, tennis coach, Richard Macci, when she became a star. There also was an agreement between Richard Williams and Reebok, which provided his family with sports gear "in return for his assistance at inner-city tennis clinics."

In that same *New York Times* article, Richard Williams fended off pressure to have Venus turn pro at age 14. "I want her to wait until she's 16," he said firmly. "I'm sick of looking around tennis and seeing these poor kids making a living for their parents."

Fortunately, Richard Williams had made his point to his children at a young age. Tennis wasn't everything. In fact, he was reported to have told his daughters that athletes are dumb. His strategy worked. As early as age ten, Venus Williams had indicated that although she loved tennis, her goal was to be an astronaut. After that, she had changed her mind, and decided she'd prefer to be an archaeologist. Later on, a report indicated she wanted to be a paleontologist. Serena initially had hoped to be a veterinarian. Both girls read quite a bit, studied languages, and obeyed their father's orders that they limit daily tennis practice. Both girls were reported to be straight A students.

The girls' three older sisters subsequently pursued professional careers. Yetunde is in the medical field, Isha is reported to be doing work for the family as an attorney, and Lyndrea is in computer services.

In 1994, it was reported that if Venus Williams could bring home a straight A report card, her father would allow her to become a professional tennis player. Later that year, Richard Williams confessed that Venus had overruled him in her desire to turn pro. "She feels so strongly about it that I feel like I should support her ideal," he told the *New York Times*.

Her decision to turn pro surprised many because it came after she hadn't played in a tournament for three years! Generally, heavier competition in junior leagues was the way most young pros move up through the ranks. The decision also came just before new rules were slated to be implemented that would have made it difficult for such a young woman to turn pro. In fact, Richard Williams later had threatened to sue the World Tennis Association if it refused to let Serena turn pro.

In addition, the family was reported to have had a falling out with Richard Macci, who had been training the girls. Reports indicated that the Williamses ultimately withdrew from his tutelage because they did not want the girls to practice quite as much as Macci desired. "If they didn't like what I was doing, why did they pay me so much for so long?" Macci responded to the *Wall Street Journal*. The girls also trained with another top tennis coach, Nick Bollettieri.

Once Venus turned pro, she signed a $12-million, five-year deal with Reebok. That was the precursor to her more lucrative $40-million deal.

You'd think that if two sisters played tennis that there would be some jealousy between them, or, at least some partiality shown by their parents. But early on, Richard Williams, when complimented on the talent of Venus, often would respond, "Wait until you see Serena!" Never, in published reports, has he shown favoritism for either daughter.

Serena is reported to be more outgoing than Venus. But the sisters also are very close and family members are extremely protective of one another.

"Family comes first, no matter how many times we play each other," Serena told *Sports Illustrated* in 1999. "Nothing will come between me and my sister." Serena has reported that Venus knew her sister would one day take a match from her and had prepared for it. In September 2001, the two sisters met in the finals of the U.S. Open, in which big sister Venus prevailed.

The two also were reported to own a home in Palm Beach Gardens. In fact, often the two would giggle to one another, as if they purposely were excluding the rest of the outside world from their jokes. They also have been criticized for being "standoffish."

It has been a subject of dispute as to whether their aloofness and personal jokes reflected a unique sense of comraderie. Some have called their withdrawal a desire not to ruin their concentration on the sport. Yet other reports indicate it reflects their disenchantment with a white sports world and white media. The two often were reported as very quiet during media interviews. Through their agent, IMG, Cleveland, they declined to be interviewed for this chapter. The reason: It was reported that it would conflict with a book deal that the Williams family had in the works.

Many have argued that the sisters are responding naturally to a difficult situation and are being unfairly judged. Their quietness merely may be a classy way of coping with innate racism in a country club sport.

At least one African American tennis father tried to put the sport's racism into perspective through a piece he wrote in the *New York Times*. "Tennis, unlike baseball, basketball, or football, is not a team sport," explained William Washington. "You must look to your family for everything. There is no support group to bring you in out of the cold."

If you play tennis, Washington complained, you must leave your neighborhood and join a country club group with which you don't belong. "They let you know it in a variety of ways, so you go in, compete, and leave."

Washington complained that even if a black tennis player has a better ranking than white peers, the same endorser that signs the white player expects the black player to continue on at "junior" level money. Then, he reports, the first question posed by the white media is whether there is any discrimination in the game. That, he claimed, is like asking, 'Is water wet?'"

The Williams sisters, though, had to overcome a double whammy. They not only are African Americans, but they also are women. They have complained repeatedly about the fact that women receive less prize money than their male counterparts. In 1999, when the men's Wimbledon winning prize money was listed as $728,000, it was reported that the women's winner was to earn $655,200.

Serena Williams told the *Palm Beach Post:* "It's pretty disappointing. I know for a fact that I'm working just as hard as Pete Sampras or whoever."

Allegations of racism permeated other areas of their lives. Richard Williams came under fire in 1998 when he called one of Venus's opponents, Irina Spirlea, "a big, tall, white turkey." The remark came after Venus collided with her. Richard Williams later apologized for the remark. But the incident has been discussed in the media for years.

More recently, Richard Williams complained that he heard the "n-word" used at least a dozen times at Indian Wells, California. The sisters had been booed there in March 2001 after Venus, citing a knee injury, withdrew from a semifinal match against Serena—giving just four minutes notice.

He also often spoke about the rude racial remarks parents of white players in junior tournaments would make concerning their young African American opponents.

Serena Williams acknowledged to the *Palm Beach Post* that although she did not hear the "n-word" at Indian Wells, racism exists. "African Americans—we've been out of slavery for just over 100 years . . . we all know there is racism in America, and that's just a fact."

Venus Williams responded that she heard "whatever" her father heard.

While the Williams sisters are successful financially, there are some downsides to their wealth. The girls, who are in tremendous demand, have little time to socialize. To excel in a sport requires much practice and often, they are under tremendous pressure to perform when they are injured or not feeling well.

It can be a traumatic experience to disappoint millions of fans by not showing up for a high-profile tournament. Venus Williams reported that she used to have to play with tendinitis in her knee. She subsequently withdrew from five tournaments in 2000 due to tendinitis in her wrists. During her downtime, she said she took a fashion course. Her mother had reported that Venus actually played tennis too long as her wrist conditions worsened. She had tried various treatments, including acupuncture, before withdrawing from competition.

Around the same time, Venus's father began publicly calling for her to retire from the sport. Thanks to the planning the family has done for the girls, he said, neither needs tennis any more.

Venus, who said she had no plans to quit, came under fire yet again when she announced in June 2001 that she would not play for two weeks at the Italian Open due to a knee injury.

Serena Williams had similar experiences. She was reported to have pulled a muscle on the right side of her neck while losing to Jennifer Capriati in the Ericsson Open in Key Biscayne, Florida, in March 2000.

Although the sisters' injuries and tournament withdrawals made their fans angry, the injuries also drew the attention of the American Academy of Pediatrics. The organization in July 2000 attacked the intensive training and sports specialization in young athletes. It warned of the health risks—including physical and mental burnout—that can affect children who focus too heavily on sports at an early age.

"Overuse injuries [such as tendinitis, apophysitis, stress fractures] can be consequences of excessive sports training in child and adult athletes," they said in their statement. "Certain aspects of the growing athlete may predispose the child and adolescent to repetitive stress injuries."

The report went on to discourage pushing children beyond their abilities and interests as well as "specialization in a single sport before adolescence."

It advised that the child athlete should be coached by people knowledgeable in proper training techniques and equipment as well as each child's unique physical and emotional characteristics. Child athletes, it claimed, never should be encouraged to "work through" injuries of repetitive stress. Rather, rest is advised. The group advised parents and trainers to be alert for signs and symptoms of overtraining, "including decline in performance, weight loss, anorexia, and sleep disturbances." Plus, it advised that pediatricians should educate the child athlete and family about the risks of heat injury and strategy for prevention.

As if the injuries weren't enough, the William sisters' increasingly frequent withdrawals from tournaments also brought charges of match fixing. There were charges that the sisters purposely were dropping out of tournaments so they would not have to compete against each other.

In 1999, when Serena dropped out of Wimbledon with the flu five days before she would have had to play, speculation was rampant. While many contended that she did so to avoid a face off early in the tournament with her sister, others charged that her father did not want the sisters to play.

The most brutal attack came in the *National Enquirer* in March 2001, which quoted the sisters' live-in nephew as saying Richard Williams had ordered Serena to lose to her sister in the Wimbledon semifinals.

The family and their attorney, Keven Davis, who has represented Tonya Harding, publicly denied the charges emphatically.

"My response is that the accusation is false; that it's not true," Venus Williams told the *Palm Beach Post*. "That my dad would never do anything like that. The magazine isn't exactly top-notch or exactly credible."

Venus Williams, though, admitted that she can't help but worry about what people think. "Naturally, you don't want someone to think bad of you, especially if you think good of yourself."

Questions have been raised about how savvy the sisters were at managing their own money. While the sisters' father has publicly stated that the girls no longer needed tennis, Venus was reported to have asked former President Clinton to lower her estimated taxes.

Both sisters, it has been reported, love to shop—a hobby that has led to the financial demise of many stars. In fact, Serena admitted to having an online shopping addiction. She'd spend as many as six hours online at a time.

Plus, we happened to notice, their Palm Beach County property tax records excluded a homestead exemption. Under Florida law, homeowners are permitted to claim a property tax exemption on the first $25,000 of assessed value of their primary residence. Although there were two properties listed under the name of Venus Williams, neither was taking advantage of this tax break. The Williams' parents' homes also listed no homestead exemption, according to Palm Beach County property records.

Despite the adversity and controversy with fans, the Williams sisters' careers were blossoming.

The two sisters also were reported to be involved in charitable activities—especially for OWL, their mother's learning foundation.

They have cast aside their earlier career aspirations for careers in fashion designing. Those careers, at this writing, already were under way. The two, as they matured, worked toward their new goal. Initially, their photographs with their hair in cornrows and beads showed up in top woman fashion magazines. Venus Williams was reported to have designed her tennis clothes herself.

But it wasn't until after 1999, when the girls signed IMG, that their careers started taking off in a big way. The two, media indicated, underwent a Madison Avenue makeover.

In the same way that Gloria and Emilio Estefan had aimed to obtain crossover from the Latin music market to the English one, Venus and Serena Williams needed crossover from tennis into other areas.

After all, the girls would not be playing tennis forever.

Stephen A. Greyser, professor of consumer marketing at Harvard Business School, told the *Palm Beach Post* that Venus

Young Tennis Stars Make Millions

Williams must next sell consumer products not necessarily tied to tennis.

"At this point, she's an absolutely terrific athlete who does have some general appeal," he reported. "Until she crosses over into consumer goods rather than sports apparel, she can't yet be seen as a female Michael Jordan or Tiger Woods."

The comment came amid announcements of a string of non-sports-related contracts with the Williams family.

Perhaps the catalyst in the Williams sisters' financial lives came in 1999. That's when the sisters signed with IMG, after agent Stephanie Tolleson had been courting the sisters for six years. The agency was reported to handle their licensing, endorsements, exhibitions, personal appearances, and literary projects.

Tolleson had been quietly trying to learn what the Williams sisters wanted from their careers over the years.

The sisters, she told the *Los Angeles Times,* are being very selective. Because they attended school, they wanted deals that did not involve major time commitments. "We're looking for a few long-term deals with the right fit," Tolleson had said.

Tolleson, a former nationally ranked tennis player herself, is reported to be very good at negotiating deals because she does whatever homework is necessary. She not only goes into negotiations armed with all the statistics she needs about the sport, but she also does research into ways the company's products can be promoted with her clients.

The girls have succeeded in boosting their fashion careers by being featured in major woman's magazines—including *Vogue, Elle,* and *Essence.*

Designer Jeremy Scott made dresses inspired by them in 1999. They also have arranged for their deals to involve what they most want to do. Venus Williams, for example, has negotiated her own design line in her deal with Wilson The Leather Experts. She was planning to design an all-leather line with the help of a company designer. She also was to design apparel and footwear collec-

Young Tennis Stars Make Millions

tions for Reebok. Serena Williams was expecting her contract with Puma to fulfill her desire to get into movies.

"Right now we're sort of famous, and while you have a name, you might want to use it," Venus told *Time* magazine. "We're going to school now, and we're seen out there looking fashionable."

EPILOGUE

So what does it really take to become a millionaire? In both our *Rags to Riches* books, we found that each person who amassed at least $1 million seems to have followed an entirely different path.

There is just one set formula we conclude that can safely guarantee you a $1 million net worth. Get your income and/or assets $1 million higher than your debt!

If that seems like a tall order, we still believe there are major lessons to be learned from the people we have interviewed that can help you in this quest.

Here are some that we have taken away from our very own interviews.

- *In the hectic throes of running your own business, be sure never to overlook payments of estimated income taxes!* In *More Rags to Riches,* we noted many instances in which a mere unawareness of this pesky government-mandated responsibility got people into a great deal of hot water. Kenneth Smaltz, B.B. King, and Anthony Parks all experienced major setbacks in their lives because they neglected to pay Uncle Sam his fair share. The Internal Revenue Service reports that in its 1999 fiscal year, more than 4 percent of the 125 million individual income tax returns filed incurred estimated tax penalties.

If you're accustomed to working for a company that pays your income taxes, it's particularly easy to overlook this responsibility once you start your own business. It's also easy to get sidetracked if you're busy. Or if like many businesses, you're having cash flow problems, it's very easy to put your income taxes on the back burner.

Don't do it!

IRS spokesman Don Roberts notes that estimated taxes, filed quarterly, are an estimate, based on a projection for income during the year. "If you find that projected income doesn't materialize, you can lower estimated tax payments later in the year," he suggests. Or, if your income is much larger than projected, you can make the appropriate adjustments in estimated tax payments. You're allowed to adjust your estimated income taxes with each payment. IRS Publication 505 gives more details.

- *Hire a well-qualified manager or agent early on if you are creative or have a skill.* Too many with major opportunities let the nuts and bolts of their finances go by the wayside for too long. You want the right person to make important deals, promote your products, and guide your career. You also want to make certain you don't miss a beat when it comes to growing your money and saving in taxes. We heard this tale repeatedly both in *Rags to Riches* and *More Rags to Riches*. B.B. King, Chi Chi Rodriguez, and Tony Hawk are among those that claimed hiring the right managers turned their financial lives around. B.B. King says he hired Sid Seidenberg, although he now is managed by Lieberman Management Ltd. Seidenberg set it up so that King, who was having a hard time getting noticed, appeared as the opening act for popular groups like the Rolling Stones and Eric Clapton. Tony Hawk, the famous skateboard champion, didn't get the ball rolling until he hired his sister, Pat Hawk, to manage his financial affairs.

Then he hooked up with the nationally known William Morris Agency to handle his endorsement deals and a big-city public relations firm, Sarah Hall Productions, to do publicity. He also linked with a former skateboarding buddy, who had a master's degree in business administration, to launch his skateboard manufacturing business.

Tennis stars Venus and Serena Williams, based upon our research, were just beginning to get the proper management team rolling.

- *If you take a job, make sure it's with the right company.* Do some homework so you can find a well-managed company where you can move up in the organization. Look through the company's annual report and talk to competitors—as if you were an investor. We credit Mary E. Foley with that advice. Foley knows. She had the farsightedness to work for America Online.

- *When it comes to a job, it's important to follow your passion.* Many told us this over and over again. Find work that you love and give 110 percent. Angela Adair-Hoy always loved writing. She worked on her high school newspaper. Later she did some TV work. After a divorce, the single mom went to work for an online company. She got the experience she needed and launched a successful online publishing company that's worth close to $5 million today. Kenneth Smaltz cut his teeth selling rare coins with several small companies. Now he's a partner in New World Rarities, a prestigious New York rare coin company. And Donna M. Auguste never let anyone discourage her from her passion—computer engineering.

- *Do not let a handicap or disadvantage stop you from making something of yourself.* African Americans Anthony Parks and Ken Smaltz did not let racial discrimination prevent them from doing a good job. The more discrimination they experienced, the more they put their noses to the grindstone. They let sales numbers do the talking for them. No one could argue with their success because money knows no color.

- *Be alert to opportunities and take decisive action.* Harlyn Riekena, a small-town Iowa farmer who eked out a living, knew rich farmland would be worth a fortune one day. So he and his wife, bought land a little bit at a time. Now the land is worth $2 million. Corporate agribusinesses are driving up land prices in the area. Paul Kieffer also knew a good opportunity when he saw one. He borrowed against his home to obtain a prime location for his now highly successful Red Wing shoe store. Joe Kruse, a retired commercial carpet salesmen, saw the opportunity for unlimited sales if he got his carpet specified by architects and designers rather than focusing on middlemen dealers. His insight paid off.

- *Don't fool yourself into thinking that money will bring you genuine friendship or solve all your family's problems.* Anthony Parks made about $5 million when he sold his Web company's stock. He lent less-fortunate friends a total of $400,000. Hardly anyone has paid him back. Although he isn't bothering them for the money, the borrowers, whom he had considered his friends, mysteriously have lost touch.

   Research by Thomas J. Stanley and William D. Danko, authors of *The Millionaire Next Door* (Times Books), seems to confirm that giving family members or friends money doesn't necessarily help. The majority of millionaires, they say, got no handouts from families.

   Giving cash can hurt in several ways, the two report. First, it depletes the gift giver's nest egg, which, in the long run, could make it more difficult to afford a comfortable retirement. Second, recipients of cash gifts rarely invest the money. Your hard-earned cash—when given as a gift—generally gets spent. Third, it fosters a lifestyle based upon buying things, which does not exactly help anyone looking to build wealth.

In *More Rags to Riches*, we continued to hear some similar themes among the wealthy that we heard in our first book. Among them:

- Many of our subjects did not necessarily set out to become wealthy. They took small but significant steps to advance themselves.

- Many told us they read a lot and/or learned from others.

- Many related stories about the evils of personal debt. However, unlike in our first *Rags to Riches* book, we actually found certain cases, such as that of B.B. King, where debt long has been a way of life. It did not necessarily stop him from ultimately building an unusually high net worth.

- Setting goals, we heard a few times, often helps. Even if you don't meet your goal, notes Paul Kieffer, at least you're further along than most people who don't set goals.

- Strong family support is important. Many of our subjects, again, cited family members who encouraged them along the way.

We enjoyed talking to these people—initially strangers—about their lives. We also thank you for the phone calls and e-mails we received as a result of our first book. One reader reported that she and her husband started buying real estate. They now have several properties and have moved from the 15 percent tax bracket into the 28 percent tax bracket. They are well on their way, we hope, to building a fortune.

Please, if you do get inspired by this book, however, do not neglect to plan for a worst-case scenario. As we learned the hard way in 2001, the stock market does not always go up. Neither does the real estate market.

While many have succeeded by taking risks, it also pays to have a backup plan in case things don't always go your way.

Diversification—or mixing up your investments—is another tactic that can help protect you from a downturn.

And patience, over the long term, with virtually any type of good well-researched investment also can help.

We sincerely hope *More Rags to Riches* has an impact on your life. Even if you don't become a millionaire, financial security is important. Sigmund Freud once said that love, work, and faith in God are the cornerstones of a healthy life. If you have all of these things, you might not become fabulously wealthy, but you will never be a loser.

REFERENCES

6. Gloria and Emilio Estefan

Ackerman, Elise. "Land of Opportunity." *Miami New Times,* 28 December 1995.

Barciela, Susana. "'The Miami Sound' Gets a Boost: Emilio Estefan, Sony to Sign Deal." *Miami Herald,* 8 January 1994, 1A.

Barciela, Susana. "The Star Maker." *Miami Herald,* 17 August 1992, Business, 20BM.

Barrett, William P. "Sweet Charity." *Forbes,* 20 March 2000, 180.

Benson, Michael. *Gloria Estefan.* Minneapolis: Learner Publications Company, 2000.

Birnbaum, Larry. "Miami Sound Machine Achieves a Crossover Dream." *New York Times,* 16 February 1986, Section 2, 27.

Bohner, Kate. "Miami's South Beach Area Is Hot, Very Hot, but Whose Judgment Would You Trust: Gloria Estefan's or David Geffen's?" *Forbes,* 16 August 1993, 50.

Cantor, Judy. "Shine On, Crescent Moon." *Miami New Times,* 7 September 1994.

Castro, Peter. "Little Glorita, Happy at Last; Once Haunted by Family Illness and Trauma, Gloria Estefan Is Seeing Rainbows but Still Wary of Storm Clouds; Her Accident a Memory, She's Back on the Road." *People,* 12 April 1996, 60.

Castro, Peter, et al. "Water Hazard; A Fatal Crash Involving Gloria Estefan Reveals the Peril of Wet Bikes." *People,* 9 October 1995, Tragedy, 65.

Cobo-Hanlon, Leila. "Latin Artists Sound Off." *Variety,* 8 June 1998–14 June 1998, M19.

Clarke, Jay. "Estefans' New Eatery Offers a Taste of Old Havana at Walt Disney." *Miami Herald,* 3 November 1997.

Delgado, Celeste Fraser. "Los Producers. The Emperor's Clothes Are Wearing Thin, As Both His Top Songwriter and the Latin Grammys Leave the Estefan Court." *Miami New Times.* 6 September 2001.

Dougherty, Steve. "One Step at a Time; Fighting to Recover From Her Broken Back, Gloria Estefan Vows to Return to the Stage 'Better Than Ever.'" *People,* 25 June 1990, 78.

Flick, Larry. "Estefan Embraces Her 'Destiny'; Epic Blitz Includes Olympic Tie-in Tour." *Billboard,* 11 May 1996.

Flick, Larry. "Latin Music: Next Stage of Success Story—Epic's Estefan Blends Caribbean Sounds on Set." *Billboard,* 6 May 2000.

Gale Research, Inc. "Gloria Estefan." *Contemporary Musicians,* 15 (1995).

Goldman, Lea. "Alien Lands in Palm Beach." *Forbes,* 16 April 2001, 153.

Gonzalez, Fernando. "Emilio Estefan Has Vision of Motown with Latin Beat." *Miami Herald,* 17 January 1994, 1C.

Graham, Jefferson. "Cutting Both Ways; Estefan's Latin Roots Sprout Pop Hits; Miami Sound Machine's '80s Lady." *USA Today,* 10 July 1989, Life, 1D.

Hobson, Louis B., Sun Media Newspapers. "Gloria Estefan Big on Miracles." *The London Free Press,* 29 October 1999, Entertainment section.

"'I Was Lucky'; The Road Back." *USA Weekend,* 24 June 1999, 4.

Kimball, Charles. "Auto Dealer Potamkin, Wife, Get Financing for Two Home Sites." *Miami Daily Business Review,* 26 June 2000, A8.

Kimball, Charles. "Emilio Estefan Firm Purchases Miami Beach Store Building for $615,000." *Miami Daily Business Review,* 8 April 1998.

La Franco, Robert. "The *Forbes* Top 40." 22 September 1997, 162.

La Franco, Robert. "Salsa, Inc." *Forbes,* 22 September 1997, 154.

"The Latin Beat." ABC News Specials, 7 September 1999.

Lopetegui, Enrique. "Q&A with Gloria Estefan; 'Mi Tierra'" Paying Tribute to Her Roots." *Los Angeles Times,* 22 June 1993, Calendar, Part F, 1.

Lyonnel, Javier. "Estefans Increase Their Miami South Beach Real Estate Portfolio." *Miami Herald,* 25 July 1998.

Martin, Lydia. "Emilio Estefan's Dedication Helped Make Latin Grammys a Reality." *Miami Herald,* 12 September 2000, Entertainment News.

Mc Donald, Kathy A. "Celeb Owners Spice Up Local Eateries." *Variety,* 1 November 1999–7 November 1999, M29.

Moon, Tom. "Inside the Miami Sound Machine." *Miami Herald,* 24 May 1987, Amusements, 1K.

Paoletta, Michael. "U.S. Warms to Latin Sounds." *Billboard,* 24 April 1999.

Perez-Feria, Richard. "Making the American Dream Work." *Variety,* 10 June 1996–16 June 1996, 49.

Pitts, Jr., Leonard. "Gloria Goes Back to Her Routes with Mi Tierra, Estefan Visits Cuba of the '30s and '40s." *Miami Herald,* 22 June 1993, Living, 1E.

Sandler, Adam. "New Estefan Imprint Takes to Miami." *Daily Variety,* 19 January 1994, News, 7.

Schneider, Karen S. "Ready, Set, Go Buy Something; For Celebrities Who Love to Shop Till They Drop, the Problem Isn't Cash Flow—It's Storage Space." *People,* 21 June 1999, 106.

"Singer Gloria Estefan Settles Accident Suit for $8.5 Million." *Miami Herald,* 28 August 1991, 1A.

Sontag, Debbie. "The Rhythm of Exile." *Miami Herald,* 18 October 1987.

Soriano, Csar and Ann Oldenburg. "Cuban Refugees Bean in Miami at Estefan's Feet." *USA Today,* 5 February 1999, 4E.

Stefoff, Rebecca. *Gloria Estefan. Hispanics of Achievement*. Philadelphia: Chelsea House Publishers, 1999.

Stieghorst, Tom. "Emilio Estefan Creates Cuban Culture Machine; As Gloria Sells Millions of Albums, Her Husband Builds an Empire." *Sun-Sentinel* (Fort Lauderdale, Florida), 2 November 1997, 1G

"Timeless Estefan." *Waikato Times* (New Zealand), 5 December 1998.

Wilker, Deborah. "Latin Pop Queen is No Diva at Home." *Variety*, 10 June 1996–16 June 1996, Special Supplement: Estefan Empire, 49.

Wilker, Deborah. "Love at 1st Sight." *Variety*, 10 June 1996–16 June 1996, 56.

Wilker, Deborah. "Pair's Charitable Efforts Make Their Mark on Miami." *Variety*, 10 June 1996–16 June 1996, Special Supplement: Estefan Empire, 58.

Willman, Chris. "Pop Music; The Last Hurdle; Gloria Estefan Says Returning to the Concert Stage Will Allow Her to Put Last Year's Wrenching Accident behind Her." *Los Angeles Times*, 27 January 1991, Calendar, 7.

9. B.B. King

Allen, Bob. "Boxscore Concerts." *Amusement Business*, 26 March 2001, 9.

"B.B. King." *The Complete Marquis Who's Who Biographies*, 6 July 2000.

"B.B. King Tours: The Grammy Award-Winner Rocks in IMAX Film, While Album Goes Double Platinum," PR Newswire, 20 April 2001.

Bragg, Rick. "The Blues Is Dying in the Place It Was Born." *New York Times*, 22 April 2001, Section 1, 1.

Brosnan, James W. "Sad to the Bone." *The Commercial Appeal* (Memphis), 24 January 1996, Metro, 1B.

Eck, Michael. "Shirley King Puts Her Blues Foot Down." *Times Union* (Albany, N.Y.), 16 December 1999, Capital Region, B15.

Ellis, Bill. "Bukka White—Essence of Blues; Brass Note on Beale to Honor Legend." *The Commercial Appeal* (Memphis), 29 May 1999, F3.

Fair, S.S. "Footnotes." *New York Times,* 21, November 1999, 6, 102.

Horowitz, Craig, et al. "Bules for B.B.'s Baby; Guitar Great B.B. King Performs for His Daughter—Imprisoned in Florida." *People,* 22 March 1993, Kin, 57.

Kagan, Daryn, et al. *In the Money,* CNNfn, 23 June 2000.

Kening, Dan. "Cancel That Cancellation, Listeners' Protests May Bring Back 'B.B. King Blues Hour.'" *Chicago Tribune,* 8 May 1990, Tempo, 2.

King, B.B. and David Ritz. *Blues All Around Me, The Autobiography of B.B. King.* New York: Avon Books, 1996.

Kinnon, Joy Bennett. "Are Whites Taking or Are Blacks Giving Away the Blues?". September 1997, Entertainment, 86.

Kramer, Louise. "B.B. King Club Is Bringing the Blues to 42nd St; Blue Note Operator behind Upscale Room." *Crain's New York Business,* 19 June 2000, 22.

Marino, Nick. "Legendary and Humble B.B. King." *Florida Times-Union* (Jacksonville, FL.), 25 January 2001, Lifestyle, C-1.

McLennan, Scott. "Daughter of the Blues; Shirley King Has Newfound Respect for B.B.'s Traditon." *Telegram & Gazette* (Worcester, Mass.), 9 December 1999, Time Out, C1.

McNeil, Liz. "Talking with B.B. King." *People,* 2 December 1996, Picks & Pans.

Minor, E. Kyle. "Music; Still a Thrill When B.B. King Comes to Town." *New York Times,* 20 August 2000, 14CN, 14.

Morse, Steve. "Music; The Making of a Guitar Prodigy Kenny Wayne Shepherd Hones His Talent through Dedication." *Boston Globe,* 10 March 2000, Arts, D15.

Nobles, Barr. "B.B. King Crowned Child of Chitlin' Circuit Highlights San Francisco Blues Fest." *San Francisco Chonicle,* 8 September 1991.

Norment, Lynn. "On Lucille's 40th Anniversary; B.B. King Talks about Love, the Blues, and History." *Ebony,* February 1992, Entertainment, 44.

Palmer, Robert. "At Mississippi Homecoming, B.B. King Unites Neighbors," 11 June 1983, Section 1, 1.

Palmer, Robert. "The Pop Life; B.B. King Hometown Proves Music Dissolves All Barriers." *New York Times,* 15 June 1983, C21.

Patton, Phil. "Who Owns the Blues?". *New York Times,* 26 November 1995, Section 2, 1.

Penn, Roberta. "At 67, B.B. King's Still Living on Blues Power." *Seattle Post-Intelligencer,* 22 January 1993, What's Happening, 5.

Salama, Sasha. *Business Unusual,* CNNfn, 25 June 2000.

Schuch, Beverly. *Business Unusual,* CNNfn, 14 October 1998.

Selvin, Joel. "Something Else." *San Francisco Chronicle,* 24 August 1991, Daily Datebook, C4.

Thompson, Art. "The King Swings, B.B. King, Jazz Musician; Interview." *Guitar Player,* 1 February 2000, 56.

Voger, Mark. "Talking with a King Blues Guitarist Reflects on Power and Path of Music." *Times Union* (Albany, N.Y.), 11 January 2001, *Asbury Park Press.*

Watrous, Peter. "B.B. King: Making the Most of a Lifetime of Experience." *New York Times,* 1990, 2 February 1990, C22.

Wolff, Cindy. "Good-time Folks Flow to B.B.'s, but King Club Suits Denote Money Jam." *The Commercial Appeal* (Memphis), 4 August 1996, Business, 1C.

Yardley, Jim. "Around the South Mississippi's Parchman Prison Has a Mean Reputation but Official Denies Violence Is Typical." *Atlanta Journal and Constitution,* 10 July 1994, A3.

Yellin, Emily. "Everybody Wants Rights to the King of the Blues." *New York Times,* 20 August 1996, D4.

"B.B. King," "Notable Black American Men," Gale Group, 1999.

B.B. King, "The Official Website," <www.bbking.com>.

King, Riley B. B.B., biography.com.

King, B.B., vh1.com

13. Tony Hawk

Antonucci, Michael, et al. "Video-Game Makers on the Hunt for Young Consumers." *San Jose Mercury News,* 16 May 2001.

Bluth, Andrew. "Jumping the Corporate Skate Ramp; PROFILE: The Extreme-Sports Hero Is Learning New Maneuvers in the Boardroom." *Orange County Register,* 20 August 2000, A01.

"Budget Gourmet Finds Home at Luigino's after Heinz Decides to Get Rid of Line. Heinz Frozen Foods Sells American Gourmet Co. to Luigino's, Inc." *Quick Frozen Foods International,* 1 April 2001, 90.

Earnest, Leslie. "O.C. Business Plus; Quiksilver Takes to the Skateboard; Apparel: The Huntington Beach Surf-Wear Maker Buys the Clothing Business of Skate Icon Tony Hawk with Plans to Expand the Line's Appeal." *Los Angeles Times,* 9 March 2000, Business, Part C, 1.

Fainaru-Wada. "Hawking His Trade; He's the Man When It Comes to the Skateboard." *San Francisco Examiner,* 24 June 1999, C-5.

Feitelberg, Rosemary. "Hawk Eyes Boarders and More; Tony Hawk's Sportswear Company." *Woman's Wear Daily,* 13 August 1998, 10.

Field, Alex. "Legend on Wheels; Skateboarder Tony Hawk Wows Young Fans in Local Stop." *Los Angeles Times,* 21 June 2000, Metro, Part B, 1.

Gallagher, Leigh. "Gen-X-tremist Pitchman." *Forbes,* 14 December 1998, 197.

Givens, Ron. "Skateboarding's Best Seller; Skateboarder Tony Hawk." *New York Times,* 11 December 2000, Upfront, 20.

Hawk, Tony. *Hawk Occupation: Skateboarder.* ReganBooks, 2000.

"Heinz Rolls out New Hot Bites." *Advertising Age,* 16 April 2001, Midwest region edition, 37.

Levine, Mark. "The Birdman." *New Yorker,* 26 July 1999.

Manning, Barbara. "Teenager Tony Hawk Soars above Everybody in the Scary Sport of Skateboarding." *People,* 23 March 1987, 48.

Mortimer, Sean. "New Pro–Just Add Water." Skateboarding.com, 24 September 1998.

Mortimer, Sean. "The Subtle Art of Shoe Sponsorship." Skateboarding .com, 30 July 1998.

Moukheiber, Zina. "Later, Skater." *Forbes,* 29 November 1999, 108.

"Photo Essay." *FSB,* February 2001, 74.

Pilgrim, Kitty. "Tony Hawk CEO." *Business Unusual,* CNNfn, 30 January 2001.

Robins, Marc. "Zap!" *Forbes,* 8 January 2001, 259.

Ruibak, Sal. "Chairman of the Skateboard X Games Star's Net Worth Soars, but Some Question the Soul of the Deal." *USA Today,* 9 March 2000, 3C.

Sabga, Patricia. "ESPN's Gigantic Skate Park Tour." *Business Unusual,* CNNfn.

Sakamoto, Ryan. "Tony Hawk Just Doesn't Fit Typical Image of Skateboarder; This Businessman, Family Man, and Champion Is the Ideal for the Sport." *Morning Call* (Allentown), 28 November 1999, C9.

Stein, Charles. "Cover Story: Can They Stay Cool? By Shrewdly Targeting 'Extreme' Sports Fans, Small Upstart Sneaker Makers Have Stomped Giant Rivals Such as Reebok. But to Survive, They Must Figure Out How to Remain." *Your Company,* 1 October 1998, 34.

"The Tony Hawk Story." <www.clubtonyhawk.com>.

"To The Top: Flyboy Chairman of the (Skate)board Tony Hawk Gets All the Breaks and Comes Back For More." *People,* 8 January 2001, 104.

Verdon, Joan. "Skateboarding Idol Hawking His Wares." *The Record* (Bergen County, NJ), 25 March 2001, 102.

Vuckovich, Miki. "Renaissance Man." Skateboarding.com, 14 August 2000.

Warth, Gary. "Chairman of the (Skate)board Tony Hawk Tells His Story." NCTimes.net, 5 November 2000.

Yabroff, Jennie. "X Games; Competing for Business; Some X Games Athletes Make a Living Running Sports-Gear Companies." *San Francisco Chronicle,* 11 August 2000, A1.

Yin, Sandra. "Going to Extremes." *American Demographics,* June 2001, Indicators, 26.

14. Venus and Serena Williams

Alex Tresniowski, et al. "Little Sister Act; Escaping Venus's Shadow with Power, Speed, and True Grit, Serena Williams Closes Her U.S. Open with Victory." *People*, 27 September 1999, 68.

Amdur, Neil. "Venus Williams Urged to Skip Year." *New York Times*, 29 March 2000, D6.

Araton, Harvey. "Sports of the Times; Venus Williams May Raise the Bar Even More." *New York Times*, 24 December 2000, 8, 4.

Bellafante, Gina. "Shopping with Serena Williams. Game, Set, Dress Me in Leather." *New York Times*, 17 October 1999, 9, 1.

Cain, Joy Duckett. "Being the Best Is a Williams Tradition." *Essence*, December 1999, 68.

Cepeda, Raquel. "Courting Destiny." *Essence*, June 2001, 124.

Chappell, Kevin. "Richard Williams: Venus and Serena's Father Whips the Pros and Makes His Family No. 1 In Tennis." *Ebony*, June 2000, 93.

Chua-Eoan, Howard. "Her Serena Highness; The Younger of the Brash Williams Sisters Is the First to Take a Major Singles Crown. What Will Daddy Say?" *Time*, 20 September 1999, 58.

Clarey, Christopher. "Tennis; Venus Williams Is Back; And She Intends to Stay." *New York Times*, 18 May 2000, D2.

Clarke, Elizabeth. "Going Big Time; Venus, Serena Take Ever-Expanding Show to U.S. Open." *Palm Beach Post*, 30 August 1998, 11C.

Clarke, Elizabeth. "Serena's Critics Wrong, Dad Says." *Palm Beach Post*, 23 July 1999, 2C.

Clarke, Elizabeth. "Venus Quiet on Racism Charge." *Palm Beach Post*, 8 September 1997, 3C.

Clarke, Elizabeth. "Williams' Rise No Surprise to Former Coach." *Palm Beach Post*, 7 September 1997, 1C.

Clark, Evan. "Avon Net Vaults 28.3 Percent." *WWD*, 30 April 2001, 16.

"Delray Beach's Williams Turning Pro at 14 Despite Her Father's Opposition." *Palm Beach Post*, 4 October 1994, 9C.

Dillman, Lisa. "Tennis; Garrison Sized Up Serena Early." *Los Angeles Times,* 12 September 1999, D15.

Dillman, Lisa. "Venus and Serena Double Fault." *Palm Beach Post,* 3 June 2001, 16C.

Downey, Mike. "A Blazing New Star Lights Tennis World." *Los Angeles Times,* 6 September 1997, A1.

Dwyre, Bill. "Tennis; Williamses Changing Attitudes On and Off the Tennis Court." *Los Angeles Times,* 6 September 1999, D3.

Elmore, Charles. "Playing the Market; Reebok, Puma Paying Court to Williams Sisters." *Palm Beach Post,* 10 October 1999, 1A.

Elmore, Charles. "Richard Williams: No Family Fix Going On." *Palm Beach Post,* 20 March 2001, C1.

Elmore, Charles. "Venus Reebok Deal out of This World $40 Million Pact Highest for Women." *Palm Beach Post,* 22 December 2000, 1A.

Elmore, Charles. "Venus to Skip Grand Slams; Play in Small Tournaments." *Palm Beach Post,* 10 May 1995, 1C.

Elmore, Charles. "Williamses Locked in One Sticky Situation." *Palm Beach Post,* 23 March 2001, C1.

Elmore, Charles. "Williams Lashes Out." *Palm Beach Post,* 27 March 2001, C1.

Feitelberg, Rosemary. "Athletes Run For Coverage." *WWD,* 27 July 2000, 8.

Finn, Robin. "Defying Her Sport's Logic, a Tennis Prodigy Emerges." *New York Times,* 7 September 1997, 1, 1.

Finn, Robin. "In Tennis, Child Prodigies Whet the Agents' Appetites." *New York Times,* 8 April 1991, A1.

Finn, Robin. "Only 14, but Groomed and Set to Be a Pro." *New York Times,* 4 October 1994, B12.

Finn, Robin. "Taking the Pro Plunge When Feet Aren't Wet." *New York Times,* 23 February 1994, B12.

Finn, Robin. "Tennis; Last of the 14-Year-Olds Will Take a First Step." *New York Times,* 27 October 1994, B17.

Finn, Robin. "Tennis; Never Too Young for Tennis Millions." *New York Times,* 10 November 1993, B21.

Finn, Robin. "Tennis: Tennis Life Begins Gloriously at 14; A Straight-Set Victory for Williams in Her Pro Debut." *New York Times,* 2 November 1994, B9.

Finn, Robin. "Williamses Are Buckled In and Rolling, at a Safe Pace." *New York Times,* 14 November 1999, 8, 1.

"Freedom of Speech." *The Reader's Companion to American History,* January 1999.

Friend, Tom. Tennis; Does Williams's Father Know Best?" *New York Times,* 16 August 1996, B12.

Gutierrez, Valerie. "Williams Sisters Open Doors, Straight Out of Compton." *Los Angeles Times,* 7 July 2000, D7.

"IMG to Market Williams Sisters." *Palm Beach Post,* 28 September 1999.

"Jehovah's Witnesses." *The Columbia Encyclopedia,* Fifth Edition, January 1993.

Jenkins, Sally. "Double Trouble, Tennis Players Venus and Serena Williams" *Women's Sports and Fitness,* 1 November 1998, 102.

Jordan, Pat. "Daddy's Big Test." *New York Times,* 16 March 1997, Magazine, 28.

Kaplan, James. "Dynamic Duo." *Vogue,* March 2001, 494.

Kennedy, Michael J. "A Tale of 2 Courts: A Wide Gulf Separates the Rolling Hills Estates Club Where Pete Sampras Trained, and the Once-Scruffy Compton Park That Produced the Williams Sisters. But Family Support and Personal Drive Made Them All Champions." *Los Angeles Times,* 28 August 2000, E1.

Klein, Frederick C. "On Sports; Dad Knows Best." *Wall Street Journal,* 31 August 1998, A17.

Lord, Mary. "Too Much, Too Soon." *U.S. News & World Report,* 17 July 2000.

Markus, Don, "13-Year-Old Tennis Prodigy Williams Waits for Her Time." *Los Angeles Times,* 23 October 1993, C6.

McCants, Leonard. "Venus Teams with Wilsons for Fall Line; Wilsons Leather Experts, Inc." *WWD,* 16 April 2001, 2.

McLachlin, Mary. "Parents of Tennis Sisters Will Bus Rich to Help Poor." *Palm Beach Post,* 27 April 1999, 1A.

Nagourney, Adam and Richard L. Berke. "President Plays Coach in First Lady's Campaign." *New York Times,* 7 October 2000, A1.

Neill, Michael, et al. "Venus Rising; It's Not Entirely a Love Match as Tennis Salutes a Confident New Talent." *People,* 27 October 1997.

Newcome, Peter. "Ad in." *Forbes,* 15 June 1998, 16.

Nobles, Charles. "Tennis; A Youngster Looks Ahead Amid Troubled Time in Florida." *New York Times,* 19 May 1994, B13.

Peyser, Marc and Allison Samuels. "Venus and Serena against the World." *Newsweek,* 24 August 1998, 45.

"Policy Statement. Intensive Training and Sports Specialization in Young Athletes." *American Academy of Pediatrics,* July 2000, 154.

Quindlen, Anna. "Public & Private; Strong Man Weeps." *New York Times,* 10 July 1991, A19.

Roberts, Selena. "On Tennis; Williams Sisters Learned to Think off Court, Too." *New York Times,* 3 July 2000, D3.

Roberts, Selena. "Tennis: US Open; Venus Williams Turns Open into Her Celebration." *New York Times,* 10 September 2000, 8, 1.

Rosenberg, Cheryl. "Spirlea a 'Racist,' Says Venus' Dad." *Palm Beach Post,* 7 September 1997, 5C.

Rosenblatt, Roger. "The Proudest Papa; Richard Williams Has a Great Time Being the Progenitor of Champions." *Time,* 20 September 1999, 92.

Rustad, Mitch. "Now the Ball Is in Tennis Court." *Business Week,* 30 October 1995, 156.

Sandomir, Richard. "Having Style Pays Off for Venus Williams." *New York Times,* 22 December 2000, D1.

Seo, Diane. "Advertising & Marketing; Off the Tennis Court, Sports Agency Exec Has Advantage." *Los Angeles Times,* 26 November 1999, C1.

"Serena Out of Wimbledon; Deion to Stay." *Palm Beach Post,* 18 June 1999, 2C.

"Serena Williams; She Claimed Center Court with Beads, Brilliance, and Brawn." *People,* 31 December 1999, 56.

"Serena Williams; Wins at U.S. Open; First Black Female Champion Since 1958." *Jet,* 27 September 1999, 51.

Smith, Doug. "Venus' $40M Deal Breaks New Ground." *USA Today,* 22 December 2000, 14C.

Smith, Thom. "Sibling Rivalry, Learning Charity a Perfect Match." *Palm Beach Post,* 15 March 2001, E1.

Stein, Joel. "Changing Courts; It's Back to Class for Venus and Serena Williams, Who Have Designs on New Careers after Tennis." *Time,* 13 November 2000, 70.

Stevenson, Samantha. "Youth Sports; The Sins of Tennis Parents." *New York Times,* 21 May 1992, B19.

Stewart, Mark. Tennis' New Wave. Venus & Serena Williams. Sisters in Arms. Brookfield, Conn.: The Millbrook Press, 2000.

Stoda, Greg. "Venus Takes Her Throne." *Palm Beach Post,* 10 September 2000, 1C.

Sullivan, Robert. "All in the Family Jewels; Now That Venus Has Her Own Grand Slam Title, the Williams Sisters Are Set to Dominate Women's Tennis." *Time,* 17 July 2000, 58.

"Tennis; Status; Undefeated. Future: Rosy: Age: 10." *New York Times,* 3 July 1990, B12.

Washington, William. "Backtalk; Accept It, America: There Is an 'I' in Tennis." *New York Times,* 14 September 1997, 8, 9.

Weintraub, Arlene. "Ad-Vantage: The Williams Sisters." *Business Week,* 5 February 2001, 71.

Wertheim, Jon L. "We Told You So; After Years of Saying They Would Dominate the Sport, Venus and Serena Williams Proved They Were on Their Way by Meeting in the Lipton Final." *Sports Illustrated,* 5 April 1999, 68.

"Wimbledon Fixed?" *National Enquirer,* 27 March 2001, 24.

"Wimbledon Rejects Plea for Equal Pay." *Palm Beach Post,* 30 April 1999, 1C.

Wolverton, Brad. "So Far, She's Not the Venus De Moola." *Business Week,* 29 September 1997, 140.

Woods, Mark. "Venus Retiring at 19? Maybe, Father Says." *Palm Beach Post,* 29 March 2000, 1C.

"World Literature, Philosophy, and Religion: Jehovah's Witnesses." *The Dictionary of Cultural Literacy,* January 1988.

ABOUT THE AUTHORS

Gail Liberman and Alan Lavine are husband-and-wife columnists and best-selling authors based in Palm Beach Gardens, Florida.

You can view their personal finance columns in the *Boston Herald* and on America Online, CNBC.com, Quicken.com, Fundsinterative.com, and numerous newspapers and Web sites.

Liberman and Lavine's latest book, *Rags to Riches: Motivating Stories of How Ordinary People Achieved Extraordinary Wealth!* (Dearborn), was featured on Oprah and hit two best-seller lists.

You may have seen or heard the couple on television and radio. They have been guests on CBS's *The Early Show*, CNN, CNBC, the *700 Club*, the *Debra Duncan Show*, and PBS's *Nightly Business Report*. They also have been quoted in the *Wall Street Journal, Money* magazine, *USA Today*, the *New York Times, Business Week, Investors Business Daily*, the *Washington Post, Redbook, First, Bride's, Elle*, and *Working Mother*.

Their other books are *Love, Marriage & Money* (Dearborn), *The Complete Idiot's Guide to Making Money with Mutual Funds* (Alpha Books), *Improving Your Credit and Reducing Your Debt* (Wiley), and *The Short & Simple Guide to Life Insurance* (Authors Choice).

The two have contributed to *Consumers Digest, Your Money*, and *Worth* magazines as well as the *Journal of the National Associ-*

ation of Personal Financial Advisors, Financial Advisor, and *Financial Planning* magazine.

Liberman, whose own column, "Managing Your Fortune," runs in the *Palm Beach Daily News,* helped found *Bank Rate Monitor* (now Bankrate.com), North Palm Beach, and was editor of the publication for 15 years. An award-winning journalist, she launched her career with the Associated Press, United Press International, and United Feature Syndicate. She also was a reporter for the *Courier-Post,* a Gannett newspaper in Cherry Hill, New Jersey. Liberman obtained her bachelor's degree in journalism from Rutgers University. She holds a Florida real estate license and Florida mortgage broker license.

Lavine, author of the nation's longest-running mutual fund column, was on the ground floor of the mutual fund industry as former director of research for IBC of Westborough, Mass. His own column, in the *Boston Herald,* has been running for 20 years. He also pens a regular column for *Accounting Today,* and has written for the *New York Times, Individual Investor, American Lawyer,* and *Financial World.* During the 1980s, his family finances research was cited by the Joint Economic Committee of Congress. A frequent guest lecturer at Cornell University, Lavine has spoken before such groups as the American Psychology Association, the American Association for the Advancement of Science, Massachusetts Psychological Association, and Morningstar, Inc.'s Mutual Fund Conference.

Prior to working on his post-graduate training in finance and economics at Clark University, Lavine worked ten years as a licensed clinical social worker in Massachusetts. He obtained his masters degree in psychology at University of Akron and trained at the Gestalt Institute.

Lavine has authored *Getting Started in Mutual Funds* (Wiley); *50 Ways to Mutual Fund Profits* (McGraw-Hill); *Your Life Insurance Options* (Wiley); *Diversify Your Way to Wealth* (McGraw-Hill), an alternate selection of the Fortune Book Club; and *Diversify: Investors Guide to Asset-Allocation Strategies* (Dearborn).

Both Liberman and Lavine are listed in Marquis' Who's Who in America and are members of the Society of American Business Editors and Writers.

MORE RAGS TO RICHES

For special discounts on 20 or more copies of *More Rags to Riches: All New Stories of How Ordinary People Achieved Extraordinary Wealth*, please call Dearborn Trade Special Sales at 800-621-9621, ext. 4455.

Dearborn™
Trade Publishing
A **Kaplan Professional** Company